W9-BVF-071

QUICKEN® 2012
QuickSteps™

About the Author

Marty Matthews has used computers for many years, as a programmer, analyst, manager, and executive. As a result, he has firsthand knowledge of how to make the most of a computer and its software, including Quicken, which he has used since its earliest days.

Also for many years, Marty and his wife Carole have been writing books on the use of computers, including ones on desktop publishing, web publishing, Microsoft Office, and Microsoft operating systems—from MS-DOS through Windows 7 SP1. Recent books published by McGraw-Hill include *Quicken 2011 QuickSteps, Windows 7 for Seniors QuickSteps, Computing for Seniors QuickSteps,* and *Microsoft Office 2010 QuickSteps.*

Marty and Carole are principals in Matthews Technology, a firm dedicated to making technology easy through books, articles, websites, and consulting. Over the last 27 years Matthews Technology has produced over 100 computer-related books, selling more than a million and a half copies. For more information, visit http://matthewstechnology.com.

About the Contributing Author

Bobbi Sandberg is an accountant and technical writer currently working in and enjoying the Pacific Northwest. A popular speaker and trainer, she has used and taught Quicken since its debut in the '80s. She is the author of *Quicken 2012: The Official Guide* and she has co-authored with her colleagues at Matthews Technology *Quicken 2011 QuickSteps* and *Computing for Seniors QuickSteps.*

She is known as the person who can make computer software understandable. One of her recent students said, "Now I can easily track my finances and before, I couldn't comfortably balance my checkbook." Bobbi combines her ability to explain complex concepts in plain language with her in-depth understanding of computers and accounting to make using financial software as easy as writing a check. She wishes for each reader a "smooth and successful" financial life!

About the Technical Editor

Mary Higgins is a long-time Quicken user, having used each version since 1999. She enjoys pushing the limits of what the software is intended to do—clicking every button, navigating every menu path, reading the help files, and so on. She reads and posts on the Quicken forums and finds it interesting to see how others are using Quicken and the different approaches to resolving issues.

QUICKEN® 2012
QuickSteps™

MARTY MATTHEWS
BOBBI SANDBERG

New York Chicago San Francisco
Lisbon London Madrid Mexico City
Milan New Delhi San Juan
Seoul Singapore Sydney Toronto

The McGraw·Hill Companies

Cataloging-in-Publication Data is on file with the Library of Congress

McGraw-Hill books are available at special quantity discounts to use as premiums and sales promotions, or for use in corporate training programs. To contact a representative, please e-mail us at bulksales@mcgraw-hill.com.

QUICKEN® 2012 QUICKSTEPS™

1234567890   QDB QDB   10987654321

ISBN   978-0-07-177824-4
MHID   0-07-177824-1

SPONSORING EDITOR / Megg Morin

EDITORIAL SUPERVISOR / Janet Walden

PROJECT MANAGER / Tania Andrabi, Cenveo Publisher Services

TECHNICAL EDITOR / Mary Higgins

COPY EDITOR / Lisa McCoy

PROOFREADER / Claire Splan

INDEXER / Valerie Haynes Perry

PRODUCTION SUPERVISOR / Jean Bodeaux

COMPOSITION / Cenveo Publisher Services

ILLUSTRATION / Cenveo Publisher Services

ART DIRECTOR, COVER / Jeff Weeks

COVER DESIGNER / Pattie Lee

SERIES CREATORS / Marty and Carole Matthews

SERIES DESIGN / Bailey Cunningham

Contents at a Glance

Contents

Chapter 7 Keeping Your Records Up to Date 159

Chapter 8 Managing Your Investments 179

9

10

Acknowledgments

The names on the cover of this book are only part of the story. This project would not have been possible were it not for the efforts of an entire team:

- **Megg Morin**, acquisitions editor at McGraw-Hill, who is always encouraging, creative, helpful, and supportive. Thanks, Megg!

- **Mary Higgins**, technical editor, who made the project better with many suggestions and creative ideas. Thanks, Mary!

- **Janet Walden**, McGraw-Hill editorial supervisor, for her quick eye, rapid response, and most gracious attitude. Thanks, Janet!

- **Tania Andrabi** of Cenveo Publisher Services, who made deadlines, pressure, and time differences disappear with her encouragement and support. Thanks, Tania!

- **Lisa McCoy**, copy editor, caught widely varied inconsistencies. Her suggested improvements to the text always added to its readability. Thanks, Lisa!

- **Valerie Haynes Perry**, indexer, adds much to the usability of the book and does so with great thoroughness. Thanks, Valerie!

- **Eddy Wu** on the Quicken 2012 team at Intuit, who helped us immeasurably and worked with us, exhibiting great kindness and patience. Thanks, Eddy!

—Marty Matthews and Bobbi Sandberg

Introduction

QuickSteps™ books are recipe books for computer users. They answer the question "How do I...?" by providing quick sets of steps to accomplish the most common tasks in a particular program. The sets of steps are the central focus of the book. QuickSteps sidebars show you how to quickly do many small functions or tasks that support the primary functions. Notes, Tips, and Cautions augment the steps, yet they are presented in such a manner as to not interrupt the flow of the steps. The brief introductions are minimal rather than narrative, and numerous illustrations and figures, many with callouts, support the steps.

QuickSteps™ books are organized by function and the tasks needed to perform that function. Each function is a chapter. Each task, or "How To," contains the steps needed for accomplishing the function along with relevant Notes, Tips, Cautions, and screenshots. Tasks will be easy to find through:

- The table of contents, which lists the functional areas (chapters) and tasks in the order they are presented

- A How To list of tasks on the opening page of each chapter

- The index with its alphabetical list of terms used in describing the functions and tasks

- Color-coded tabs for each chapter or functional area with an index to the tabs just before the table of contents

Conventions Used in This Book

Quicken® 2012 QuickSteps™ uses several conventions designed to make the book easier for you to follow:

- A 🔍 or a 🖊 in the table of contents or the How To list in each chapter references a QuickSteps or a QuickFacts sidebar in a chapter.

- **Bold type** is used for words on the screen that you are to do something with, such as click **Save As** or open **File**.

- *Italic type* is used for a word or phrase that is being defined or otherwise deserves special emphasis.

- Underlined type is used for text that you are to type from the keyboard.

- When you see the command, **CTRL/CMD,** you are to press the **CTRL** key in Windows or the **CMD** key on the Mac; **ALT/OPT**, press the **ALT** key in Windows or the **OPTIONS** key on the Mac.

- SMALL CAPITAL LETTERS are used for keys on the keyboard such as **ENTER** and **SHIFT**.

- When you are expected to enter a command, you are told to press the key(s). If you are to enter text or numbers, you are told to type them. Specific letters or numbers to be entered will be underlined.

How to...

- *Determine the Version for You*
- *Upgrading Quicken*
- *Get Quicken*
- *Install Quicken*
- *Start Quicken*
- *Creating a Quick Start Shortcut for Quicken*
- *Set Up Quicken for the First Time*
- *Understand the Home Tab*
- *Add Accounts Manually*
- *Using the Ticker Symbol Lookup*
- *Find Help*
- *Using the Address Book*
- *Importing from Microsoft Money*
- *Exit Quicken*
- *Recognize Quicken Terms*
- *Use Windows Tools*
- *Finding More Keyboard Shortcuts*

Chapter 1
Stepping into Quicken

Welcome to Quicken 2012! Quicken is a personal financial program that provides an easy way to account for all of your income, expenses, assets, and debt, as well as do financial planning, budgeting, and handling your investments. Much more than a digital check register or a financial organizer, Quicken can give you peace of mind and a way to control your money instead of letting your money control you. With Quicken, you can print checks; pay bills online; reconcile your bank, credit card, and investment account statements; track your expenses; and plan your financial future.

This chapter introduces you to the various versions of Quicken, shows you how to install it on your computer, explains some Quicken terms, reviews some Windows concepts, walks you through Quicken Setup, and shows you how to close the program when you have finished using it. Even if you are an experienced user of Quicken, it might be good to review this chapter to see some of the new features of Quicken 2012.

Meet Quicken

Quicken 2012 helps you set up your checking, savings, investment, asset, debt, and credit card accounts; enter transactions into those accounts; balance or reconcile the accounts to the institution's records; print checks; create reports; design and print graphs; manage your debt; and see tips to help save your hard-earned dollars. If you have an Internet connection, you can download information from your bank, investment house, and credit card company. Quicken also makes it quick and easy to transfer your data to TurboTax at year-end to make tax preparation less stressful.

Determine the Version for You

Quicken 2012 for Windows comes in several versions: Starter, Deluxe, Premier, Home & Business, and Rental Property Manager. There is also a single version for the Mac. This book describes the Windows product and shows the Premier version in figures and illustrations. The version you select will depend on the tasks you want Quicken 2012 to perform:

- **Quicken 2012 Starter Edition** is a basic package for new users, but it has a number of limitations and does not include any investment functionality. It lets you track your checking, savings, credit card, and cash accounts. With an Internet connection, you can work online with any of the mentioned accounts and produce banking, spending, income and expense, and tax reports.

- **Quicken 2012 Deluxe** is the mainstream version used by most users. It lets you manage a broader array of financial accounts and gives you more power to make future financial decisions. It includes all of the features in the Starter edition, plus it provides the ability to track investments, property, assets, loans, and other liabilities and offers planning tools for budgeting, taxes, college, and other major financial events. It features detailed investment tracking, including downloading information from your broker, as well as lifetime and tax planners and debt reduction tips.

NOTE

For the automatic stock updating every 15 minutes to work, the Quicken file has to be open and the Quicken program must be the active window. The updates do not occur if Quicken is open, but minimized, or if the computer is in standby mode.

QUICKSTEPS

UPGRADING QUICKEN

If you purchase any version of Quicken 2012 and later want to upgrade, you can do so easily with your Internet connection.

1. Click **Help** on the menu bar.

2. Depending on the Quicken version you have, you will see one or more of the following options for upgrading. Click the one that is correct for you:

   - **Which Quicken Is Best For You?** In either Quicken Starter or Deluxe edition, you can read about the other versions and decide if you want to upgrade.

   - **Add More Investing & Tax Tools** In either Quicken Starter or Deluxe edition, you can read about Quicken Premier and decide if you want to upgrade.

   - **Add Business Tools** or **Add Rental Property Tools** In Quicken Starter, Deluxe, Premier, and Home & Business editions, you can read about additional versions for your home business or rental property and decide if you want to upgrade.

3. The window displayed by your choice in step 2 shows the features of the upgrades available to you. Select the upgrade you want. A Quicken webpage opens where you can order your upgrade. Click **Products** to choose the upgraded product you want. Complete the order form, which will require a credit card for payment.

Continued . . .

- **Quicken 2012 Premier** is for more advanced users and includes everything in Deluxe plus additional investment reports, automatic stock updating every 15 minutes, and Morningstar ratings. It also provides income tax Schedules A (Itemized Deductions), B (Interest and Dividends), and D (Capital Gains and Losses).

- **Quicken 2012 Home & Business**, in addition to everything in Premier, helps you run your small business by providing payables and receivables account; letting you create, track, and report estimates, invoices, vendor bills, vehicle mileage, and a host of other features. It prints business financial statements in the proper form, creates customer and vendor lists, helps you track specific projects and jobs, and prepares income tax Schedule C for business income and expense.

- **Quicken 2012 Rental Property Manager** adds to Quicken 2012 Home & Business the ability to track income and expense by property, track tenants, track rent payments, and identify tax-deductible property expenses.

You can upgrade any of the first four versions directly from your computer with an Internet connection. See the "Upgrading Quicken" QuickSteps.

Install Quicken 2012

Quicken 2012 can be installed on your computer for the first time, or it can update an earlier version. Either way, you need only follow the directions in a series of windows and dialog boxes to complete the task.

Get Quicken

You can get Quicken in several ways. Quicken Starter edition comes already installed on some new computers, or you can buy it from retailers such as Amazon.com, Best Buy, Office Depot, and Wal-Mart either online or in a store. When you buy online, you can have the retailer ship you a CD in the mail, or in some cases you can download the program over the Internet, sometimes at a discount. Quicken Deluxe, Premier, Home & Business, and Retail Property Manager can be purchased new from Intuit (www.quicken.intuit.com) or from a retailer such as Amazon.com and others by having the seller send you a CD or by downloading the program over the Internet. Often, retailers such as Amazon .com sell Quicken at a discount rather than at Intuit's price.

UICKSTEPS

UPGRADING QUICKEN (Continued)

4. After your order has been accepted, you will see a link to download an installer for the upgraded product you have purchased. Intuit will send you an email to confirm your order. This download will be available in your online account in case you need to reinstall later.

5. Double-click the link to download the installer to your computer, close Quicken if it is open, and double-click the installer to install your upgraded Quicken features.

TIP

To assist in finding a downloaded file at a later date, it is recommended that you save a copy of the downloaded file on your computer or save the email with the instructions for accessing the download so that it will be easy to reinstall later. If a file is downloaded automatically, look in the C:/Users/*your name*/Downloads folder.

NOTE

If you have a previous version of Quicken already installed, your Quicken data will not be removed by the installation process. The previous version's data files will be saved in a folder named QXXFiles, where XX is the previous year's version.

Install Quicken

To install Quicken:

1. If you get Quicken 2012 on a CD, put it in a CD or DVD drive and follow the installation instructions that appear on the screen. Your installation should start automatically.

2. If you download Quicken 2012, you should have a recent version of your web browser installed; follow the online instructions. Click **Save** so you have a copy of the program on your hard disk. You may also want to back up this file in case your hard disk goes bad. When downloading is complete, click **Run** to start installation.

3. With a CD, if you do not see the installation instructions, browse to the appropriate CD/DVD drive letter, and double-click the **install.exe** file. With a download, if you don't see the Run option, browse to your download folder (see the accompanying Note) and double-click the Quicken application file. In Microsoft Windows Vista or Windows 7, you may be asked if you want to allow this software to make changes to your computer. Given that you want to install Quicken, click **Yes**.

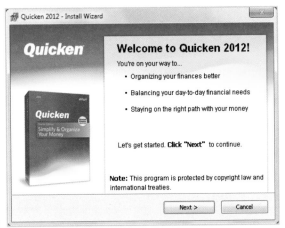

4. Click **Next** to begin the installation. The license agreement appears. Use the vertical scroll bar (see "Use Windows Tools" later in this chapter) to read through the license agreement, and click **I Agree To The Terms Of...** if you agree to its terms, and click **Next**. If you do not accept the license agreement, you cannot go forward and Quicken 2012 will not be installed.

5. If you want to install the program to its default location, click **Next** again. If you want to install the program in a location other than the default folder, click **Change**, and then:

   a. The Change Current Destination Folder dialog box appears. The default is a folder named "Quicken" in your Program Files folder, which displays at the bottom of the dialog box. Click the **Up One Level** icon to change the location of your Quicken folder. The Program Files folder appears in the Look In field.

NOTE

In Windows Vista and Windows 7, most downloads including Quicken 2012, are automatically stored in the C:\users*username*\download\ folder. We recommend that you move the Quicken 2012 file to its own folder and then back it up on a CD.

NOTE

Quicken 2012 does not allow more than one version of Quicken on your computer. You may install the Deluxe or Premier edition, 2011 or 2012 version, but not more than one of those.

b. Click the **Up One Level** icon again to create a folder in another location. Click the **New Folder** icon to create a Quicken folder at your chosen location. Click **OK** when you have completed the task. You are returned to the Destination Folder dialog box. Click **Next**.

6. In all cases, the Ready To Install Quicken 2012 dialog box appears. If you want to make any changes before installation begins, click **Back**. Otherwise, click **Install** to continue. If you have a previous version of Quicken installed on your computer, it will be uninstalled before Quicken 2012 is installed. Quicken will install any current updates during the installation process.

> Quicken 2012 - Install Wizard
>
> **Ready to Install Quicken 2012**
> The wizard is ready to begin installation.
> **Quicken**
>
> Before you can use Quicken, the wizard needs to:
>
> 1.) Install Quicken 2012
> 2.) Update Quicken 2012
>
> If you want to review or change any of your installation settings, click Back. Otherwise click Install to proceed.
>
> Note: We recommend turning off your anti-virus program while you install Quicken. This is because anti-virus programs can sometimes cause conflicts with the installation files.
>
> < Back   Install   Cancel

Installation takes a few minutes, depending on the speed of your computer and the speed of your Internet connection. A progress bar displays to let you know how it is proceeding.

7. When the installation and any updates are complete, the Installation Complete dialog box appears. Note the **Launch Quicken 2012** check box, which should be selected by default. To start Quicken now, click **Done**. The Quicken Home tab's Main View window appears.

8. If you clear the **Launch Quicken 2012** check box and click **Done**, the wizard closes and you return to your desktop.

When the installation has finished, remove the CD from its drive, if you used one, and store it in a safe place. Should you ever need to reinstall the program, you will need the disk.

QUICKSTEPS

CREATING A QUICK START SHORTCUT FOR QUICKEN

Depending on the version of Windows you have (7, Vista, or XP), you can create a quick way to start Quicken without opening the Start menu or locating its icon on the desktop.

CREATE A SHORTCUT IN WINDOWS 7

In Windows 7, you want to "pin" Quicken to the taskbar at the bottom of the window.

1. Start Quicken in any way described earlier.

2. Right-click the **Quicken** icon on the taskbar, and click **Pin This Program To Taskbar**.

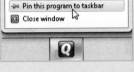

When you close Quicken, the icon will stay on the taskbar; to start it again, you only need to click the icon.

CREATE A SHORTCUT IN WINDOWS VISTA AND WINDOWS XP

In Windows Vista or Windows XP, you want to add Quicken to the Quick Launch toolbar. The Quick Launch toolbar, located just to the right of the Start button on the Windows taskbar, allows you to cover your desktop with programs you are running and still quickly access your important programs with a single click. To create a shortcut on your Quick Launch toolbar:

1. Right-click a blank area of the Windows taskbar to display the taskbar menu.

2. Click **Toolbars**, and if it is not already selected, click **Quick Launch** to activate the Quick Launch toolbar.

Continued . . .

Get Started with Quicken

As part of the installation, Quicken places a number of icons on your desktop. With them, you may be able to order a free credit report, apply for a credit card through Quicken, and get one month of Quicken Bill Pay for free. You will also have a shortcut to start the program.

Start Quicken

You can start Quicken 2012 in several different ways:

- Double-click the **Quicken** icon on the Windows desktop.
- Click the **Start** button on the Windows taskbar, click **All Programs**, click **Quicken 2012**, and then click **Quicken 2012** again.

- Click the **Quicken 2012** icon on the taskbar (Windows 7) or on the Quick Launch toolbar (Windows Vista or XP) on the Windows taskbar, as explained in the "Creating a Quick Start Shortcut for Quicken" QuickSteps.

Whatever method you use, whether you click an icon or use the Start menu, Quicken 2012 opens.

Set Up Quicken for the First Time

After starting Quicken for the first time, if you do not have a recent Quicken dataset on your computer, the Welcome To Quicken 2012 window appears

QUICKSTEPS

CREATING A QUICK START SHORTCUT FOR QUICKEN (Continued)

3. Ensure that **Lock The Taskbar** is unchecked. If the check mark appears, click **Lock The Taskbar** to clear the check mark.

4. Drag the **Quicken** icon from the desktop to the Quick Launch toolbar. A small I-beam appears along with a shadow of the Quicken icon.

5. Drag the I-beam to where you want the Quicken icon, and then release the mouse button. Your icon appears on the Quick Launch toolbar.

NOTE

While all major changes to Quicken are made on an annual basis, small changes are made throughout the year. As a result, you may see slight differences between what you see on your screen and what is shown in this book.

Add your Primary Checking Account

Enter the name of your bank

wells

MOST COMMON
Wells Fargo Bank
Wells Fargo CEO Basic Banking
Wells Federal Bank

(otherwise, your most recent Quicken data will appear). If you have never used Quicken before:

1. Accept the default, **I Am A New User**, and click **Get Started** to begin.

2. You are asked to register Quicken. Click **Register Now**, fill in your name and address and answer the questions, and click **Register**. Quicken will open with the Home tab displayed, as you see in Figure 1-1.

SET UP A BANK ACCOUNT WITH ONLINE SERVICES

Begin by setting up your main checking account.

1. From the Home tab, click **Get Started** to open the Add Your Primary Checking Account dialog box. (You may see a pop-up window that refers to updating financial institutions here.)

2. If you want Quicken to automatically set up your account, click your bank's name or enter the first few letters of its name. Otherwise, click **Advanced Setup** at the bottom of the screen, and jump to the next section "Set Up a Bank Account Manually."

3. Using the automatic setup and entering the first few letters of your bank's name, a list appears. Click your bank from the list, or if your institution is not listed, look for another spelling or alternate name. For example, you might consider your bank's name to be Maintown Bank, while it is listed as Main Town Bank.

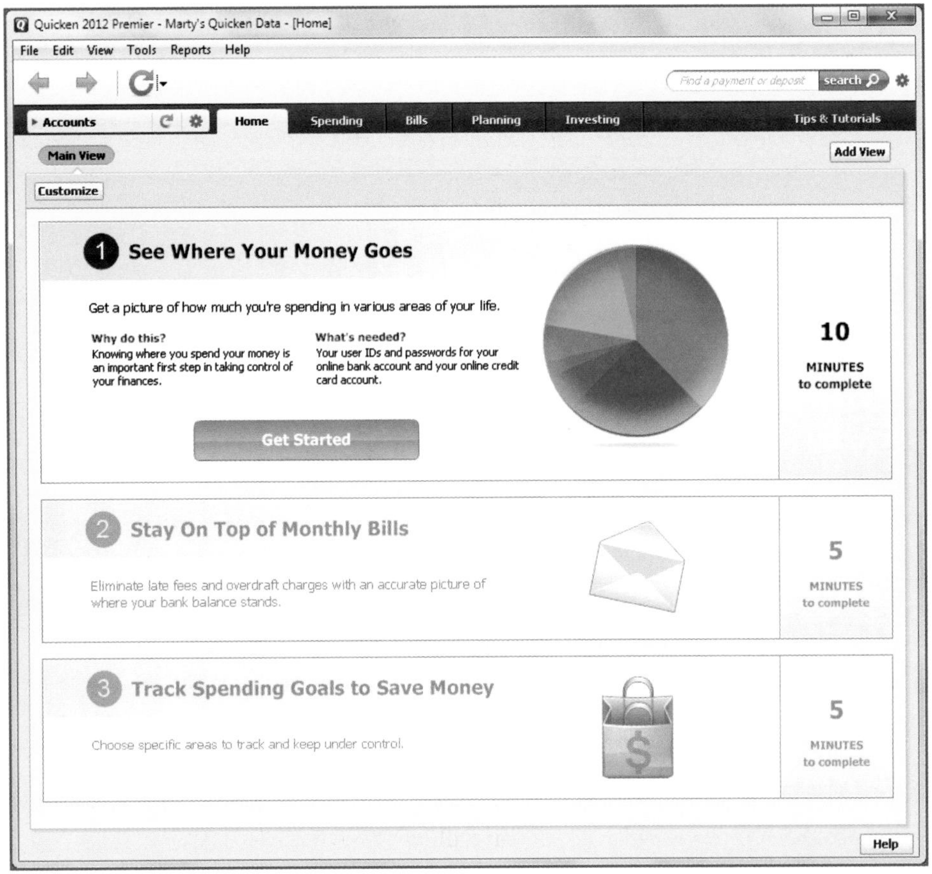

Figure 1-1: *If you have not used Quicken before, you are led through the setup of your data.*

4. If asked, select your account type and click **Next**. You are prompted to log in to your account by entering the user name or ID and password or PIN issued to you by your bank. Fill out the information that identifies you to your bank to activate the account for downloading into Quicken, and click **Connect**. Depending on your financial institution and your accounts, you may be asked for additional information here.

5. Quicken connects to your financial institution, downloads the initial information, and enters transactions into a new Quicken account. The number of transactions that are downloaded depends on your bank. Some banks will download transactions for the last 60 days, while others download up to a year's worth of transactions. After the download is complete, you are told the Quicken accounts that were added and the bank accounts and number of days of transactions in each.

6. You may add another bank or credit card account by clicking **Add Another Account**, or start using Quicken by clicking **Finish**.

SET UP A BANK ACCOUNT MANUALLY

You can set up accounts manually if you choose or if your bank does not offer online services or you do not have an Internet connection. Follow

---

NOTE

You can add more accounts at a later time by clicking the **Tools** menu and clicking **Add An Account**. Once you have completed the initial process of adding accounts using the Get Started button in the See Where Your Money Goes section, the Get Started button is removed.

NOTE

If your bank is a large institution with many branches, you may see a dialog box indicating that Quicken needs to know the correct branch.

NOTE

Quicken protects your privacy by using secure Internet technology and encryption during any online transmission.

NOTE

Some financial institutions have user names and passwords for online activity, such as online bill pay, that are different from the passwords required for web access. Ensure that you have the correct user name and password for both activities. If you are unsure, check with your financial institution.

NOTE

The Stay On Top Of Monthly Bills section will be grayed out if you have not added at least one account.

steps 1 and 2 in "Set Up a Bank Account with Online Services" earlier in this chapter. Then:

1. If your bank offers online services and you want to download transactions, keep the default to select the connection method to download transactions, enter the name of the bank, and click **Next**. Choose the connection method for your bank, and click **Next**. Enter your user ID and password, and click **Connect**.

2. If you cannot or do not wish to use online services, click **I Want To Enter My Transactions Manually**, and click **Next**. Enter the name you would like to use for this account. By default, Quicken uses the type of account

   Add Checking Account

   Enter the name you'd like to use for this account in Quicken.
   For example: "Family Checking" or "Mary's Household Account"

   Account Name/Nickname Checking

   as the account name. For example, if you are setting up your first checking account, Quicken will call the account "Checking." Click **Next**.

3. Enter the date of your last bank statement and the ending balance shown on it. Click **Next**.

4. You may add another bank or credit card account or start using Quicken. To start using Quicken, click **Finish**.

ADD RECURRING BILLS

Quicken helps you stay on top of monthly bills by allowing you to set up reminders that pop up on or before the bills are due. Quicken uses the downloaded transactions to display a set of suggested recurring bills and help you schedule your payments so you will never have another late fee. If you have not downloaded your transactions from your bank, you can still add reminders for your monthly bills.

1. From the Home tab, click **Get Started** in the Stay On Top Of Monthly Bills section to enter the bills you pay every month, as well as edit, remove, or schedule potential bills Quicken has found in downloaded transactions, as you see in Figure 1-2.

2. Review the list of suggested recurring transactions and, for those you don't want to be reminded about or automatically entered in your register, click **Remove**. For the bills you want to change in some way, click **Edit**, make any desired changes to the name of the payee, and use the following instructions for adding a new bill beginning with step 4.

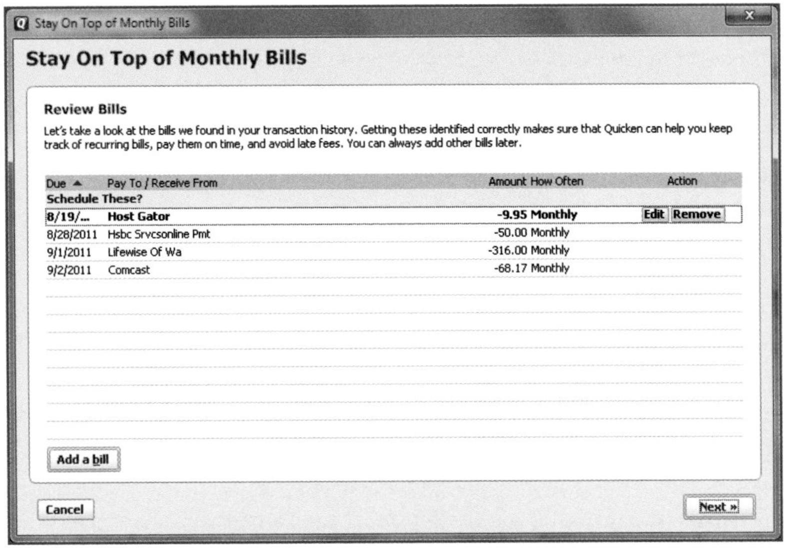

Stay On Top of Monthly Bills

Review Bills

Let's take a look at the bills we found in your transaction history. Getting these identified correctly makes sure that Quicken can help you keep track of recurring bills, pay them on time, and avoid late fees. You can always add other bills later.

Due ▲	Pay To / Receive From	Amount How Often	Action
Schedule These?			
8/19/...	Host Gator	-9.95 Monthly	Edit Remove
8/28/2011	Hsbc Srvcsonline Pmt	-50.00 Monthly	
9/1/2011	Lifewise Of Wa	-316.00 Monthly	
9/2/2011	Comcast	-68.17 Monthly	

Add a bill

Cancel

Next »

Figure 1-2: Quicken will look at your downloaded transactions and suggest recurring ones that you may want to be reminded about.

TIP

Categories are organizational tools to group similar information. For example, all payments to the phone company could be put into the Telephone category. Quicken supplies a number of categories with the program, but you can add new ones or delete those you don't want to use. Categories are handy for preparing taxes, budgeting, and analyzing where you are spending and receiving money. Categories are discussed in depth in Chapter 2.

NOTE

Once you open Optional Settings it will remain open in future bill reminders until you close it and then it will be closed in the next bill reminder you open.

3. To add recurring bills, click **Add A Bill** to display the Add Bill Reminder dialog. Type the name the bill is to be paid to, and click **Next**.

4. Enter the next due date and amount, select the account from which to pay the bill, and click **Add Category, Tag, Or Memo**. Click the down arrow and select a category; add a memo you want to appear on your check, if you used one, such as your account number, or other note about the payment; and click **OK**.

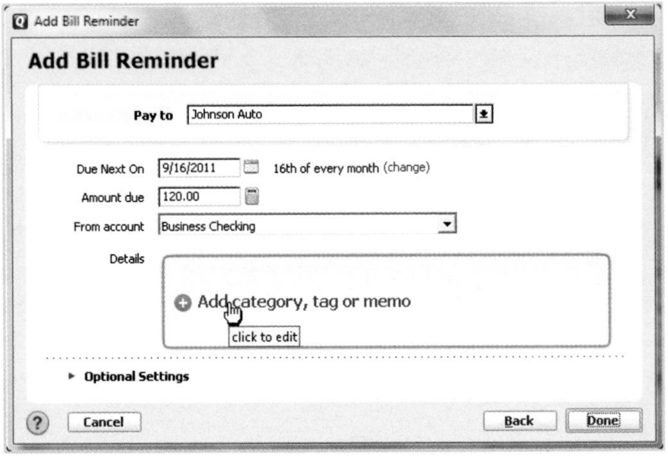

Add Bill Reminder

Pay to: Johnson Auto

Due Next On: 9/16/2011   16th of every month (change)

Amount due: 120.00

From account: Business Checking

Details

⊕ Add category, tag or memo
click to edit

▶ Optional Settings

Cancel   Back   Done

5. Click **Optional Settings**:

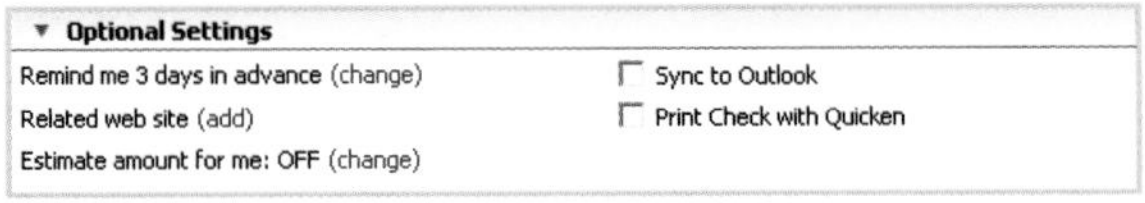

▼ Optional Settings	
Remind me 3 days in advance (change)	☐ Sync to Outlook
Related web site (add)	☐ Print Check with Quicken
Estimate amount for me: OFF (change)	

a. If you want Quicken to remind you of the bill other than three days in advance, click **Change** opposite that question and either enter the number of days in advance you want in the Remind Me field or use the spinner to select a number. Alternatively, you can automatically enter the transaction in the register a number of days in advance if it is automatically taken from your account, and you can choose to count only business days. Click **OK** when you are finished.

Quicken can help you estimate variable payments.

| $150.00 No estimate | ⊛ | Fixed amount ▾ | 150.00 |

Fixed amount
Previous payments
Time of year

OK   Cancel

---

b. If you want to go to an organization's website to pay a bill on a recurring basis, click **Add** opposite Related Web Site, enter the website's address (URL), and click **OK**.

c. If you want Quicken to estimate an amount for a payment that varies, click **Change** opposite Estimate Amount For Me. In the dialog box that opens click the down arrow in the middle drop-down list and choose from among the following:

- **Previous Payments** if you want Quicken to enter an amount based on what you've paid the last few times. You can change the number of payments from which Quicken estimates by using the spinner or entering a number.

- **Time Of Year** if this is a seasonal payment and you want Quicken to find the amount based on periodic payments in the last year.

d. Click **OK** when you have completed estimating a variable payment.

e. Click **Sync To Outlook** if you want this bill to appear in your Outlook calendar.

f. Click **Print Check With Quicken** if you want to do that with this bill.

6. Click **Done** when you have completed entering all the information you want for a bill reminder.

7. Click **Next** in the Stay On Top Of Monthly Bills dialog box to display the Review Income dialog box and continue in the next section.

ADD RECURRING INCOME

The Review Income dialog box displays the income that was downloaded with your transactions. If you chose not to download or didn't have any income, you can enter your paycheck or other income information now.

1. Review the income information that was downloaded. Click **Remove** to delete those you don't want to be reminded about or have automatically entered in your register. Click **Edit** opposite those you want to change, and follow the instructions beginning with step 3.

2. To add a new source of income, click **Add Other Income**. The Add Income Reminder dialog box will open. Type the name of the organization from which you get the income, and click **Next**. The full Add Income Reminder dialog box will appear.

3. Type the date you next expect the income (usually your next pay date) in the **Due Next On** field. You may also click the small calendar icon to the right of

---

NOTE

Until some payments have been made, Quicken cannot create an accurate Estimate From Last *n* Payments figure and Quicken will give you a message to that effect.

CAUTION

Some window envelopes allow memo information to be seen. If you mail checks in window envelopes, it is better not to put your account number in the memo line to ensure your privacy.

Add Income Reminder

Add Income Reminder

From   Martin Engineering

Due Next On 10/15/2011   Twice per month on the 15th and 30th (change)
Amount due 0.00
To account Business Checking ▾
Details

  ⊕ **Add category, tag or memo**

▼ **Optional Settings**

Remind me 3 days in advance (change)   ☐ Sync to Outlook
Related web site (add)
Estimate amount for me: OFF (change)

⑦ Cancel   To track your payroll taxes and deductions, use the Paycheck Setup wizard.   Back   Done

TIP

You can also track payroll taxes and deductions from paychecks in Quicken using the Paycheck Setup Wizard, as you will see in Chapter 3.

the field and choose a date. If it is not that date every month or is on a period other than monthly, click **Change** to open the pay date dialog box.

Martin Engineering

Start date: 3/15/2011

How often: Monthly   Every 1   month on the   15th   Day

End date: No end date

OK   Cancel

4. Click the **How Often** down arrow, select the period, and then select the period modifiers as needed. Change the End Date field if appropriate, and click **OK**.

5. Type the amount of income you receive. If you do not receive the same amount each time, enter an average, which you can adjust as needed.

6. Click the **To Account** down arrow to see the list of your Quicken accounts, and select the one into which this income is to be deposited.

7. Click **Add Category, Tag, Or Memo**. Click the **Category** down arrow, click **Personal Income**, and click the income category you want to use. Type a tag if desired, and type any additional information in the memo field, for example, if you receive two checks, one for base pay and one for commissions. Click OK to close the Category, Tag, And Memo dialog box.

8. Click **Optional Settings**:

   a. If you want Quicken to remind you of the income other than three days in advance, click **Change** opposite that question and either enter the number of days in advance you want in the Remind Me field or use the spinner to select a number. Alternatively, you can automatically enter the transaction in the register a number of days in advance if it is automatically deposited to your account, and you can choose to count only business days. Click **OK** when you are finished.

   b. If you want to go to the paying organization's website on a recurring basis, click **Add** opposite Related Web Site, enter the website's address, and click **OK**.

   c. If you want Quicken to estimate an amount for income that varies, click **Change** opposite Estimate Amount For Me. In the dialog box that opens click the down arrow in the middle drop-down list and choose from among the following:

   - **Previous Payments** if you want Quicken to enter an amount based on what you've been paid the last few times. You can change the number of payments from which Quicken estimates by using the spinner or entering a number.

   - **Time Of Year** if this is a seasonal payment and you want Quicken to find the amount based on periodic payments in the last year.

d. Click **OK** when you have completed estimating a variable payment.

e. Click **Sync To Outlook** if you want this income to appear in your Outlook calendar.

9. Click **Done** when you have completed entering all the information you want for an income reminder.

SET GOALS

Quicken can help you track goals for spending and saving money, starting out with budgeting.

1. Click **Get Started** in the Track Spending Goals To Save Money section. The Budget section opens. Click **Get Started** again.

2. Type a name for your budget. Accept Automatic Budget, where Quicken builds a budget based on your transactions, and click **OK**. The Planning tab will open and show you your budget for the current month, as shown in Figure 1-3.

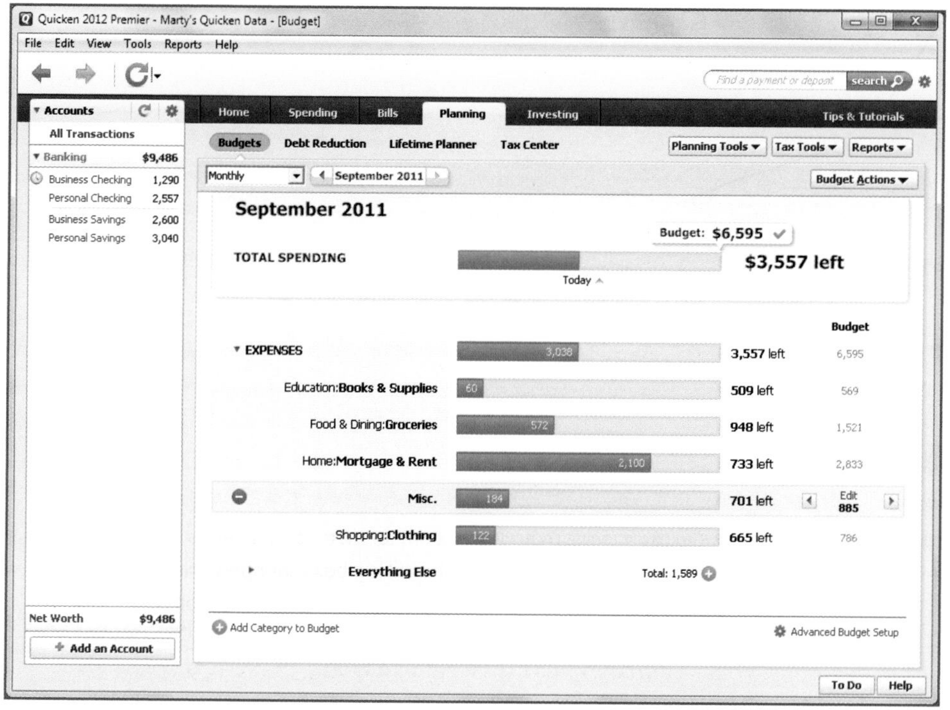

3. To add categories, click **Add Category** in the lower-left corner to open the Add A Budget Category dialog box.  🟢 Add category

4. Click the down arrow, and select a category to budget. Click **Next**. Type an amount you plan on spending in that category. If not monthly, click the down arrow and select a frequency. Click **Done**. Repeat this for as many categories as you want to add.

5. Click the **Home** tab to return to the Main View window.

Understand the Home Tab

The Quicken Home tab's Main View provides a summary of all the information you have entered into Quicken. Figure 1-4 shows the default display of the Home page. You

Figure 1-3: *Quicken can help you set goals that make budgeting easy.*

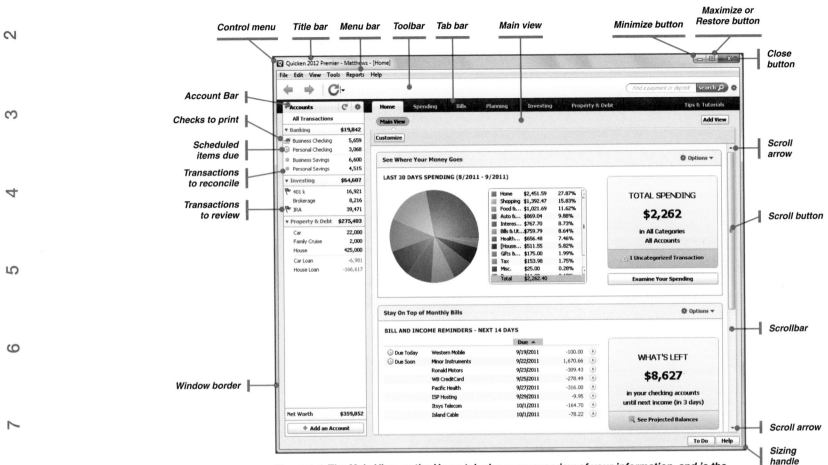

Figure 1-4: The Main View on the Home tab shows an overview of your information, and is the starting place when you first open Quicken.

will learn how to customize it in Chapter 2. The Quicken Home page has two major sections: the Account Bar on the left that shows the summary of your accounts, and the Main View on the right. In the Main View pane, you determine what information is displayed. By default, the view displays the spending, bills, and budgeting information that you entered when you began using Quicken. You can change the items that appear in this section of the window and add account registers, transaction lists, and several other items. You will learn how to customize and create additional views in Chapter 2. Around these panes are a number of objects that are common to other Windows programs and include the following:

- The **Control menu** allows you to move, size, and close the window.
- The **title bar** contains the name of the program or folder in the window and is used to drag the window around the screen.
- The **menu bar** contains the menus that are available in the window. Click a menu to open it, and then click one of its options.
- The **Minimize button** decreases the size of the window so that you see it only as a task on the taskbar.
- The **Maximize button** increases the size of the window so that it fills the screen. When the window is maximized, the Maximize button becomes a Restore button to return the window to the size it was before being maximized.
- The **Close button** closes the window and any program it contains.
- The **scroll arrow** moves what is viewed in the window by one line in the direction of the arrow.
- The **scrollbar** moves what is viewed in the window by the height of the window in the direction of the arrow.
- The **scroll button** moves what is viewed in the window by the amount dragged in the direction of the arrow.
- The **sizing handle** allows you to size a window diagonally by increasing or decreasing its height and width.
- The **window border** separates the window from the desktop and other windows, and can be used to size the window horizontally or vertically by dragging either the vertical or horizontal border.

Add Accounts Manually

Quicken 2012 separates your accounts into three specific centers on the Accounts bar: Banking, Investing, and Property, as shown on the Account Bar at the left

Add Account

Primary Accounts (for managing your finances)

Spending
- ⦿ Checking
- ○ Savings
- ○ Credit Card
- ○ Cash

Investing
- ○ Brokerage
- ○ IRA or Keogh Plan
- ○ 401(k) or 403(b)
- ○ 529 Plan

Property & Debt (for net worth tracking)

Property
- ○ House
- ○ Vehicle
- ○ Other asset

Debt
- ○ Loan
- ○ Other liability (not a credit card)

(?) [Cancel]   [Next]

TIP

For more info about the connection methods, such as where your login data is stored for each connection type, click the **Learn More About How Quicken Connects To Your Bank** link in the lower-left corner of the dialog box.

NOTE

Depending on your financial institution, you may only be able to download the last 60 or 90 days' worth of transactions. If that is true, you will need to enter the balance at the beginning of that time period.

---

of the Home tab in Figure 1-4. If you chose not to enter accounts as part of the See Where Your Money Goes section, you can still add new accounts.

1. Click **Add An Account** at the bottom of the Quicken Account Bar.   **+ Add an Account**

2. The Add Account dialog box appears. Select an account type from the list, and click **Next**. The most common accounts are checking, savings, credit card, and cash accounts. These accounts appear in the Banking Center on the Account Bar.

3. Select one of the banks listed, or type the name of the bank where this account is held, or click **Advanced Setup** if you choose to manually set up an account at this time.

4. If you selected or entered your bank, your bank offers download services, you have your user name or ID and password or PIN from that bank, and you wish to download your transactions, go to the "Set Up a Bank Account with Online Services" section earlier in this chapter.

5. If you clicked Advance Setup, choose whether you want to select your connection method, in which case type the name of the financial institution and click **Next**, or choose to enter your transactions manually and click **Next**.

6. If you want to select a connection method and Quicken can't find the bank you entered, you will be shown a list of banks to choose from. Otherwise, you can keep the bank name you chose, but you won't be able to automatically download your transaction. Click **Next**. Skip to step 8.

7. If you want to select a connection with a bank Quicken recognizes, select one of the connection methods shown and click **Next**. Skip to step 10.

8. Fill in the **Account Name/Nickname** fields, and click **Next**. Type or select the statement ending date, type the ending balance, and click **Next**.

9. If you choose a manual downloading method, Quicken will give you some steps to get started. Review them, use any links that might help you, click **Finish**, and skip to step 12.

10. If you choose an automated downloading method, enter your user ID and password or PIN, and click **Connect**. The connection is verified and depending on the type of connection, Quicken either will automatically download all your accounts or will display the accounts found at your

Accounts Added

Wells Fargo Bank
WEB: www.wellsfargo.com | TEL: 1-800-956-4442

✓ BUSINESS CHECKING
Downloaded and categorized 88 days of transactions.

✓ BUSINESS MARKET RATE SAVINGS
Downloaded and categorized 68 days of transactions.

✓ CUSTOM MANAGEMENT(RM)
Downloaded and categorized 90 days of transactions.

✓ SAVINGS
Downloaded and categorized 88 days of transactions.

Add another account | Finish

Investing
○ Brokerage
○ IRA or Keogh Plan
○ 401(k) or 403(b)
○ 529 Plan

bank and ask you which you want to download. For each account that you want to download, leave the default **Add** selected if it is a new account to Quicken, click **Link** if it is an account that already exists in Quicken and choose the existing name from the drop-down list, or click **Ignore** if you don't want to download that account. Click **Next**.

11. If you have said you want to download transactions, a connection will be made with your bank and transactions will be downloaded to Quicken. At the Account Added dialog box, note the account names, the number of transactions that were downloaded, and any warnings that might appear. Click **Finish**.

12. From the Account Bar, click the account into which you just downloaded to open the register. Review each of the transactions. You may need to add new categories or change the payee name. Each financial institution has a slightly different format for downloaded transactions. See Chapter 2 for more information about online banking.

ADD INVESTMENT ACCOUNTS

To enter an investing account:

1. Click **Add An Account** at the bottom of the Account Bar. In the Add Account dialog box, choose one of the categories under Investing, and click **Next**.

2. Select or type the name of the financial institution, or click **Advanced Setup**.

3. If you entered a financial institution that provides downloading services, type the user name or ID and password or PIN, and click **Connect**. The account(s) will be displayed. Either click **Add Another Account** or click **Finish** and skip to the next section.

4. If you clicked Advanced Setup, choose whether to download transactions or to do so manually. If you choose to download transactions, type the name of the institution, click **Next**, and go back to step 3.

5. If you clicked Advanced Setup and chose to enter transactions manually, click **Next**. Enter an account name or nickname for this investment account, and click **Next**. Depending on the type of investment account you chose, you may be asked if this is a tax-deferred account or if you wish to track loans against this account. If so, answer **Yes** to the questions, and click **Next**.

6. Enter the date of the last paper statement you received, or, if you are entering information from a brokerage website, the date the information was posted to the website. Enter the cash in the account and then the amount in a money market or sweep account, and click **Next**.

Quicken Account Setup

What securities are in this account?

Enter a ticker symbol for each security in your account.

- If your computer is connected to the Internet, Quicken uses the ticker symbol to download security details for you. If you don't know the ticker symbol, click Ticker Symbol Lookup.
- If you are not connected to the Internet, just enter a security name. You can add more details later.

	Ticker*	Security Name (optional)
1.	F	Ford
2.	AAPL	Apple
3.	Cat	Caterpiller
4.	IBM	IBM
5.		

[Ticker Symbol Lookup] [Add More...]

*Required for downloading security details. Do not include bonds--add bond purchases later (in the transaction list, click Enter Transactions.)

[?] [Cancel]   [Next]

7. Enter the ticker symbol for securities (if any) in this account. Click **Next** and enter the number of shares you own of each security; choose whether the security is a stock, a mutual fund, or other; and click **Next**. (You will have a chance to enter your cost information later in the process.)

8. The information you entered is displayed in a Summary window. Click **Done** to close the Summary window.

9. If you are entering an IRA or Keogh, select the owner and type of IRA, and click **Next**. Review the suggestions in the Account Added dialog box, and then click **Finish**. The account is displayed in the Investing tab and also shown on the Account Bar.

Quicken Account Setup

Summary

IRA-c holdings as of 7/29/2011

Ticker	Security Name	Total Shares	Security Type
F	Ford	100	Stock
AAPL	Apple	20	Stock
CAT	Caterpiller	50	Stock
IBM	IBM	30	Stock

	Cash Balance:	6,250.00

For complete performance and tax tracking, be sure to enter complete transaction history or cost basis information for each security. Click Done, and then click the Transactions tab for this account.

[?] [Cancel]   [Back]   [Done]

You can read more about investment accounts in Chapter 8.

ADD PROPERTY & DEBT ACCOUNTS

You use accounts in the Property & Debt tab to give Quicken information about your house, your car, or other major assets. (An asset is something you own that has significant value, like a rare painting or a stamp collection.)

1. Click **Add An Account** at the bottom of the Account Bar. In the Add Account dialog box, click the type of asset or liability you want to add. If you are adding your house, click that and click **Next**.

Property & Debt (for net worth tracking)	
Property	**Debt**
○ House	○ Loan
○ Vehicle	○ Other liability (not a credit card)
○ Other asset	

TIP

If you pay most of your bills with a check rather than paying them online, consider using checks you can print on your printer. You can order these checks directly from Quicken or from a number of other check printers you can easily find on the Internet.

QUICKSTEPS

USING THE TICKER SYMBOL LOOKUP

When setting up your investment accounts, you may not know the ticker symbol for a particular security. You can use Ticker Symbol Lookup if you have an Internet connection. From the What Securities Are In This Account? dialog box:

1. Click **Ticker Symbol Lookup**. You are connected to the Internet, and the Quicken Symbol Lookup window will open.

Quicken
INVESTING

Close ✕

Symbol Lookup

Not finding the company or fund you're looking for on Quicken Investing? Start by typing part or all of the company or fund name in this form to begin your search. Stocks, Mutual Funds, ETFs, and Indices matching your query will appear in the table below. From there, simply select the result of your choice.

Amazon   **Search**

Stocks (4)	Mutual Funds (0)	ETFs (0)	Indices (1)		
Symbol	Company Name		Exchange	Country	
AMZO	Amazon Biotech Inc		OTC	US	
AMZN	Amazon.com Inc		NASDAQ	US	
AMZN.DG	Amazon.com Inc		Direct Edge Holdings - EDGX - Global Select Marke	US	
AMZN.DY	Amazon.com Inc		Direct Edge Holdings - EDGA - Global Select Marke	US	

Continued . . .

2. Type an account name and, if asked, indicate if it is used for personal or business transactions.

3. Click **Next** and enter the date you acquired the asset, its purchase price, and an approximate current value, as well as any other needed information. You can enter approximate values and change them later.

4. Click **Next**. Quicken asks if there is a mortgage or loan on this asset. If so, tell Quicken how you'd like to track the information. If you do not want to track the mortgage or loan, choose that option and click **Next**.

5. If you choose to track the mortgage or loan, Quicken prompts you to set up the liability account and leads you through the steps. Chapter 6 has more detailed information about property and debt accounts. When you have entered all the necessary information for the mortgage or loan, click **Done** to open the Edit Loan Payment dialog box. Enter the loan payee, and click **OK** to return to the Account Added dialog box.

Q Loan Setup ☐ ✕

Balloon Information
- ⦿ No Balloon Payment
- ○ Amortized Length: [ ] Years ▾
- ○ Calculate

Current Balance
- ⦿ Current Balance: 68,000.00   as of: 8/8/2011
- ○ Calculate

Payment
- ○ Payment Amount (P+I): 365.04   due on: 8/9/2011
- ⦿ Calculate   Interest Rate: 5.0%

(?) **Cancel**   **Back**   **Done**

6. Click **Finish** to return to the Home page.

**USING THE TICKER
SYMBOL LOOKUP** *(Continued)*

2. Type either the full name or part of the security name.

3. Click **Search**. A list of choices will appear, with what Quicken considers to be the best match shown at the top of the list.

4. Drag across the symbol for your security to select it. Press **CTRL+C** (based on Quicken's default shortcut preferences) to copy the symbol. You can also right-click to display a menu. Click **Copy** from the menu.

5. Close the Quicken Symbol Lookup window and return to Quicken. Click the **Ticker** field, right-click, and click **Paste** (or press **CTRL+V** based on default preferences) to copy the information into the Ticker field.

NOTE

The Help button at the lower-right corner of the Quicken screen does not open Quicken Help; it opens a search pane for the Quicken Live Community.

Find Help

The Quicken Help window, shown in Figure 1-5, provides a ready reference to answer your questions about Quicken and show you how to accomplish tasks. At any point in the program, pressing the **F1** key brings up the Help window with information about the current Quicken window. You also can click the **Help** menu and click **Quicken Help** to open the Help window for a broad range of information about Quicken.

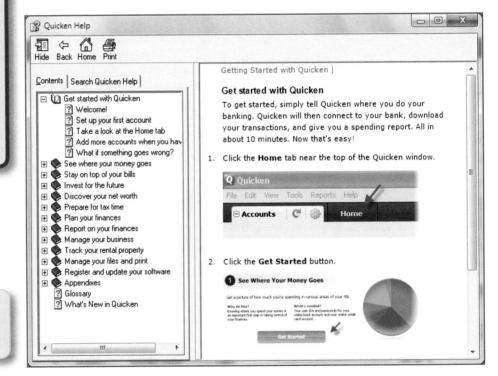

Figure 1-5: Quicken Help gives answers to many of your Quicken questions.

QUICKSTEPS

USING THE ADDRESS BOOK

You can use the Quicken Address Book to keep track of addresses for your payees, contact information, secondary address information (such as physical addresses), personal information (including the name of the payee's spouse and/or children), and up to three other types of miscellaneous information.

1. To access the Address Book, click **Tools** on the menu bar, and then click **Address Book**.

2. Click **New**. The Edit Address Book Record dialog box will appear. You see this same dialog box when you click the Address button when entering a bill reminder.

3. Enter the payee's name in the relevant field.

4. Press **TAB** to move to the Street field, enter the information, and continue through the fields using the **TAB** key.

5. Click the **Contact** tab to enter information about the person to contact, his or her work phone, work fax, website, and other contact information.

6. Click **OK** when you have entered all of the information you want to record, and click **Done** to close the Address Book.

Edit Address Book Record

Payee:	Edward Bloom
Street:	254 Old Saw Rd
City:	Ferryville
State:	WA
Zip Code:	98456
Country:	
Attn Line:	
E-mail:	

Include this Payee in
☐ QuickFill List ☐ Customer List ☑ Vendor List

Groups: <Vendors>

Group... | Format... | OK | Cancel

USE HELP

The Help window gives you two ways to find information:

- The **Contents** tab in the left pane of the Help window allows you to open a topic by clicking the plus sign on its left, open subtopics in the same way, and eventually click and view an article with the information you want.

- The **Search Quicken Help** tab allows you to enter a word or phrase in the text box at the top of the left pane and be given a list of articles, which you can click to display and read in the right pane.

USE OTHER HELP RESOURCES

The Help menu in the primary Quicken window provides a number of other resources to assist you, which you can access by clicking one of the following options:

Help
Getting Started Guide
Quicken Help   F1
Quicken Live Community
Quicken Support
Submit Feedback on Quicken
Join the Quicken Inner Circle
Privacy Statement
Log Files
About Quicken
Unlock Again...
Add Business Tools
Add Rental Property Tools...

- **Getting Started Guide** Provides a tour of Quicken and a review of many of the basic tasks you need to perform to start using Quicken.

- **Quicken Live Community** Connects to an online forum where Quicken users can exchange ideas, get answers to their questions, and participate in discussions.

- **Quicken Support** This opens the support page on the Quicken website.

- **Submit Feedback On Quicken** Allows you to give Intuit feedback on Quicken. It is through feedback from users such as you that Quicken improves its products. Your input is important, and Quicken encourages you to contact them.

QUICKSTEPS

IMPORTING FROM MICROSOFT MONEY

In June 2009, Microsoft announced that their financial software product, Microsoft Money, was being discontinued. If you are a former Microsoft Money user and are new to Quicken, you can quickly import transactions into Quicken (Microsoft Money 2007 or 2008 must be installed on your computer).

1. Back up your Microsoft Money file. After the backup, check the last few transactions in your checking account to ensure the file is up to date. Make a note of these transactions.

2. Create a new Quicken file. Do not enter any transactions.

3. Click **File** on the menu bar, and choose **File Import**.

> Web Connect File...
> QIF File...
> Quicken Transfer Format (.QXF) File...
> Import security prices from CSV file...
> TurboTax File...
> Microsoft Money® file...

4. Click **Microsoft Money File**. Browse to locate your .mny file in the Import From Microsoft Money File dialog box.

5. Select the file you want to import. Click **Open** and the transactions will be imported into your Quicken file.

6. Verify that your transactions have been imported by opening your checking account in Quicken and checking the last few transactions. They should be the same transactions you noted in step 1.

7. That's all there is to it. Welcome to Quicken!

- **Join The Quicken Inner Circle** The "Inner Circle" is a group of both new and veteran Quicken users who are willing to work with Intuit to ensure that Quicken stays viable in today's marketplace.
- **Privacy Statement** This tells you how Quicken protects your personal information.
- **Log Files** Provides links to log files that may be requested by Quicken Support for troubleshooting purposes.
- **About Quicken** Shows you which version of Quicken you are using should you need to contact customer support.
- **Add Business Tools** and **Add Rental Property Tools** These options provide a fast way to upgrade your edition over the Internet.

Exit Quicken

When you have completed a Quicken session, you should exit the program. You will usually be encouraged to back up your work before you close it.

That is always a good idea. Hard drive crashes, power outages, and computer malfunctions happen to all of us at one time or another. Backing up your files is discussed in more detail in Chapter 2.

You can exit Quicken in several ways:

- Click the **Close** button on the right side of the title bar.
- Click **File** on the menu bar, and then click **Exit**.
- Hold down your **ALT** key and press the **F4** key.

The Quicken Backup dialog box will appear and ask if you want to back up your Quicken data file. If you do, click **Backup** and see Chapter 2. Otherwise, click **Exit**.

Use Quicken and Windows Basics

If you are new to Quicken, take a few minutes to read this section. It discusses terms used with Quicken, as well as some that are used with all Windows-based programs. The dialog boxes and windows make more sense when you understand their contents.

Recognize Quicken Terms

Quicken is meant to be intuitive. You do most tasks with one or two clicks, and the design of each window is intended to be easy to use and understand. The terms defined here are used throughout Quicken and this book:

- **Accounts** in Quicken represent the separate checking, savings, credit card, and brokerage accounts you have, as well as your mortgage and car loans, as you can see in Figure 1-4. Quicken considers each of these an account. The information about all of the accounts of any type that relate to you is kept within one Quicken data file. In Table 1-1, you can see the different account types used by Quicken, the location in which Quicken stores them, and some examples of each account type. There are standard accounts within each account type.

- **Data files** (or just "files") are how Quicken stores the information about your financial records. Just as a word-processing document is stored as a document file in a folder on your hard disk, Quicken stores your data file in a folder on your hard disk. A data file contains information about all of your accounts, assets, liabilities, financial goals, and tax plans. Each family's or person's information is stored in a separate file. For example, if you are taking care of Aunt Harriet's financial matters, it is a good idea to store her information in a file separate from your personal data file. You can do that by clicking the **File** menu and clicking **New Quicken File** and naming it "Aunt Harriet," or something like that.

ACCOUNT TYPE/LOCATION	EXAMPLES
Banking Accounts	These accounts track your checking, savings, and credit card accounts. You can even set up cash accounts for each member of your family to track allowances for the kids or cash kept in a cookie jar.
Investment Accounts	These track your investments. You can track your individual brokerage accounts, your individual retirement accounts (IRAs), your mutual funds, or any other investment. If you have Quicken 2012 Deluxe, Premier, Business, or Rental Property edition, you can keep track of your 401(k) or 403(b) plans offered by your employer.
Property & Debt Accounts	Here is where you keep track of your home mortgage and any other mortgages, your car and any loans on it, or any other property you own. You can track loans owed to you or by you. You can even record the value of your stamp collection or your son's baseball card collection. Assets and liability accounts are shown in the Property & Debt tab.

Table 1-1: Types of Accounts in Quicken

- **Folders** are similar to the manila folders you store in a filing cabinet. Data files for your documents, spreadsheets, and Quicken files are stored in folders. Compare your hard drive to the filing cabinet in which you store paper files in folders to see the relationship with digital files and folders.

- **Registers** are similar to the paper check register used with a checking account, and show the checks you write and the deposits you make. Each noninvestment account in Quicken has its own register, and investment accounts have transaction lists, which are the equivalent. Clicking the account in the Account List opens its register or transaction list. The menu items accessed from the Account button on the top-right corner of the register let you locate and delete transactions, write checks, and reconcile the account to a statement.

- **Transactions** are the checks you write, the payments you make, and all of the other individual financial events in your life. Quicken stores each event in either an account register or on an investment account transaction list.

- **Transaction lists** are used with investment accounts, such as a brokerage account or a 401(k) account, in place of a register. Quicken designed these lists to look like a brokerage statement, showing every transaction that has taken place.

- **Categories** are used to group similar transactions. Every time you enter a transaction into a Quicken register, you have the option of assigning it to a category. Categories help you understand where you are spending your money and prepare for income taxes.

- **Windows** are used to display related information on the screen. In addition to the basic Quicken window shown previously, there are several other types of windows used by Quicken to display various types of information:

  - An **Internet window** uses the built-in Quicken web browser to display a Quicken webpage.

  - **List windows** display information about related items, such as tags or categories.

  - **Report windows** let you create customized reports from your accounts and organize the data in a way you can more easily understand.

- **Menus** and the **menu bar** are the tools Quicken and many other Windows-based programs use to give you access to the commands and features within the program. Click a menu name in the menu bar to open the menu, and then click one of the options in the menu to select it. Some menu options have a right-pointing arrow to the right of the option. When you move the mouse pointer over that type of option, a submenu, or flyout menu, will open. When you right-click some objects within a window or dialog box, a context menu will open. Context menus show options specific to the item clicked.

NOTE

By default, Quicken uses the Windows shortcuts. You can tell Quicken to use Quicken Alternative shortcuts in the Setup section of Quicken Preferences.

- **Toolbars** are rows of buttons, frequently directly below the menu bar. Click a button to perform its task, open a window, or display a dialog box. While the Quicken Toolbar displays by default, you can choose to turn it off. Click the **View** menu and click **Show Toolbar** to turn off your Quicken Toolbar or to turn it back on.

- **Keyboard shortcuts** allow you to perform tasks from the keyboard rather than use the mouse and menus or toolbars. Table 1-2 lists the more frequently used keyboard shortcuts. If the shortcut is **CTRL+P**, for example, you are to hold down the **CTRL** key while pressing the **P** key on the keyboard. Then let go of both keys.

ACTION (WINDOWS/QUICKEN ALTERNATIVE)	KEYBOARD SHORTCUT
Copy to the Clipboard/Open the Category List	CTRL+C
Paste from the Clipboard/Void a transaction	CTRL+V
Print	CTRL+P
Open the Account List	CTRL+A
Create a backup file	CTRL+B
Open the Split Transaction dialog box	CTRL+S
Delete a transaction or a line in a split transaction	CTRL+D
Help	F1
Go to the next field or column	TAB

Table 1-2: *Keyboard Shortcuts in Quicken*

Use Windows Tools

Quicken 2012 has a familiar feel if you are used to working with other Windows-based programs. For example, the Minimize, Maximize, and Close buttons appear in the title bar on the upper-right corner of every window.

As with all Windows programs, if you have more than one window (or program) open at the same time, the *active window* is the one with the brightest title bar.

- **Windows** are areas of the screen in which you can see a program that is running and they provide primary control of that program. When Quicken starts, it opens in its own window. Windows generally have menus and can be sized.

QUICKSTEPS

FINDING MORE KEYBOARD SHORTCUTS

To see additional keyboard shortcuts:

1. Click the **Help** menu, and then click **Quicken Help**.

2. Click the **Search Quicken Help** tab, type keyboard shortcuts, and then click **Seek**.

3. Click **Tell Me About Keyboard Shortcuts** in the Selected Topic list to see the upper part of the list of shortcuts shown in Figure 1-6.

4. Click the scroll bar on the right side of the window to see the remainder of the shortcuts list.

5. When you are done, click Close in the title bar to close the Quicken Personal Finance Help window.

● **Dialog boxes** are used by Quicken and other Windows programs to communicate with you, the user, and for you to communicate with the program. They can be message boxes that require no action other than clicking OK, or smaller areas of the screen with check boxes, options, drop-down lists, text boxes, and other controls that let you add information and control what is happening in a program, as you can see in Figure 1-7.

The primary parts of dialog boxes are as follows:

● The **title bar** contains the name of the dialog box, and is used to drag the box around the desktop.

● A **drop-down list box** opens a list from which you can choose one item that will be displayed when the list is closed.

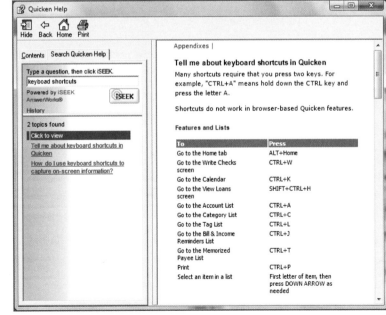

Figure 1-6: Keyboard shortcuts help you get around Quicken without removing your hands from the keyboard.

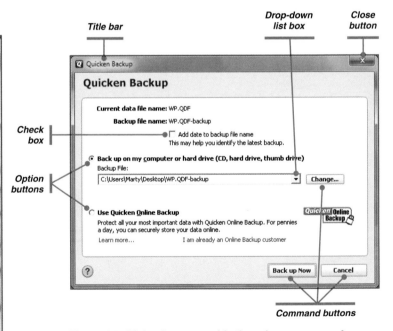

Figure 1-7: Dialog boxes provide the primary means of controlling what is happening in a program.

- A **list box** (not shown) lets you select one or more items from a list; it may include a scroll bar.

- A **check box** lets you turn features on or off.

- A **text box** (not shown) lets you enter and edit text.

- **Command buttons** perform functions such as closing the dialog box and accepting the changes (the OK button) or closing the dialog box and ignoring the changes (the Cancel button).

- **Tabs** (not shown) let you select from among several pages in a dialog box.

- **Option buttons**, also called *radio buttons,* let you select one among mutually exclusive options.

- A **spinner** (not shown) lets you select from a sequential series of numbers.

- A **slider** (not shown) lets you select from several values.

How to...

Chapter 2
Personalizing Quicken

In Chapter 1 you saw how to install Quicken and how to establish your initial accounts. When you were finished, however, the look and feel of Quicken is the default style built into the product. For many people, this is fine, and their whole experience with Quicken is with the default style. However, Quicken provides a number of ways that you can customize it—both in how it looks and how it operates—allowing you to tailor the program to meet your specific needs. Quicken most likely will become an important program that you use often. As a result, it should reflect what you want. In this chapter you will see how to customize the Home tab so that it reflects you, how to add and change accounts, how to set up online banking, and how to add and delete categories so that they provide the level of organization you want for your finances.

Customize the Home Page

After you have completed Quicken's installation, the default Quicken Home page is displayed, as shown in Figure 2-1. You can customize the Home page by modifying the Main View, showing or hiding the Quicken toolbar, changing the location of the Account Bar, creating additional views, and setting your preferences for the way various elements on the page are used.

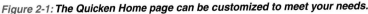

Figure 2-1: *The Quicken Home page can be customized to meet your needs.*

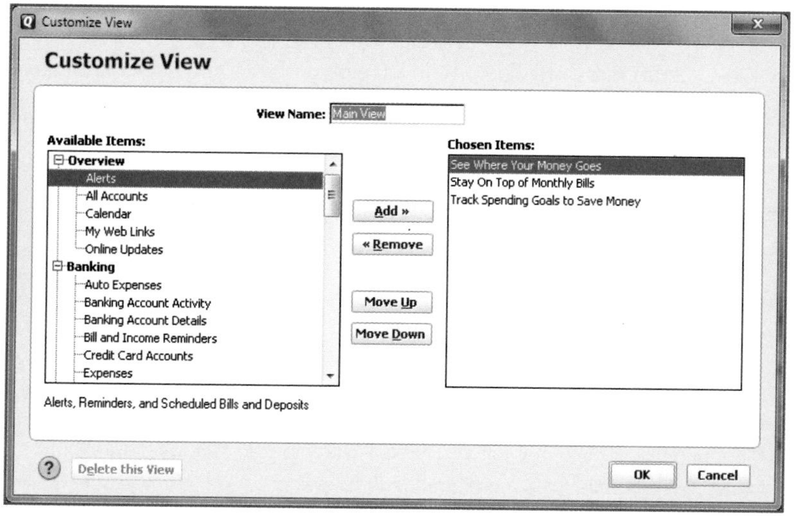

Customize View

Figure 2-2: *The Customize View dialog box allows you to personalize your Quicken Home page.*

NOTE

By default, the Available Items list displays only a few commands. Use the scroll bar to display the more than 40 available items.

Modify the Main View

In the Home tab Main View, the Customize button allows the view to be changed to display any of the many available snapshots of your finances. To customize the Main View:

1. Click the **Customize** button below Main View. The Customize View dialog is displayed, as seen in Figure 2-2. The Chosen Items area on the right contains the items that are currently being displayed. The Available Items area on the left shows what can be displayed.

2. To add an item to the Main View, select the item in the Available Items list on the left, and then click **Add**.

3. To remove an item, select the item in the Chosen Items list on the right, and then click **Remove**.

4. To change the order in which items are displayed on the page, select the item in the Chosen Items list on the right, and click either the **Move Up** or **Move Down** button. One click moves the item up or down one place.

5. If you want to stop the process, click **Cancel**.

6. When finished, click **OK** to set the changes and close the dialog box.

ADD A CUSTOM VIEW

To create your own view, click **Add View** in the upper-right corner of the Main View. In the Customize View dialog that appears, type the name of the view and follow steps 2 through 6 in the previous section.

DELETE A VIEW

After you have created a new view, it appears to the right of the Main View. To delete a view, select the view you want to delete, click **Customize**, and click **Delete This View**. A message box opens asking if you are sure you want to delete this view. If you are, click **Yes**.

Change the Account Bar

By default, the Account Bar is docked on the left side of the Home page. It displays your accounts in the various activity centers, as you see on the left of Figure 2-1.

At the top of the Account Bar you see a downward-pointing arrow to the left of the word "Accounts." When you click the down arrow the Account Bar closes. When the Account Bar is closed, the down arrow turns into a right-pointing arrow. To reopen the Account Bar, click the right arrow. ▸ **Accounts**   C ☼

The Account Bar can be changed in the following ways:

- Right-click anywhere within the Account Bar to view the Account Bar context menu. If you click over an account, even to the right of the account name, you get one additional item on the context menu, Edit/Delete Account, which opens the Account Details dialog box. With this menu you can do the following:

✓	Expand all accounts
✓	Show amounts
	Show cents in amounts
✓	Show Current Balance in Account Bar
	Show Ending Balance in Account Bar
	Account List (Account Bar Options)

▾ **Accounts**   C ☼

All Transactions

▸ Banking	**$8,125**
▸ Investing	**$45,799**
▸ Property & Debt	**$596,786**
Net Worth	**$650,711**

✚ **Add an Account**

- Click **Expand All Accounts**, when it is selected (the default), to show only the totals in each center. Click it when it is not selected to show the amounts in each separate account within each center.

- Click **Show Amounts**, when it is selected (the default), to show the account name only. Click it when it is not selected to show the balance in each account.

- Click **Show Cents In Amounts**, when it is not selected (the default), to display the cents in each balance. Click it when it is selected to display amounts rounded to the nearest dollar.

- Click **Show Current Balance In Account Bar** (the default) to display the balance in each account as of today's date.

- Click **Show Ending Balance In Bar** to display the balance after any future transactions have been entered.

- Click **Account List (Account Bar Options)** to open the Account List dialog box.

▼ **Accounts**	⟳	⚙
All Transactions		
▼ **Banking**		**$8,125**
Business Checking		2,404
🚩 Personal Checking		2,147
Cash		216
Business Savings		2,100
Personal Savings		1,840
Business Credit Card		-367
Personal Credit Card		-215
▼ **Investing**		**$45,799**
Brokerage ...		479
IRA-a		24,175
IRA-b		21,145
▼ **Property**		**$596,786**
Cotttage		180,000
House		485,000
Pickup		3,500
Prius		18,950
Net Worth		**$650,711**
✛ Add an Account		

NOTE

The additional menus available when you choose the Classic Menus option under View are similar to the choices available with each of the tabs.

- A right arrow to the left of each activity center name indicates that there are minimized accounts within that center. A down arrow indicates either that there are no accounts set up in that center or that all accounts are displayed. Click the right arrow to display individual accounts.

- Use the scroll bar that appears in the Account Bar if not all of the accounts are displayed at one time.

- Click **Customize** (the small gear icon) at the top-right corner of the Account Bar to display the Account List. See "Manage Accounts" later in this chapter.

- Click **Add An Account** to set up a new account as described in Chapter 1.

Change Your Views

When Quicken opens, the menu bar appears just under the title bar. Click each menu on the menu bar to see the options or commands on the menu. You can change from the recommended Standard menus to Classic menus and add other items with the View menu. From the View menu, you can also choose to use pop-up registers, show or hide the Quicken toolbar, set the location of the Account Bar and side bar, and tell Quicken which tabs to display.

View	Tools	Reports	Help
✓ Standard Menus (recommended)			
Classic Menus			
Use Large Fonts			
Use Pop-up Registers			
✓ Show Toolbar			
Customize Toolbar...			
Account Bar			▶
Dock Help and To Do Bar			
Tabs to show			▶
Full Screen			F11

1. From the menu bar, click **View**. Click **Classic Menus** to display additional menus. See the "Using Classic Menus" QuickFacts elsewhere in this chapter for more information about Classic menus.

2. Again open the View menu, and click **Use Pop-Up Registers** to make pop-up registers available. Normally, when you choose an account from the Account Bar, the register opens within its center, as shown in Figure 2-3. Pop-up registers appear in a new window on top of the Quicken window, as shown in Figure 2-4. These register windows can be moved around and placed anywhere on the screen that you choose. Click **Close** (the red X) on the pop-up register window title bar to close the register.

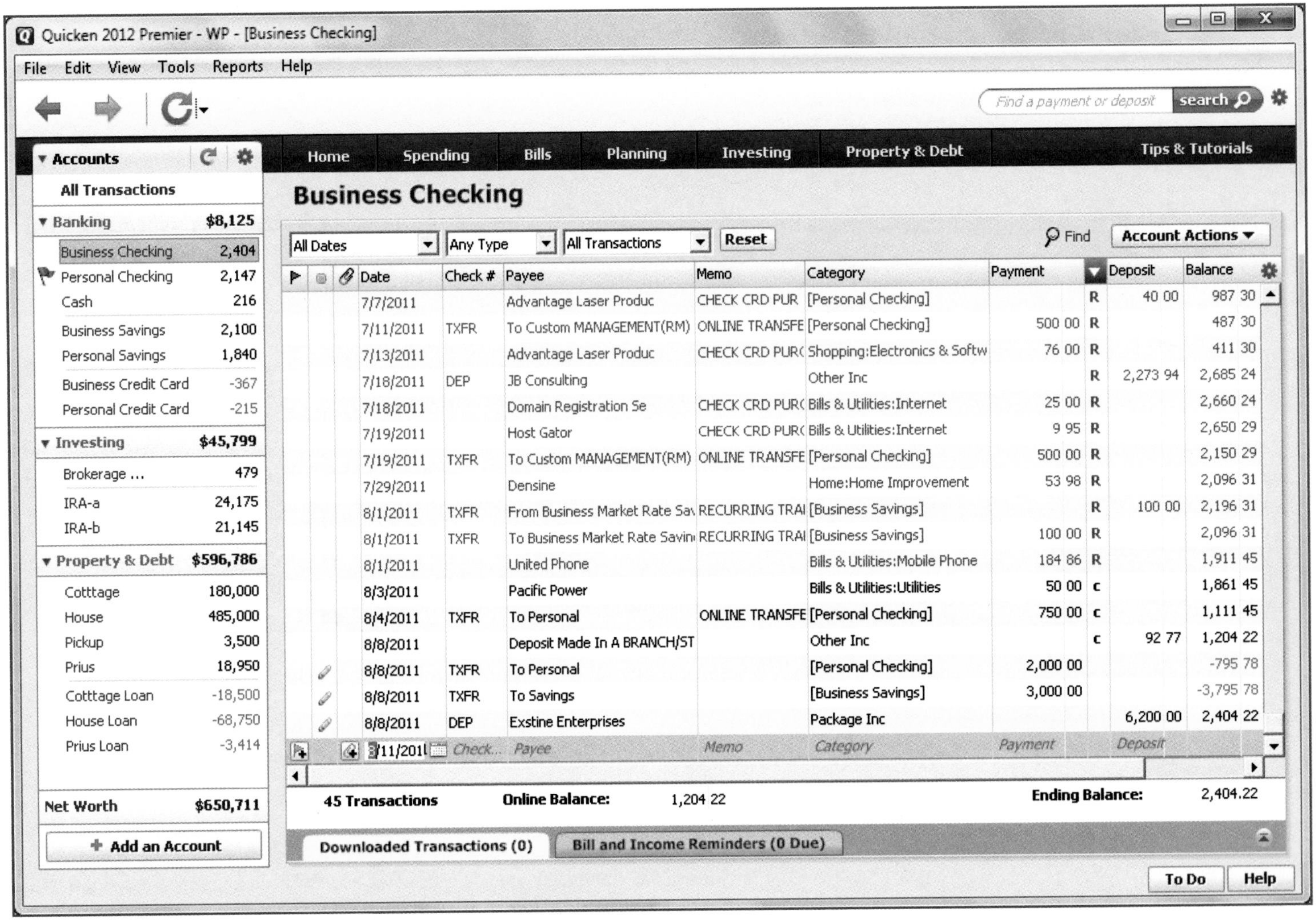

Figure 2-3: *This account register displays transactions within Banking.*

Business Checking

Business Checking

			Date ▲	Check #	Payee	Memo	Category	Payment	Clr	Deposit	Balance	⚙

All Dates ▼ | Any Type ▼ | All Transactions ▼ | Reset | 🔎 Find | Account Actions ▼

Date ▲	Check #	Payee	Memo	Category	Payment	Clr	Deposit	Balance
7/5/2011		Advantage Laser Produc	CHECK CRD PUR(	Shopping:Electronics & Softw	40 00	R		1,774 21
7/5/2011		Www Newegg Comcheck	CHECK CRD PUR(	Shopping:Electronics & Softw	59 98	R		1,714 23
7/5/2011		Pacific Power		Bills & Utilities:Mobile Phone	130 91	R		1,583 32
7/5/2011		Microsoft	CHECK CRD PUR(	Shopping:Electronics & Softw	270 66	R		1,312 66
7/5/2011		Bob's Electronics	CHECK CRD PUR(	Bills & Utilities:Home Phone	379 36	R		933 30
7/7/2011		Advantage Laser Produc	CHECK CRD PUR	[Personal Checking]		R	40 00	973 30
7/7/2011		Www Newegg Comcheck	CHECK CRD PUR	Shopping:Electronics & Softw		R	14 00	987 30
7/11/2011	TXFR	To Custom MANAGEMENT(RM)	ONLINE TRANSFE	[Personal Checking]	500 00	R		487 30
7/13/2011		Advantage Laser Produc	CHECK CRD PUR(	Shopping:Electronics & Softw	76 00	R		411 30
7/18/2011	DEP	JB Consulting		Other Inc		R	2,273 94	2,685 24
7/18/2011		Domain Registration Se	CHECK CRD PUR(	Bills & Utilities:Internet	25 00	R		2,660 24
7/19/2011	TXFR	To Custom MANAGEMENT(RM)	ONLINE TRANSFE	[Personal Checking]	500 00	R		2,160 24
7/19/2011		Host Gator	CHECK CRD PUR(	Bills & Utilities:Internet	9 95	R		2,150 29
7/29/2011		Densine		Home:Home Improvement	53 98	R		2,096 31
8/1/2011	TXFR	From Business Market Rate Sav	RECURRING TRAI	[Business Savings]		R	100 00	2,196 31
8/1/2011	TXFR	To Business Market Rate Savin	RECURRING TRAI	[Business Savings]	100 00	R		2,096 31
8/1/2011		United Phone		Bills & Utilities:Mobile Phone	184 86	R		1,911 45
8/3/2011		Pacific Power		Bills & Utilities:Utilities	50 00	c		1,861 45
8/4/2011	TXFR	To Personal	ONLINE TRANSFE	[Personal Checking]	750 00	c		1,111 45
8/8/2011	DEP	Exstine Enterprises		Package Inc			6,200 00	7,311 45
8/8/2011	TXFR	To Personal		[Personal Checking]	2,000 00			5,311 45
8/8/2011	TXFR	To Savings		[Business Savings]	3,000 00			2,311 45
8/9/2011	Check...	Payee	Memo	Category	Payment		Deposit	

44 Transactions	Online Balance:	34.51	Ending Balance:	2,311.45

Figure 2-4: Pop-up registers can be moved around the window by dragging the title bar.

3. From the View menu, click **Show Toolbar** to turn off the display of the Quicken toolbar, which is displayed by default. Initially the toolbar provides the following features:

- Use the left-pointing arrow to return to a previous page in Quicken, or the right-pointing arrow to go to the next page. These arrows are not available until you have gone to several pages within the Quicken program.

- Click the **One Step Update** icon to update your accounts directly from their financial institutions. See more about online banking later in this chapter.

4. From the View menu, click **Customize Toolbar** to open the Customize Toolbar dialog box. The Your Toolbar Buttons area on the right shows the items that are currently being displayed. The Available Toolbar Buttons area on the left shows what can be displayed.

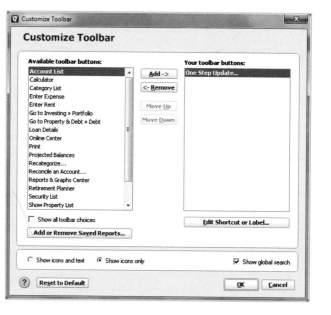

NOTE

By default, the Available Toolbar Buttons list displays only a few commands even when scrolled. Click **Show All Toolbar Choices** to display many more buttons.

TIP

I don't find the toolbar very useful and so I keep it turned off. Many of the remaining figures and illustrations in this book will show it turned off.

a. To add an item to the toolbar, select the item in the Available Toolbar Buttons list on the left, and then click **Add**.

b. To remove a button, select it in the Your Toolbar Buttons list on the right, and then click **Remove**.

c. To change the order in which buttons are displayed on the page, select the item in the Your Toolbar Buttons list on the right, and click either the **Move Up** or **Move Down** button. One click moves the button up or down one place.

d. If you want to stop the process, click **Cancel**.

e. When finished, click **OK** to set the changes and close the dialog box.

5. In the View menu, click **Account Bar** to open the flyout menu with these options:

- **Dock Account Bar**, when it is selected, which it is by default, displays the Account Bar. When it is not selected, the Account Bar is minimized.

- **On Left** (the default) or **On Right** places the Account Bar on that side of the Quicken window.

6. Click the View menu's **Dock Help And To Do Bar** option to *allow* the semipermanent docking of either the Help or To Do window; however, this selection doesn't open either of those windows. *After* clicking **Dock Help And To Do Bar**, you must click either **Help** or **To Do** in the lower-right corner of the Quicken window to open either of those panes. The View menu option will then keep them visible while you do other things within the Quicken window. When you are ready, click the View menu's **Dock Help And To Do Bar** option again to remove those bars from the windows (only one is displayed at a time).

7. Click **Tabs To Show** to open the list of seven tabs. You may choose the tabs to display by clicking the check box before their name. However, if you have entered transactions in any of the centers, the tab for that center will display by default.

8. If you opened Classic menus, pop-up registers, the toolbar, and the side bar and don't want them permanently displayed, open the View menu and deselect these items.

Dock Help and To Do Bar		
Tabs to show	▸	✓ Home
Full Screen	F11	✓ Spending
		✓ Bills
		✓ Planning
		✓ Investing
		✓ Property & Debt
		✓ Tips & Tutorials

Manage Accounts

You manage your accounts and determine how they are displayed using the Account List dialog box, which appears when you click **Customize** (the small gear icon) at the top-right corner of the Account Bar or by pressing CTRL+A. The Account List dialog, shown in Figure 2-5, allows you to review and manage your accounts in more detail.

NOTE

If you have only created accounts in one area, like Banking, you won't see the All Accounts and other headings on the left side of the Account List.

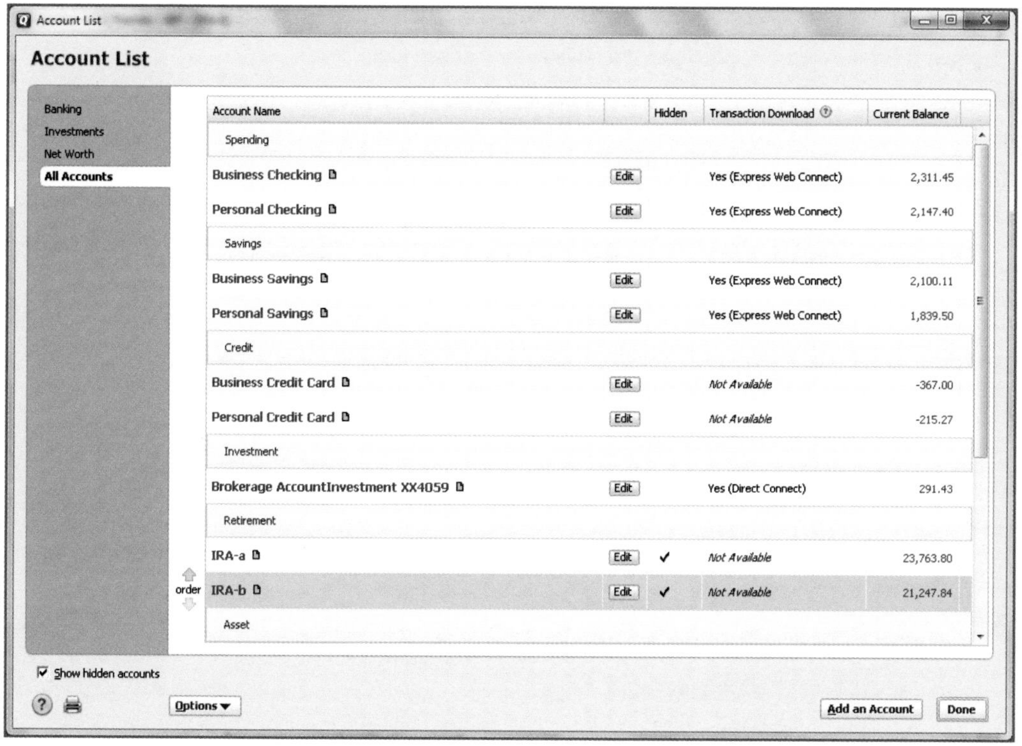

Account List

Account Name		Hidden	Transaction Download ⑦	Current Balance
Spending				
Business Checking ⓑ	Edit		Yes (Express Web Connect)	2,311.45
Personal Checking ⓑ	Edit		Yes (Express Web Connect)	2,147.40
Savings				
Business Savings ⓑ	Edit		Yes (Express Web Connect)	2,100.11
Personal Savings ⓑ	Edit		Yes (Express Web Connect)	1,839.50
Credit				
Business Credit Card ⓑ	Edit		Not Available	-367.00
Personal Credit Card ⓑ	Edit		Not Available	-215.27
Investment				
Brokerage AccountInvestment XX4059 ⓑ	Edit		Yes (Direct Connect)	291.43
Retirement				
IRA-a ⓑ	Edit	✓	Not Available	23,763.80
order IRA-b ⓑ	Edit	✓	Not Available	21,247.84
Asset				

☑ Show hidden accounts

⑦ 🖨   Options ▼   Add an Account   Done

Figure 2-5: *You can manage your various accounts from the Account List dialog.*

To show all of your accounts, click **All Accounts** on the left side of the dialog. To see only the accounts in each activity center, choose that center. For example, to see all of your Investment accounts, click **Investments** on the left side of the Account List dialog.

By default, there are four columns in the Account List (five if you have hidden accounts):

- **Account Name** shows the name of each account. Click the name of the account with which you want to work.

- The **Edit** column allows you to open the Account Details dialog box and edit the settings for the account.

- The **Hidden** column indicates if an account is hidden from Quicken's totals. The Hidden column doesn't appear until you hide an account and you select Show Hidden Accounts.

- The **Transaction Download** column indicates what type of online connection is associated with this account. See "Use Quicken Online" later in this chapter for more information about online connections.

- The **Current Balance** displays the current balance in that account.

Within the Account List you can do the following:

- Click **Edit** for an account within the list to open the Account Details dialog box for that account, as seen in Figure 2-6. See "Edit an Account" elsewhere in this chapter. Click **OK** to close the Account Details dialog.

- Click the **Order** arrow on the left of the accounts to change where the account appears in the Account Bar.

TIP

When you hide an account, the account will not appear in the Account Bar or as a transfer account even if the Show Hidden Accounts box is checked. You have to unhide the account to get it to show up again in the Account Bar.

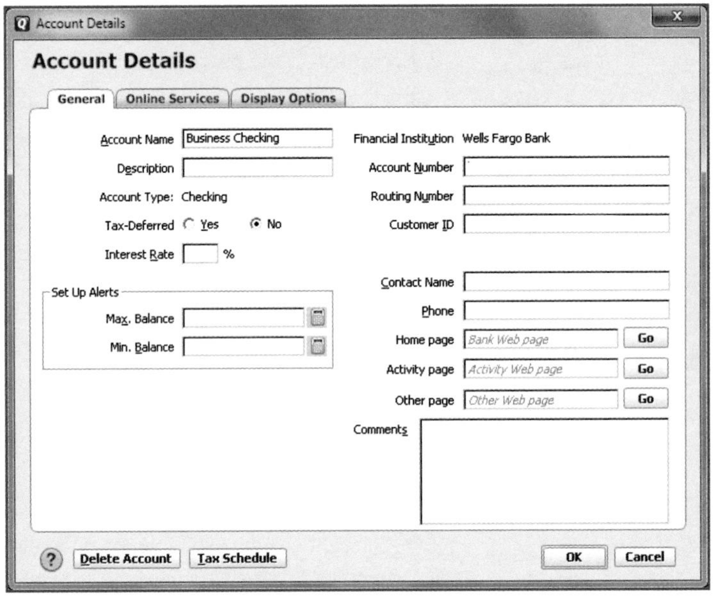

Figure 2-6: *You can edit, hide, or delete an account from the Account Details dialog box opened from the Account List.*

- Click the **Account Name** or the **Current Balance** amount for an account to open the register for that account.

- If any accounts are hidden, click the **Show Hidden Accounts** check box at the lower-left corner of the Account List window to display all of your Quicken accounts. This is not displayed if you haven't hidden an account.

- Click the question mark icon to open Quicken Help; click the printer icon to print the Account List.

- Click **Options** to see display options for your accounts. The Include Additional Info When Printing option provides some worthwhile information when printing the Account List.

- Click **Add An Account** to open the Account Setup dialog.

- Click **Done** when you have completed your changes.

TIP

Accounts are shown in alphabetical order *until* you first move an account. As you first add accounts, they automatically sort themselves alphabetically. If you later decide to change the order and then add more accounts, the newly added accounts are inserted at the bottom of the section.

TIP

A common question is how to edit the financial institution, routing number, or customer ID fields. Once online access is set up, these fields are not accessible and you must deactivate online access to change them.

Edit an Account

You can edit information about each account from the Account List dialog box. Select the account you want to edit, and click the **Edit** button to display the Account Details dialog box, as you saw in Figure 2-6.

1. Open the Account Details dialog box by clicking **Edit** in the Account List as described earlier, or right-click an account in the Account Bar and click **Edit Account**. Use the **TAB** key to move between the fields in this dialog.

2. Click in the **Account Name** text box to change the name of the account, and click in the **Description** text box to add or change the account description.

3. Click **Yes** if the account is tax-deferred (credit card, liability, and cash accounts don't have the tax-deferred selection). **No** is chosen by default.

4. Enter any interest rate in the **Interest Rate** field (investment and cash accounts do not have the Interest Rate field).

USING CLASSIC MENUS

While most people use the recommended Standard menus, Classic menus offer familiar choices for those who have used earlier versions of Quicken. To use Classic menus:

1. From the Quicken menu bar, click **View** and then click **Classic Menus**.

Quicken 2012 Premier - WP - [Business Checking]

File Edit View Tools Home Bills Spending Investing Property & Debt Planning Tips & Tutorials Reports Help

▼ Accounts   C ⚙   Home   Spending   Bills   Planning   Investing   Property & Debt

2. Additional menus appear. You see Home, Bills, Spending, Investing, Property & Debt, Planning, and Tips & Tutorials menus added to the menu bar.

3. By default, the Show Tabs option is chosen, even though this duplicates the Classic menu options. However, you can turn off the tabs by clicking **Show Tabs**.

4. Each Classic menu item has its own commands:

- Click **Home** to open the Home tab's Main View and any custom views you have created on the Home tab, as well as to customize that view or add or delete a view.

- Click **Bills** to display upcoming bills or the projected balance after paying those bills, and to add and manage reminders.

Bills Spending Investing Property & Debt Plann
   Go to Bills
     Upcoming
     Projected Balances
   Add Reminder   ▶
   Manage Bill & Income Reminders   Ctrl+J

Continued . . .

5. Enter any minimum or maximum balances in the **Set Up Alerts** fields (only spending accounts have this field, although credit card accounts have a Credit Limit field in the Set Up Alerts area of the Account Details dialog box).

6. When you enable online services, the financial institution, account and routing numbers, and customer ID will fill in automatically. In the remaining text boxes, type any additional information about the account, such as a contact name, the institution's phone number, and so on.

7. Click the **Online Services** tab to amend the online banking information. See "Use Quicken Online" later in this chapter for more information about online banking.

8. Click the **Display Options** tab to determine how and when to display this account:

Account Details

Account Details

General | Online Services | Display Options

Hide or Show Accounts
☐ Hide this account in Quicken (lists, menus, reports)
☐ Hide this account in Account Bar
☐ Don't include this account in net worth total

Account Intent
[Spending ▼]

Account Intent determines:
- How accounts are grouped in the Account Bar and other Account Lists
- What accounts are considered in certain Cash Flow features
(For Example: "Spending" accounts are typically included in cash flow)

(?) [Delete Account] [Tax Schedule]   [OK] [Cancel]

- Click **Hide This Account In Quicken** to remove the account and its balance from lists, menus, and reports. Selecting this option automatically selects the next two options.

- Click **Hide This Account In Account Bar** to hide the name of the account but include the total in a section called "Other Accounts."

- Click **Don't Include This Account In Net Worth Total** to tell Quicken not to add this account's balance into the total net worth shown on the Account Bar.

- Click the down arrow under **Account Intent**, and select how the account will be grouped in the Account Bar and Account List.

USING CLASSIC MENUS (Continued)

- Click **Spending** to open the Spending tab, the Account List, any of your spending account registers, and a number of spending and banking reports.

- Click **Investing** to open the Investing tab and handle a number of investing activities. This is discussed in Chapter 8.

- Click **Property & Debt** to open the Property & Debt tab and work with the property, debt, and loan accounts, as well as with the property and loan tools. This is discussed in Chapter 6.

- Click **Planning** to open the Planning tab and work with budgets, debt reduction, the Lifetime Planner, and the Tax Center, as well as a number of planning tools. This is discussed in Chapter 9.

- Click **Tips & Tutorials** to open the Tips & Tutorials tab, which offers Using Quicken and Quicken Services pages.

Each menu item in the Classic menus takes you to the tabs of the same name and provides many of the links that are available in each center's tab. These menus simply offer another way of navigation for previous users of Quicken.

To return to the Standard view, which is what is used throughout this book, open the **View** menu and choose **Standard Menus**.

Planning	Tips & Tutorials	Reports	Help

Go to Planning
 Budgets
 Debt Reduction
 Lifetime Planner
 Tax Center

Update Planning Assumptions ▶

Projected Balances
Debt Reduction Planner
Savings Goals

Calculators ▶

Tax Planner
Deduction Finder
Itemized Deduction Estimator
Capital Gains Estimator
Tax Withholding Estimator

Online Tax Tools ▶
TurboTax ▶

Spending Reports ▶

9. Click the **Delete Account** button at the bottom to open the Delete dialog box:

- If you want to delete this account, you must type Yes to confirm the deletion. Then, click **OK**.

- Click **Cancel** to close the dialog if you choose not to delete the account. A message will appear telling you the account was not deleted and you need to click **OK**.

10. Click **Tax Schedule** to select the tax schedules for transfers in and/or out of this account. Click the relevant down arrow to display a drop-down list of tax schedules from which you can choose.

11. Click **OK** or **Cancel** to close the Account Details dialog.

Set Preferences

Preferences are the ways in which you make Quicken behave to your liking. For example, when you start Quicken, instead of displaying the Home tab, you can choose to display the Spending tab. This is a startup preference. Other types of preferences in Quicken include backup preferences, register preferences, and report preferences. This section will discuss startup and setup preferences. The remaining preferences will be discussed elsewhere in this book. To change the startup and setup preferences:

1. Click the **Edit** menu and click **Preferences**. The Quicken Preferences dialog box appears with the startup preferences displayed, as shown in Figure 2-7.

2. In the Startup Preferences section on the right side of the dialog box:

- Click the **On Startup Open To** down arrow, and choose what you want to appear when you start Quicken. Be sure to scroll down and see the many options that are available for your startup window. (I like to have my personal checking account appear when I start up because that is where I do the most work in Quicken.)

- Click **Download Transactions When Quicken Starts** to automatically download all of the transactions in your online accounts.

QUICKSTEPS

USING THE QUICKEN CALENDAR

From the Quicken Calendar, you see at a glance the bills and income items for each day of a month. To open the Quicken Calendar:

1. Click **Tools** and then click **Calendar**. You can also use the keyboard shortcut **CTRL+K**. Either action will open the Quicken Calendar shown in Figure 2-8.

2. Enter the date in the **Go To Date** field, and click **Go** to focus on that date.

3. Use the arrows to the right and left of the current month to see earlier or future months.

4. Click **Add Note** to open the Add Note dialog. You can quickly add a note to any date on the calendar. A small note icon will appear next to the numeric date on your calendar. Click the icon to open it.

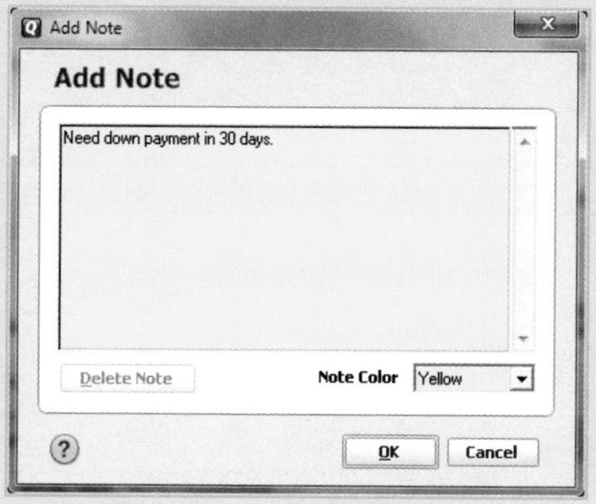

Add Note

Need down payment in 30 days.

Delete Note   Note Color [Yellow ▼]

OK   Cancel

Continued . . .

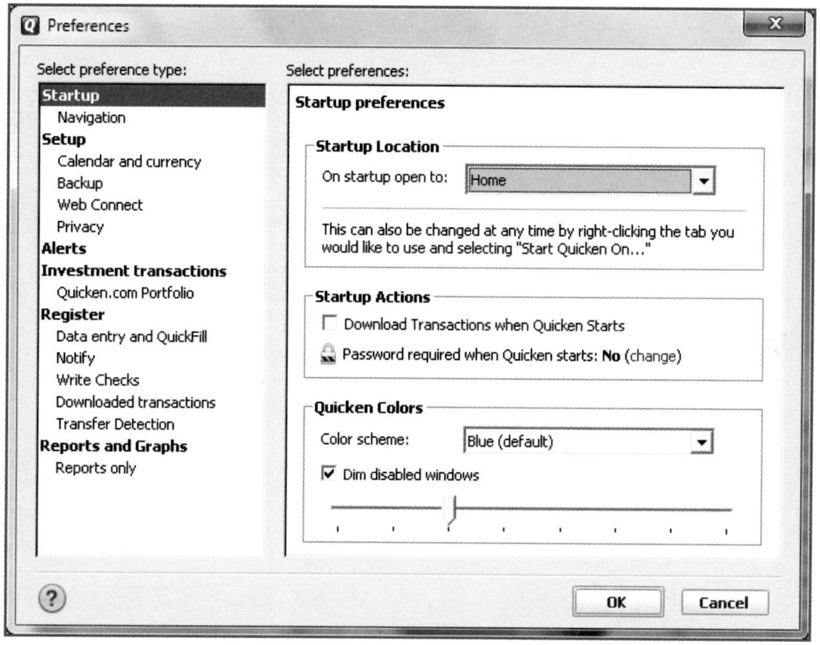

Preferences

Select preference type:

- **Startup**
  - Navigation
- **Setup**
  - Calendar and currency
  - Backup
  - Web Connect
  - Privacy
- **Alerts**
- **Investment transactions**
  - Quicken.com Portfolio
- **Register**
  - Data entry and QuickFill
  - Notify
  - Write Checks
  - Downloaded transactions
  - Transfer Detection
- **Reports and Graphs**
  - Reports only

Select preferences:

Startup preferences

Startup Location

On startup open to: [Home ▼]

This can also be changed at any time by right-clicking the tab you would like to use and selecting "Start Quicken On..."

Startup Actions

☐ Download Transactions when Quicken Starts

🔒 Password required when Quicken starts: **No** (change)

Quicken Colors

Color scheme: [Blue (default) ▼]

☑ Dim disabled windows

OK   Cancel

Figure 2-7: You can control many of the nuances of Quicken through the Quicken Preferences dialog box.

- In the Password Required When Quicken Starts section, click **Change** to use or change a Quicken password. See "Manage Your Passwords" later in this chapter.

- Click the **Color Scheme** down arrow to choose another color scheme for Quicken.

- By default the Quicken window is dimmed when a dialog box is opened. You can turn that off by removing the check opposite **Dim Disabled Windows**, and you can drag the slider beneath to change the opacity of the disabled window.

3. Click **Navigation** in the top of the left column to tell Quicken how you want to move around within the program:

- Click **Use Classic Menus** in the Main Navigation section to use Classic menus. Classic menus are discussed elsewhere in this chapter.

QUICKSTEPS

USING THE QUICKEN CALENDAR

(Continued)

5. Click **Options** to open a menu from which you can determine what is shown on the calendar:

- Choose one or more of the three **Show** options to show transactions, reminders, and balances in each day's box on the calendar, as seen in Figure 2-8.

- Click **Show Snapshots Below Calendar** to display the Bill And Income Reminders and Account Balance Graph tabs below the calendar. If you do not want these tabs available, clear the check mark.

- Click **Show Memorized Payee List** to display the list of your memorized payees at the right of the calendar.

- Click **Edit Memorized Payee List** to open the list and make changes. See Chapter 5 for more information about memorized payees.

- Click **Select Calendar Accounts** to choose which accounts to include in your calendar.

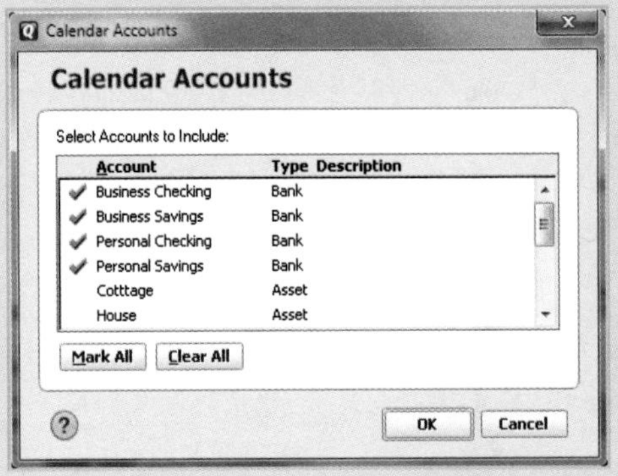

Continued . . .

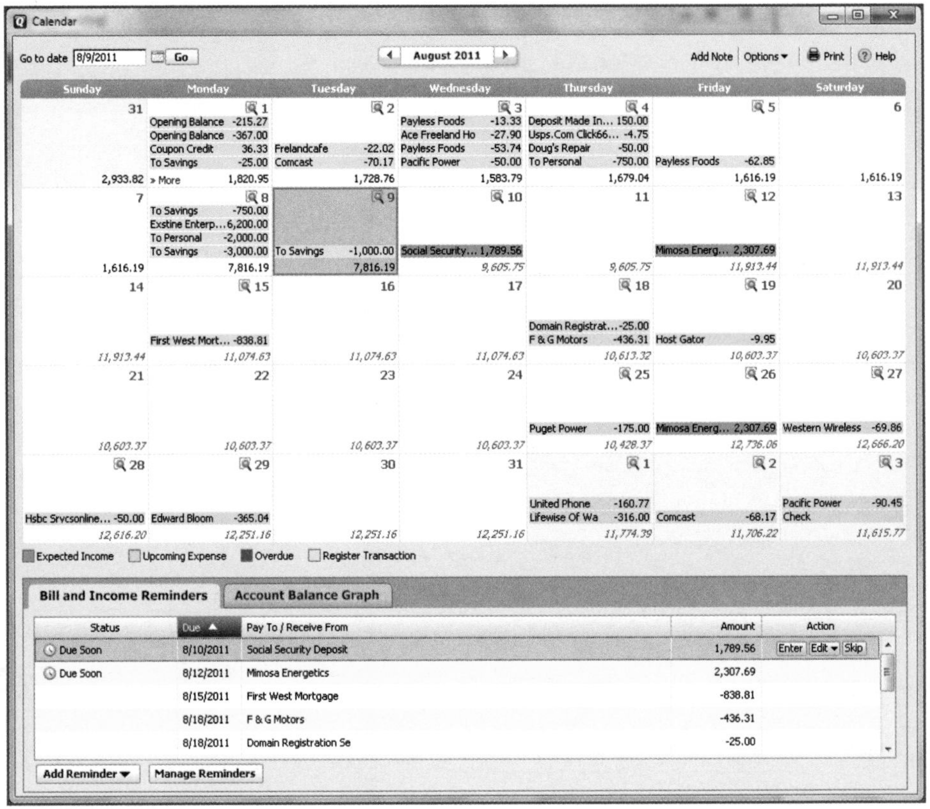

Figure 2-8: *The Quicken Calendar gives you a visual picture of when you will receive income and have to pay bills.*

- Choose whether and how your Account Bar, the Quicken toolbar, and the side bar display in Quicken.

4. Click **Setup** in the left column. The setup preferences are displayed:

- Choose whether to map keyboard shortcuts to Quicken or Windows standards. See Table 2-1 for what these shortcuts do in each case. The Windows standard is the default (see Chapter 1 for more information).

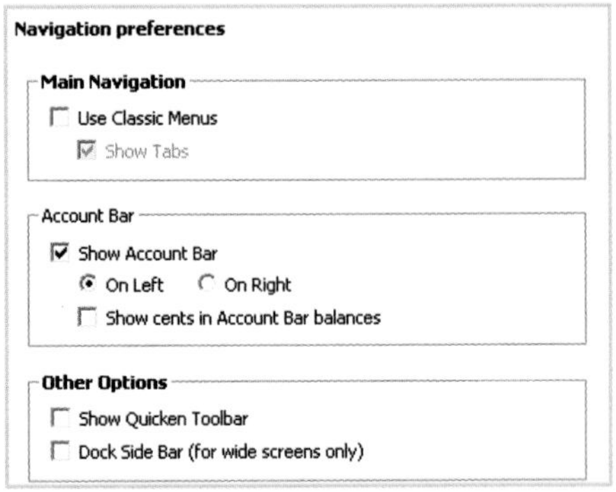

QUICKSTEPS

USING THE QUICKEN CALENDAR
(Continued)

6. Click **Print** to open the Print dialog and print the calendar.

7. Click **Help** to open the Quicken Help window.

8. If you have chosen to display the "snapshots" below the calendar, you can manage your reminders from the Bill And Income Reminders tab. See Chapter 5 for information on working with reminders.

9. The Account Balance Graph tab displays a graph showing account balances for one or multiple accounts.

10. When you are ready, click **Close** to close the Calendar window.

Transactions on each day of the month are color-coded per the legend on the bottom of the calendar. Close the calendar to return to the Quicken Home page and the current month's information.

NOTE

You can display the Quicken Calendar from the Bill And Income Reminders window by double-clicking the small calendar at the bottom of the window. The small calendar is not visible if the Show Calendar check box is unchecked.

SHORTCUT KEYS	WINDOWS	QUICKEN
CTRL+C	Copy	Open the Category List
CTRL+V	Paste	Void a transaction
CTRL+X	Cut	Show the matching entry, for example, in a liability register
CTRL+Z	Undo	Recalculate all the investment transactions in the selected investment account

Table 2-1: Alternative Mappings of Shortcut Keys in Windows and Quicken

- Choose whether to turn on or off the Quicken sounds—for example, the "ka-chung" sound that plays every time you enter a transaction—by clicking that option to select it.

- Choose to turn on or off animation within the program by clearing that check box.

- Choose whether or not to automatically minimize pop-up windows by clicking that option.

5. Click **Calendar And Currency** to open those preferences:

   - Choose how you want your calendar displayed. You may choose either a calendar year or a fiscal year.

   - If you choose to display your calendar as a fiscal year, choose the month the fiscal year begins.

   - Click **Multicurrency Support** if you use more than one currency in Quicken.

6. Click **Backup** to open the backup preferences. Choose **Automatic Backups** or **Manual Backup Reminder**, or both (which is the default). See "Protect Your Quicken Data" later in this chapter.

7. Click **Web Connect** to set how you want Quicken to manage Web Connect data. Normally you do not need to separately save the downloaded data because it is saved by Quicken and by your financial institution but you want to keep Quicken open so you can reconcile your accounts.

NOTE

Most people keep the Windows standard for the **CTRL+C**, **CTRL+V**, **CTRL+X**, and **CTRL+Z** shortcut keys because the Windows commands are heavily used in many Windows programs, while the Quicken commands are infrequently used.

8. The **Privacy** option informs you that by default Quicken sends anonymous product statistics to Intuit without any personal information to help make Quicken better. You can turn this off and not send feature usage and/or banking connectivity statistics. I see no harm in sending this useful information to Intuit.

9. Click **OK** to close the dialog box when you are finished.

Add and Change Accounts

Accounts are central to Quicken's operation, whether they are checking, investment, or property and debt accounts. In Chapter 1 you saw how to get started setting up accounts with Quicken New User Setup. As you use Quicken, it is likely that you will want to add accounts and modify the accounts you already have. This section will look at adding and modifying checking and savings accounts. In later chapters you'll see how to add and modify accounts in other centers.

Add Spending Accounts

If you need to create additional checking, savings, or credit card accounts, you can do that with the following steps:

1. Click **Add An Account** in the Account Bar.

–Or–

Click the **Tools** menu, and click **Add Account**.

In either case, the Add Account dialog box will appear and prompt you to select an available account type.

2. Click the spending account you want to add, and click **Next**.

3. For all but cash accounts, you are asked to enter the institution at which this account is held. You are shown a list of popular financial institutions from which you can make a selection, and this list is updated based on what you type. If you see your institution, click it. Otherwise, click **Next** to continue. If the name is not on the list, or if you prefer not to download, or if you are

TIP

Many Quicken users find that using the ten-key pad on their computer keyboard is the easiest way to enter numbers.

CAUTION

You can enter dates into Quicken 2012 in any format *except* those that use dashes, such as 10-8-12.

Add Account

Primary Accounts

Spending
- ⦿ Checking
- ○ Savings
- ○ Credit Card
- ○ Cash

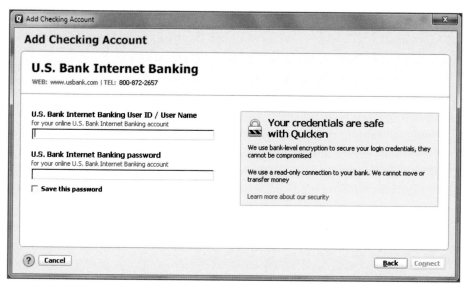

Add Checking Account

U.S. Bank Internet Banking
WEB: www.usbank.com | TEL: 800-872-2657

U.S. Bank Internet Banking User ID / User Name
for your online U.S. Bank Internet Banking account

U.S. Bank Internet Banking password
for your online U.S. Bank Internet Banking account

☐ Save this password

🔒 **Your credentials are safe with Quicken**

We use bank-level encryption to secure your login credentials, they cannot be compromised

We use a read-only connection to your bank. We cannot move or transfer money

Learn more about our security

(?) Cancel   Back   Connect

*Figure 2-9: **Log in to your financial institution to enable transaction downloads to Quicken.***

NOTE

Some financial institutions ask for additional information as you are signing in. If so, simply enter that information during the connection process.

TIP

For the account name, you can use any combination of letters, numbers, and spaces, except the following characters: right and left brackets ([ ]), the forward slash (/), colon (:), caret (^), and vertical bar (|). If you do not type a name, Quicken uses the type of account as the default name.

interested in advanced setup, click **Advanced Setup**. If you are setting up an institution without online banking, go to step 7.

4. If you have selected a name of a financial institution Quicken recognizes, a connection window opens and moves to a login dialog, as seen in Figure 2-9.

5. If you have chosen an institution for which you have a user name or ID, enter that, press **TAB**, and then enter your password or PIN provided by or used with your bank. Click **Connect**. If you do not have a user name or ID and password or PIN and wish to use your bank's online services, apply to your bank for them.

6. When the download is complete, check the accounts you want to add to Quicken.

7. Enter an account name, and click **Next**.

8. If you have downloaded transactions, the Setup Complete dialog appears, as you saw in Chapter 1.

9. If you have not downloaded, you are prompted for the date of the last bank statement and its ending balance.

10. Click **Finish**.

ADD A CASH ACCOUNT

Cash accounts are useful for tracking where your money goes. You can set up cash accounts for each member of the family. To set up a cash account:

1. Click **Add An Account**, click **Cash**, and then click **Next**.

2. Type a name for the account, such as Nick's Allowance, and click **Next**.

3. If you want to start keeping track of your cash spending as of today, leave the default of today's date. If you want to use another date, enter the one you want.

4. Press **TAB**, enter the amount of cash you are starting with, and click **Next**. The Account Added dialog appears.

5. Click **Finish** to close the dialog. Your new cash account appears under Banking on the Account Bar.

TIP

When you use a cash account, make sure you include ATM withdrawals and deposits to and from your cash account. You could even set up a cash account just for ATM withdrawals.

TIP

Recording each credit card charge helps you prevent errors and credit card fraud. If a charge appears that you have not made, you can notify your credit card company at once. If your credit card company offers a Quicken download service, you can download the information directly into your Quicken register.

NOTE

With Express Web Connect, Intuit systems access your financial institution and retrieve your transaction data. When you download from within Quicken, you are retrieving the transactions from the Intuit server, *not* your institution. You may notice a day or two delay in transactions being available on your bank site and transactions downloaded to Quicken because of the two-step process. This delay is a fairly frequent complaint in the Quicken community.

Tracking your spending with cash accounts allows each member of the family to see exactly where his or her money goes. It can be a valuable tool for anyone, but especially for young people as they learn to handle money.

Use Quicken Online

Most banks and credit unions, as well as brokerages, mortgage lenders, and insurance companies, give you the option of connecting to them online and potentially interfacing with Quicken. With banks and credit unions, at least two services are usually offered: online account access and online bill paying. With the online account access service, you use an Internet connection to connect to your financial institution's computer to see what checks have cleared, what deposits have been posted, and what service charges or other *automatically recurring* transactions have been posted to your account. (Automatically recurring transactions are transactions that you have agreed to be automatically deducted from or added to your account on a regular basis, such as property tax and car loan payments, or Social Security receipts.) Online banking also allows you to transfer between accounts—from checking to savings, for example, or from your savings account to your credit card account to pay your credit card bill.

The online bill-paying service lets you pay bills electronically rather than by writing a check. You tell the bank the name of the payee, the address, and the amount to pay, and the bank facilitates the payment, either electronically or by writing the check. You can usually set up regularly scheduled payments, such as insurance or mortgage payments, so that those payments are never late.

Quicken also offers bill-paying services through Quicken Bill Pay. Available for any U.S. checking account, the service stores payee information for you, so whenever you make a new payment, account numbers and payee information appear automatically. You just fill in the correct amount to pay. As with some banks, but not all, there is a charge for this service.

SERVICE	DESCRIPTION
Online Account Access	This service allows you to sign on to your financial institution's website and look at your account. You can see which checks or deposits have been posted and any fees charged to your account. Some institutions allow you to transfer money between accounts. Some also allow you to transfer funds from your banking account to your credit card account to pay your bill. This type of access is now available through many types of companies. Firms as diverse as insurance, utility, telephone, and even gasoline companies are beginning to offer forms of online account access.
Online Bill Payment	With this service, your bank or credit union pays your bills from your existing account. Working with information you give them, the institution will either electronically transfer money from your account to your payee's account or actually prepare a check they send to your payee. While not all institutions support this service, you can get the same service by subscribing to Quicken Bill Pay.
Transaction Download	With this service, you can *download* (copy from the bank's computer to Quicken) all of your account activity. There are three ways to download transactions. Which type you use will depend on your financial institution: • **Web Connect** This service requires that you log on to the institution's website, enter your identifying information, and indicate which items you want downloaded to Quicken. With this method, you can usually specify a date range for the download. • **Express Web Connect** With this method, you can access all of the institution's services directly from within Quicken and there is no need to log on to the institution's website. One Step Update uses this method, and Quicken remembers your login information from session to session. • **Direct Connect** If your institution offers this service, you can create two-way communication with your financial institution instead of the one-way communication available with Express Web Connect. You can transfer from account to account from within Quicken and use the institution's online bill-paying services if available. Unlike the other two methods, some institutions charge a fee for some services when using the Direct Connect method.

Table 2-2: Online Services Offered by Many Financial Institutions

Understand Online Services

Today, most financial institutions offer some type of online financial service. This saves them money and offers consumers a valuable tool. All such online services require an Internet connection. Some institutions charge a fee for these services, although many do not. Over time, your costs may be less than working with paper statements, paying bills by check, mailing payments, and buying stamps. Check with your institution to determine the costs for the services they provide. Table 2-2 explains these services.

Working online can save you time and money, and as more financial institutions are going online, their security procedures are becoming more stringent. Many institutions discuss these procedures on their websites, and others provide brochures about maintaining security online. You can help by ensuring that you keep your user name or ID and password or PIN secure, by keeping your antivirus program up-to-date, and by using a good firewall. When using any online service, remember that with any benefit comes some risk.

TIP

Quicken provides a virtual "vault" where you can store your password or PIN for many different organizations. Click **Tools** from the Quicken menu bar, click **Password Vault**, and then click **Set Up New Password Vault**.

TIP

In many, if not most, instances, if you have an existing Internet connection that you use for email and web browsing, your Quicken Internet connection is automatically set up when you install Quicken, and you need to do nothing further to use Quicken's online features.

NOTE

Many programs labeled "Internet Security," such as Norton Internet Security, Kaspersky Internet Security, and BitDefender Internet Security, include antivirus, antimalware, antispam, and other protective features when using the Internet. Other products labeled "Anti-Virus" provide a more limited protection.

UNDERSTAND INTERNET SECURITY

As the Internet has gained in popularity, so have the risks in using it. Viruses, worms, spyware, and adware have become part of our vocabulary. As you start to work online, take a moment to understand what each problem is and how to guard your computer and data, as described in Table 2-3.

PROBLEM	DEFINITION	SOLUTION
Virus	A program that attaches itself to other files on your computer. There are many forms of viruses, each performing different, usually malevolent, functions on your computer.	Install an antivirus program with a subscription for automatic updates, and make sure it is continually running.
Worm	A type of virus that replicates itself repeatedly through a computer network or security breach in your computer. Because it keeps copying itself, a worm can fill up a hard drive and cause your network to malfunction.	Almost all antivirus programs also protect against worms.
Trojan horse	A computer program that claims to be one thing, such as a game, music, or a story, but has hidden parts that can erase files or even your entire hard drive.	Almost all antivirus programs also protect against a Trojan horse.
Adware	The banners and pop-up ads that come with programs you download from the Internet. Often these programs are free, and to support them, the program owner sells space for ads to display on your computer every time you use the program.	Install an anti-adware program.
Spyware	A computer program that downloads with another program from the Internet. Spyware can monitor what you do, keep track of your keystrokes, discern credit card and other personally identifying numbers, and pass that information back to its author.	Install an antispyware program.

Table 2-3: *Security Issues Associated with the Internet and How to Control Them*

DECIDING TO USE
ONLINE BANKING SERVICES

In making the decision whether to use online banking services, consider the following points:

- While electronic banking has become very common, not all financial institutions make it available through Quicken—or even offer it at all. Ensure your bank or credit union has the service available.

- You need an Internet connection to use these services.

- To ensure security, carefully protect your user name or ID and password or PIN for your financial institution. Most financial institutions transmit using *encrypted* data. That means anyone intercepting the transmission would see only gibberish. Quicken uses the same method to send information to your financial institution.

- Your records should be up-to-date and your last paper statement reconciled before you start the service.

- You should understand how to use Quicken to record a check, create a deposit, reconcile your accounts, and transfer between accounts before you use the electronic services.

- Financial institutions may charge a fee for some of their online services. Compute the cost of doing it yourself (postage, gas to go to the post office, envelopes, and your time). Compare those costs to the fees charged by Quicken or your financial institution.

Before you start your online financial transactions, understand the online security issues and take steps to protect your computer. Your financial institution is working to protect your information on its end, but you need to do your part as well.

Set Up Online Banking

Before you can use online banking services, you must have a working Internet connection. You get such a connection through an *Internet service provider*, or ISP. Ask your friends and neighbors, check your phone book, or call your local telephone company or cable TV company to find an ISP in your area.

The ISP will give you the information you need to get an Internet connection and set it up in Windows. Once you have established your Internet connection, you are prepared to contact your bank to sign up for their online services. Many financial institutions allow you to sign up on their website, while others require that you call your local branch. Either way, most institutions need you to fill out an application, send a voided check or complete other paperwork, and agree to their fees. Then, you may need to wait a few days to get your identification number, password, or PIN sent to you by regular mail.

CONNECTION METHODS

There are several methods by which Quicken can update your transactions and balances. Depending on your financial institution, Quicken chooses the best method. Table 2-4 explains the differences. An X under a connection service indicates that the feature applies to that service.

IMPLEMENT ONLINE BANKING

For an account that is not already online, once you have received the login information from the financial institution, you can implement the online service.

1. For an existing account, click its name in the Account Bar to see its register.

2. Click **Account Actions** and click **Set Up Online** to open the Add Account dialog box.

3. Continue with the steps under "Add Spending Accounts" earlier in this chapter, beginning with step 3.

FEATURE	DIRECT CONNECT	EXPRESS WEB CONNECT	WEB CONNECT
You must set up this service in Quicken even if you already log on to your financial institution's website.	X	X	
Quicken can remember your logon information for you. This can include user name or ID, password or PIN, and, in some cases, supplemental information.	X	X	
Two-way communication with your financial institution is possible. You can access account information, transfer money from one account to another, pay bills, and so forth.	X		
All services are available from within Quicken. You don't need to log on to your financial institution's website.	X	X	
You can use One Step Update to update multiple accounts during one session on the Internet.	X	X	
You can usually specify a date range for transactions you want to download.			X
Downloaded transactions are automatically matched with existing transactions, and new transactions are entered into your register.	X	X	X
Your financial institution may require a monthly fee for this service.	X	X	

*Table 2-4: **The Three Ways Quicken Can Update from Your Financial Institution***

Activate One Step Update

Once you have set up your accounts for online services, you can update all of your transactions and balances at once with One Step Update.

1. Click the **One Step Update** symbol ⟳ in the upper-right corner of the Account Bar. The One Step Update Settings dialog appears, as seen in Figure 2-10.

2. Click the check boxes to select the institution and information you want to download, enter your passwords, and click **Update Now**.

3. You are asked if you want to save your passwords in Quicken so that you don't have to re-enter them each time. This uses Quicken's Password Vault. If you don't want to do this initially, you can come back at a later time and do it through the Tools menu (see "Manage Your Passwords" later in this chapter). Click **Yes** or **No**.

4. Your balances will be updated and transactions downloaded for the accounts you chose. While the information is being downloaded, you can continue to work in other parts of Quicken.

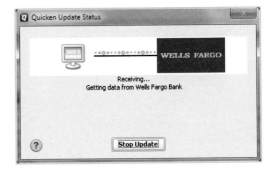

TIP

One reason to use Web Connect is that you can see electronic bills and messages from your bank that way. By logging on to the bank site for Web Connect, you can review electronic bills, schedule payments, and read any messages from the bank.

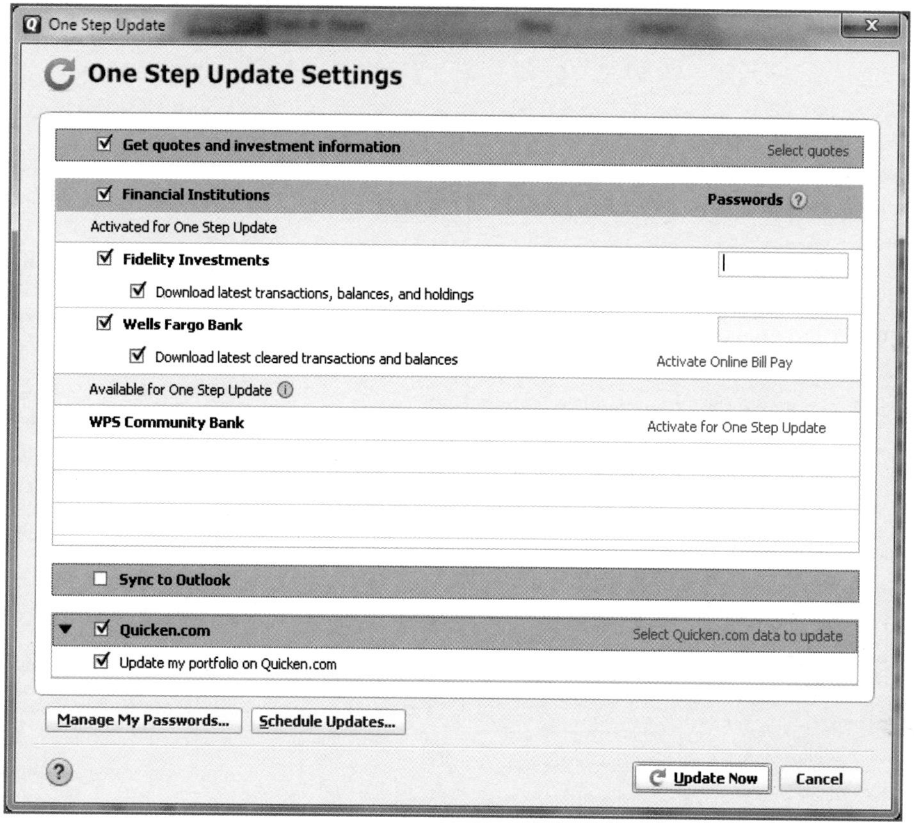

Figure 2-10: *The One Step Update dialog lets you tailor your download to meet your requirements.*

TIP

If your preferences are set to only display the One Step Update Summary when there is an error and no errors occur, you will not see the One Step Update Summary. You can access the One Step Update Summary from the Tools menu, if needed.

5. If you want to change how Quicken manages your passwords, click **Manage My Passwords**. For further information, see "Manage Your Passwords."

6. When the update has completed, the One Step Update Summary is displayed showing you what the update has accomplished. You can click the right-pointing arrows to see further information for those accounts. When you are ready, click **Close**.

Manage Your Passwords

Two types of passwords are available for use within Quicken itself. You can set a password for the overall Quicken data file that is currently open so that others cannot access the file without the password. You can also set a password that is required if transactions are modified. This type of password is especially useful after you have filed your income tax and other financial reports for a specific year and want to ensure changes are not made to the data.

- To set a password for your Quicken data file, click the **File** menu, click **Set Password For This Data File**, type and confirm the password you want, and click **OK**.
- To create a password so that existing transactions cannot be modified without it, click the **File** menu, click **Set Password To Modify Transactions**, type and confirm the password, and click **OK**.

In addition, most financial institutions require passwords to access your information. There are two methods of managing your passwords. The first is the least convenient—entering each password individually. The most secure and convenient method is to store your passwords in the Quicken Password Vault. To do that:

1. Click **Manage My Passwords** from the One Step Update dialog; or click **Tools** in the Quicken menu bar, click **Password Vault**, and then click **Set Up New Password Vault**. Either way will open the Password Vault Setup wizard. Click **Next** to begin.

2. Select the financial institution from the drop-down list. Click **Next**. If you have several accounts with different user names or IDs for this financial institution, select the relevant user ID for the password you want to store. Enter and confirm the password you use for this account. The fields may not be left blank. Click **Next**.

3. If you have multiple accounts with different financial institutions or multiple accounts with the same institution but with different user names or IDs, you are asked if you want to enter additional passwords. If so, click **Yes** to repeat the process.

   If you are finished storing passwords, click **No** and then click **Next**.

4. Enter a master password. The master password protects your Password Vault. It must contain at least six characters with both numbers and letters. Enter the master password again to confirm it.

Password Vault Setup

Welcome | Select Bank/CC | **Summary**

Vault Password

Enter a password to protect your Vault. [Change Vault Password]

PASSWORDS

Financial Institution	Password Stored
Wells Fargo Bank	
	Yes
Fidelity Investments	
	Yes

[Add Password]
[Change Password]
[Delete Password]

Access to Business Checking, Business Savings, Personal Ch...

(?) 🖨 [Cancel]   [Back] [Done]

5. The password summary displays, showing the passwords that have been stored for each of your accounts. Click **Done**.

CHANGE YOUR MASTER PASSWORD

It is a good idea to change your master password every six months or so. To change it:

1. Click **Tools** in the menu bar, click **Password Vault**, and click **Add Or Edit Passwords**. If you haven't used your Password Vault since you started your current Quicken session, you will be asked to enter your password and click **OK** to open the Edit Password Vault dialog box.

2. Click **Change Vault Password**, enter and confirm a new password, and click **OK** to change the Vault password.

3. Click the user name or ID whose password you want to change, click **Change Password**, enter and confirm a new password, and click **Change** to change the password for your individual accounts.

4. Click **Done** to complete the changes.

DELETE A PASSWORD VAULT

If you have changed banks or want to start over, you can do so. To completely reset the Password Vault, delete the existing Password Vault and set it up again. To delete the current Password Vault:

Click **Tools**, click **Password Vault**, and click **Delete Vault And All Saved Passwords**. You are asked if you are sure you want to delete the Password Vault. If so, click **Yes**.

Understand Categories

A *category* is a description or label for an expense or a source of income. For example, payments to your telephone company might use the Telephone category. You can create subcategories for each category. For example, your trash pickup service might be a subcategory of Utilities. There are at least two types of categories: Income and Expense. Another set of category types might be Business and Personal. As you set up your accounts and prepare to enter

CAUTION

Deleting the Password Vault removes all stored passwords and erases the current Password Vault master password.

TIP

When you create a password, make it a *strong* password. A strong password is at least eight characters long and contains *all* of the following: uppercase and lowercase letters, numbers, and one or two special characters, such as !, @, #, $, %, ^, &, or *. A strong password should not be recognizable as any kind of name, an address, a date, a telephone number, or a word in any language. Also, it is important to change passwords at least two to four times a year.

NOTE

The four sets of available categories in Quicken are Standard, Business, Investment, and Rentals & Royalties.

TIP

You can also open the Category List by pressing **CTRL+SHIFT+C**.

transactions, it is a good idea to set up categories at the same time. Categories are used to group your transactions for budgeting, taxes, and managing your money.

Quicken supplies a number of preset categories for you to use. It also remembers the category you assign for each payee. Quicken customizes your list of categories in response to your answers in Quicken New User Setup. You can add categories and delete any of the preset categories that do not apply to you.

Work with Categories

To view the preset Category List and add and remove categories:

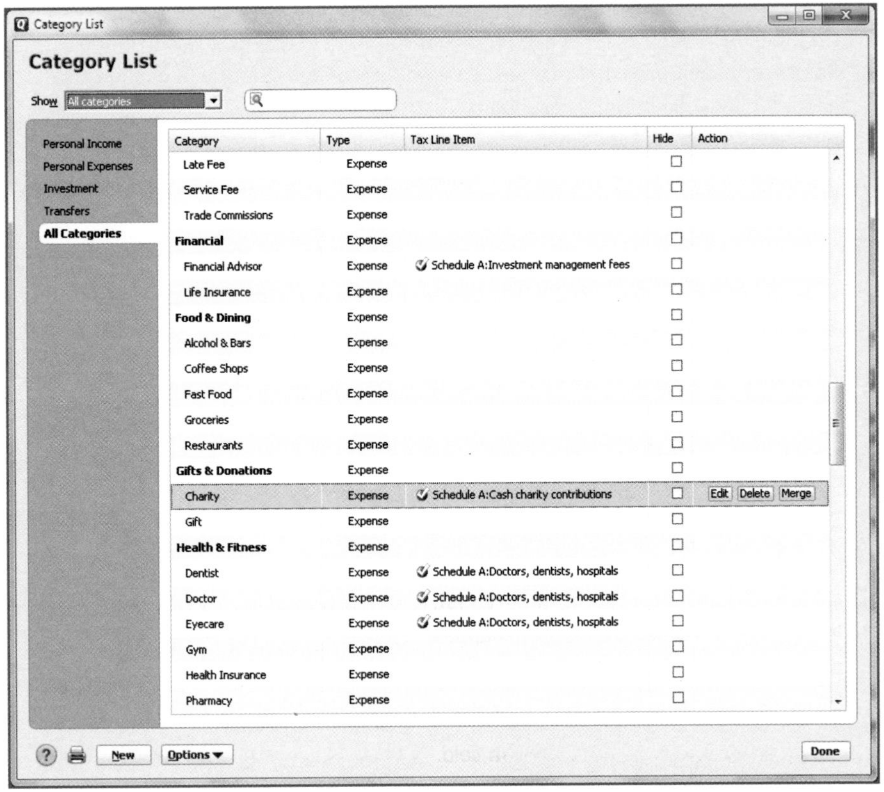

Figure 2-11: ***The Category List displays the categories you can use to organize your finances.***

1. Click the **Tools** menu, and then click **Category List**. Your Category List is displayed, as shown in Figure 2-11. The list shows all of the Income and Expense categories in alphabetical order.
2. Click the **Show** drop-down list to choose the categories you want to display, or click a name from the list on the left side of the window.
3. Click **New** to add a new category. See "Add a New Category" later in this chapter.
4. From the bottom-left area of the Category List, click the **Help** icon to open the Quicken Help dialog; click the **Print** icon to print the list.
5. Click **Options** at the bottom of the Category List to tell Quicken how to display your list. Clicking each of the first five of the following items will enable them if they are disabled, and vice versa:
   - **Show Category Usage** displays the number of transactions in that category.
   - **Show Descriptions** displays the description entered for each category.
   - **Show Category Group** displays the group into which you've put this category. See "Assign Category Groups" later in this chapter.

- **Show Type** tells Quicken to include the type of category each item is. For example, Bonus is usually a Personal Income item.
- **Show Tax Line Item** includes the tax information you've entered about the category.
- **Assign Category Groups** opens a dialog box where you can assign categories to custom groups that you create (if you start with a new file, Quicken 2012 does not start with any custom groups).
- **Manage Categories** opens the Manage Categories dialog box where you can select categories from each of the four groups and add them to your list of categories.

Add a New Category

To add a new category:

1. Click the **Tools** menu, click **Category List**, and click **New** in the lower-left corner of the list. The Set Up Category dialog box appears.

2. In the Details tab, type a name for your new category. Click whether it is an Income, Expense, or Subcategory item; and select the category it is subordinate to.

3. Press **TAB** or click in the **Description** field. Type the description, such as <u>Part-time job</u> or <u>Annual homeowner dues</u>.

TIP

Do not combine alimony payments you receive with child support payments you receive. Instead, create a separate category for each item. Check with your tax professional for further information.

Set Up Category

Details | Tax Reporting

Complete this form to use the category in tax related features. (learn more)

☑ Tax related category
  ◉ Standard line item list
  ○ Extended line item list

Tax line item for this category (optional)
Schedule C:Gross receipts or sales

Tax Line Item Description:
Gross receipts or sales from a business before deducting adjustments for returns and allowances and cost of goods sold.

? | OK | Cancel

TIP

Assigning tax-line items to categories makes it easier to create tax reports and plan for tax time.

TIP

When selecting categories in the Add Categories dialog box, you can select multiple contiguous categories (categories that are next to each other) by holding down the **SHIFT** key while clicking the first and last categories.

4. Press **TAB** or click in the **Group** field *if* you have added groups (the Group field does not appear at the bottom if you have not done this). With the Group field you have the option to assign this category to a group.

5. If this category is tax-related, click the **Tax Reporting** tab, click **Tax-Related Category**, and select whether it is a **Standard Line Item** or an **Extended Line Item**. Then choose the tax-line item to which it applies.

   a. Click the **Tax Line Item** down arrow to display a list of possible tax lines from which to choose.

   b. Click the relevant line, or you may choose to leave this field blank. A small explanation appears in the box below when a tax-line item is chosen.

6. Click **OK** to finish adding the category and close the dialog.

ASSIGN CATEGORY GROUPS

Quicken allows you to group categories of transactions to better match how you manage your finances and for tax purposes, although groups are optional and you do not have to use them.

1. From the Options menu on the Category List, click **Assign Category Groups**. The Assign Category Group dialog box appears.

Assign Category Groups

1. Find the category you'd like to re-assign

Categories in: Personal Expenses

Parking	Personal Expenses
Public Transportation	Personal Expenses
Registration	Personal Expenses
Service & Parts	Personal Expenses
Tolls	Personal Expenses
Bills & Utilities	Personal Expenses
Credit Card Payment	Personal Expenses
Home Phone	Personal Expenses
Internet	Personal Expenses
Mobile Phone	Personal Expenses
Television	Personal Expenses
Utilities	Personal Expenses
Cash & ATM	Personal Expenses
Deposit to Savings	Personal Expenses
Education	Personal Expenses
Books & Supplies	Personal Expenses

Add ->
<- Remove

2. Assign it to a custom category group

No custom Category Groups

You haven't added any custom category groups.

Add Custom Groups

Note:
Custom category groups are completely optional. You can add as many as you'd like, or delete them at any time.

☐ Show hidden categories

Done

QUICK**FACTS**

USING TAX-LINE ASSIGNMENTS

While Quicken does not require that you include tax information in categories, entering this information can save a lot of time when planning for and preparing your taxes. By using them, Quicken can

- Display up-to-date tax information on your taxes. By knowing your tax position, you can talk to your tax professional about options well before year-end.

- Prepare tax reports by tax schedule or form. These reports will assist your tax professional and perhaps save you money in tax-preparation fees.

- Create reports that describe taxable and nontaxable dividends, interest, and other items separately.

- Help you use the Tax Planner within Quicken (see Chapter 10).

- Export your data directly into Intuit's TurboTax to help you prepare your income tax return.

The time you spend assigning tax-line items to your categories can save a lot of time and money at the end of the year.

2. Click the down arrow on the category type drop-down list in the upper-left corner, and select a category type.

3. Click **Add Custom Group** on the right. In the Custom Category Group dialog box that opens, click **New**. Type the group name, click **OK**, and, if you don't want to add another group, click **Done**.

4. Click a category from the category list on left.

5. Click the **Category Group** down arrow, and click the category group you want to use in the drop-down list in the upper-right area. Click **Add**.

6. Repeat the process for all the assignments you want to make. Click **Add/Rename Custom Groups** to add or change category groups.

7. Click **Done** to close the dialog box when you are finished.

RENAME A CATEGORY

You can rename a category to make it more meaningful.

1. In the Category List window, click the name of the category, and click **Edit** on the right of the category. The Set Up Category dialog box appears.

2. The Name field should already be selected. If not, click in it to select it, and type a new name.

3. If this category is tax-related, review the tax-line item to ensure it is still correct.

4. Click **OK** to close the Set Up Category dialog box.

USE SUBCATEGORIES

Expense categories are the best way to find out just where you are spending your money. You can use any of the predefined categories or add your own. You can also create subcategories to show more detail. When you categorize each item, you can create reports and graphs that show spending patterns and habits. You can even create budgets for categories or groups of categories.

1. Follow the instructions in the "Add a New Category" section earlier in this chapter to add a category to which you want to add subcategories.

2. To add a subcategory to your new category, right-click any category in the Category List, and click **New** from the context menu. The Set Up Category dialog box appears.

3. Type the name of your subcategory. Click the **Subcategory Of** option. Type the name of the parent category, or choose it from the drop-down list.

TIP

Just because Quicken includes a specific category or subcategory does not mean you have to use it in the same way. For example, if you want all of your insurance expenses to be in one category, use the parent category and hide or delete the subcategories.

TIP

You can choose to hide a category by clicking the **Hide** check box. Hidden categories appear on the Category List and are still included in the Quicken data file, but are not in the list of categories available for attachment to a transaction.

QUICKSTEPS

DELETING CATEGORIES

As you are working with your Category List, you may see some items that you will not use and want to delete.

1. Click the **Tools** menu, and click **Category List**, or press **CTRL+SHIFT+C**, to display the Category List.

2. Select the category you want to delete, and click the **Delete** button on the right of the category.

HOA Dues	Expense		☐	Edit	Delete	Merge

–Or–

Right-click the category you want to delete to display a context menu. Click **Delete**.

Continued . . .

4. Press **TAB** to move to the Description field, and type a description if you want.

5. If it appears, leave the **Group** field blank; or click the **Group** down arrow, and make a selection from the drop-down list.

6. If this expense has tax implications, click the **Tax Reporting** tab, click **Tax-Related**, and choose the tax-line item from the drop-down list. Otherwise, leave the **Tax-Related** field unchecked.

7. Click **OK** to close the dialog box.

You will see the new category as a subcategory on the Category List. The Category List displays the categories in alphabetical order. Subcategories are displayed in alphabetical order indented underneath the parent category.

Set Up Category

Details | Tax Reporting

Category Name:
Mobile Phone

○ Income
○ Expense
● Subcategory of: Utilities

Description: (optional) Mobile Phone

Group: (optional) Personal Expenses

OK | Cancel

Protect Your Quicken Data

Computers have been a great asset to many people. However, like any machine, they are prone to failures of many kinds. Once you have started using Quicken regularly, it becomes important to protect your information and store it in another location should your hard drive fail or something else happen to your computer.

Quicken offers an easy solution to this problem called Quicken Backup. *Backup* (or back up—the verb form) is a computer term that means storing a copy of your information in a location other than on your computer.

You can back up your information to a CD, another drive that is connected to your computer (such as a USB flash or thumb drive), or to an external hard drive or one on another computer. You might choose to alternate your backup between two different flash drives each time you use the program, and then back up all of your data to a recordable CD and store it in your bank safety deposit box a couple of times a year.

QUICKSTEPS

DELETING CATEGORIES (Continued)

3. A warning message appears, notifying you that this category is about to be deleted. Click **OK** if you want to delete the category, or click **Cancel** if this was an error.

4. If you click **OK**, the category disappears from the Category List.

5. Click **Done** to close the Category List.

TIP

You may want to back up your data before performing category surgery so you can revert to the backup file should anything go awry.

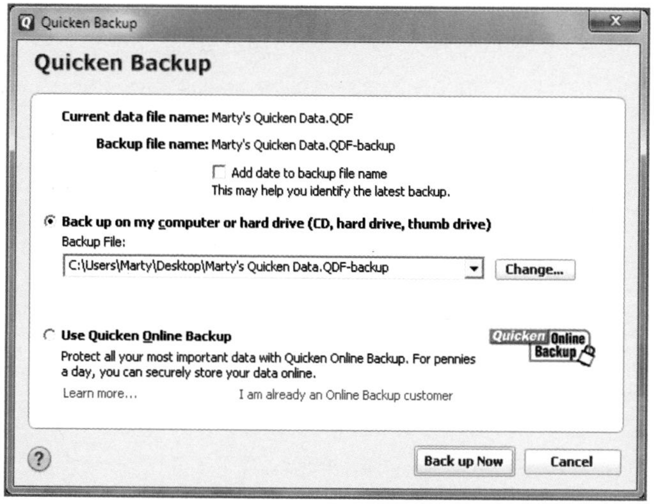

Back Up Your Data to External Media

To create a backup data file to a disk on your computer:

1. Click **File** on the Quicken menu bar, and then click **Backup And Restore**.

2. Click **Back Up Quicken File** to display the Quicken Backup dialog box.

   –Or–

   Press **CTRL+B**.

3. The Quicken Backup dialog appears, as seen in Figure 2-12.

4. The current data file information and the default backup filename assigned by Quicken are displayed.

5. Click the **Add Date To Backup File Name** check box if you want to add the date to your backup filename.

6. Click **Back Up On My Computer Or Hard Drive (CD, Hard Drive, Thumb Drive)**.

7. The location to which this data file will be backed up appears in the Backup File text box. Click **Change** to back up your information to another location.

8. If you have signed up for the fee-based Quicken Backup service (click **Learn More** to better understand the Quicken Online Backup), click **Use Quicken Online Backup** instead of the Back Up On My Computer option.

9. Click **Back Up Now**.

10. When the backup is complete, a message box appears telling you that your data file has been successfully backed up.

11. Click **OK** to close the message box.

*Figure 2-12: **Quicken Backup protects your data.***

Chapter 3

Adding More Accounts

In the first two chapters, the focus was on setting up the checking, savings, and credit card accounts. In this chapter you'll look at the Investing and the Property & Debt tabs, learn how to set up their accounts, and examine some of the Quicken tools that are available in those areas. Both areas are optional, depending on how much detail you want to maintain in Quicken.

Understand Financial Terminology

Before you begin working with the Investing and Property & Debt accounts, review the terms that are used in these areas, as explained in Table 3-1.

TERM	DEFINITION
Asset	Something you own that you expect to increase in value
Brokerage	A company that buys and sells stocks and bonds for a fee on behalf of their clients
Default	A setting or other value used by a computer program; Quicken names an account "Asset" by default if you do not choose another name
Depreciation	A decrease or loss in value due to age, wear, or market conditions
Equity	The market value of an asset, minus any debt owed on that asset
Interest	Rent or payment for borrowed money
Interest rate	The percentage of a debt charged for borrowing money
Investment	Something you expect to increase in value or to generate income
Market value	The amount for which an asset can be sold today
Mutual fund	An investment portfolio that contains the securities of other companies and sells shares of the portfolio
Performance	How a specific investment behaves over time—for example, how much money it earns
Portfolio	A set of investments
Principal	The original amount of a debt or investment on which interest is calculated
Real property	Assets that consist of land and/or buildings
Securities	Documents that show ownership, such as a stock certificate or a bond
Stock	Capital raised by selling portions (*shares*) of the ownership of a corporation; stockholders may receive a share of profits, called *dividends,* based on the number of shares they own

Table 3-1: Definitions Pertaining to the Investment and Property & Debt Accounts in Quicken

Use the Investing Tab

The Investing tab can contain four types of investment accounts:

- **Standard brokerage accounts** allow you to track stocks, bonds, mutual funds, and annuities. You can download information directly from your brokerage company or enter items manually to keep track of your capital gains or losses, cash balances, market values, performance, and shares for one or more securities.

INVESTMENT	USE THIS ACCOUNT TYPE
401(k) and 401(b)	401(k) or 403(b).
Annuities	Standard brokerage account.
Brokerage account	Standard brokerage account.
CD or money market account	Standard brokerage account (Note: You can also set these up as standard savings accounts in the Banking area of the Account Bar.)
Dividend reinvestment program	Standard brokerage account.
Employee stock options or employee stock purchase plans (ESPP)	Standard brokerage account.
IRA (any type)	IRA or Keogh account.
Real estate investment trusts (REIT)	Standard brokerage account.
Real property	Asset account.
529 Educational Plan (can be an IRA in some states)	529 Plan.
Stocks and bonds (certificates that you hold, including U.S. savings bonds)	Standard brokerage account.
Treasury bills	Standard brokerage account.

Table 3-2: **Types of Quicken Investment Accounts to Use with Various Investments**

TIP

If you hold bonds or stock certificates in a safe deposit box or other secure location, you can still track your information in a standard brokerage account.

TIP

Review your portfolio, at a minimum, at the end of the year.

- **IRA or Keogh accounts** track your retirement plans.
- **401(k) and 403(b) accounts** track your pre-tax contribution investment accounts for your retirement. It is important to set up a separate account for each plan.
- **529 Plan** tracks this educational savings plan to ensure your children's college tuition.

Table 3-2 describes which type of account to use for a particular type of investment.

Track Investments

Using Quicken to track your investments allows you to consolidate all of your investment information so that you can easily see the value of your total portfolio at any time. Understanding the performance history of several different types of investments and being able to calculate capital gains quickly can be extremely helpful throughout the year, as well as at year-end for tax purposes.

If you have several accounts, possibly with various dividend-paying stocks, it would be a great deal of work to keep track of the cost basis of all the lots of all the securities. Quicken makes it simple. At any time and for any use you can get a complete history and exact cost basis for the portfolio.

You open the Investing tab by clicking it. Figure 3-1 shows the Investing tab Portfolio view before you have set up any investing accounts.

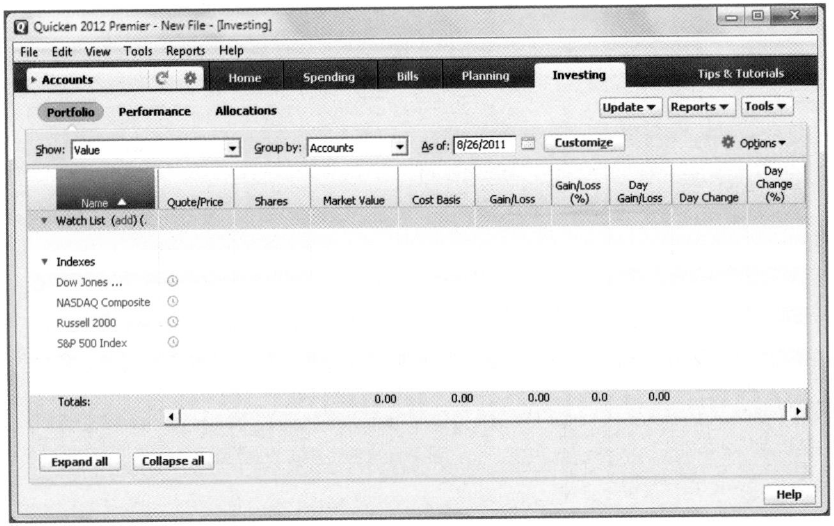

Figure 3-1: ***You can add new accounts and manage all of your investing activities with tools found by clicking the Investing tab.***

Set Up an Investment Account

Setting up an account in the Investing tab is similar to setting up an account in the Banking tab. To set up your first investing account:

1. Click **Add An Account** at the bottom of the Account Bar.

   –Or–

   Click the **Tools** menu, and click **Add Account**.

2. In all cases, the Add Account dialog box appears.

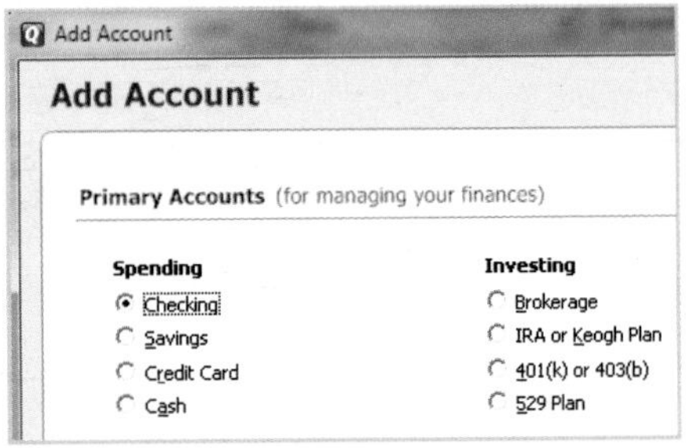

3. Choose the type of account you want to set up, and click **Next**.
4. Select your financial institution if you see it in the list of popular institutions. Otherwise, type the first few letters of the name of your institution. A drop-down list appears as Quicken tries to match the name you are typing. Select the name of your financial institution from the list. If you don't see the name of your institution, or if you don't want to or can't use online services, click **Advanced Setup** at the bottom of the dialog box and skip to step 8.
5. If you have selected or entered the name of your financial institution and are connected to the Internet, a brief message appears stating that Quicken is connecting to the institution. If your institution has download services available, enter your user name or ID and password or PIN information, and click **Connect**.

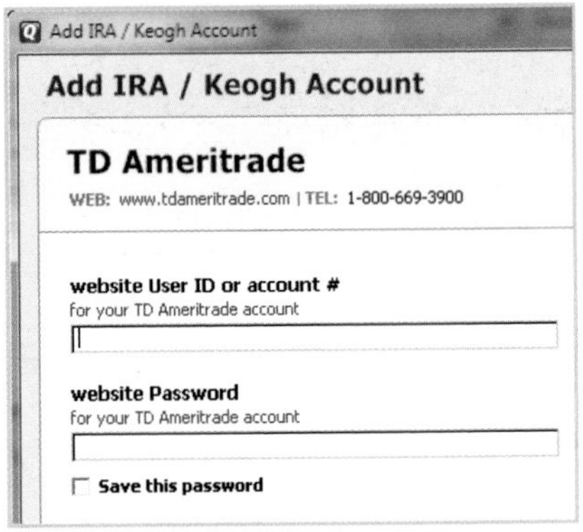

TIP

If the Investing tab is not displayed, click **View**, click **Tabs To Show**, and click **Investing**.

NOTE

Some financial institutions require that you sign up for their download service prior to using the Quicken download. Most institutions require an account number or ID and a password or PIN that they assign.

6. You may be asked if this is a single mutual fund account. If so, click **Yes** or **No**, as appropriate, and then click **Next**.

7. You are connected to your financial institution and your transactions are downloaded. When this process is done, click **Finish**.

8. Click your new account in the Account Bar. Verify or enter your cash balance, click **Done**, and skip to the next section of this chapter.

9. If your brokerage is not on the list or you are using manual entry, you may be prompted to use a different institution on Quicken's list or to keep the institution you entered. If you choose one on Quicken's list, jump back to step 5. Otherwise, click **Next**.

10. Type a name that you will use for this account in Quicken. You can type any name that identifies the account for you. You might consider using the name of the brokerage firm or other institution. Depending on the type of investment account you are setting up, you may also be prompted for information about your holdings. See "Enter Your Holdings" later in this chapter for more information.

11. If this account is an IRA or Keogh account, you are asked if this is for you or your spouse. You are also asked to choose the type of IRA from a drop-down list. Choose one and click **Next** to continue.

12. Using either your last statement or your account on the firm's website, enter the last statement date (or the "as of" date), the ending cash balance in the account, and any money-market fund balances in the account, and then click **Next**.

QUICK**FACTS**

UNDERSTANDING PLACEHOLDERS IN INVESTMENT ACCOUNTS

You may see a note in an investment account that says "Placeholder entries for missing data are used in these calculations." Quicken uses these entries when you have not entered either the purchase date or purchase price of a security. Placeholder entries simply record the name and number of shares in an investment account transaction. When you enter all of the information about a security, including purchase date and price, Quicken can track the performance of these securities.

If you want to let Quicken correctly reflect the data, either download the information from your financial institution, if it is available, or enter the information directly from the original purchase information statement. As you enter each transaction, Quicken subtracts what you enter from the placeholder entry until all of the current shares have been entered.

CAUTION

Transactions dated prior to a placeholder will not affect the account's cash balance.

13. You may be prompted for additional information, such as the securities that are in the account. If you want Quicken to download current information about each security, type its symbol. If you do not have an Internet connection, you can just type the name of the security. You can add more information later (see "Enter Your Holdings").

14. Click **Next** to continue. You are shown a summary of your holdings. Click **Done**.

15. You may be asked if this a single mutual fund account (one containing a single mutual fund with no cash balance). If it is, click **Yes** and click **Next**; otherwise, since No is the default, just click **Next**.

16. After you have entered all of the information about this new investing account, click **Finish** to complete the account setup.

Refer to Table 3-2 for some suggestions as to which Quicken investment account you should use for each of your investments.

Enter Your Holdings

As you create your new investment account, at some point you may be prompted to enter information about each of the securities that are held in it. The point at which this prompt appears will vary according to the type of account you are creating. With your Internet connection, Quicken can help you find the ticker symbols for your securities.

1. In the Quicken Account Setup: What Securities Are In This Account dialog box, select the first text box to enter the ticker symbol for the first security. If you do not know the symbol and have an Internet connection, click **Ticker Symbol Lookup** to open the Quicken Investing Symbol Lookup page, as you saw in Chapter 1.

2. Use your TAB key to move through the text boxes, entering each of the securities in the account. You do not have to enter the name—Quicken will do that for you—just the ticker symbol. If you need to add more than five, click the **Add More** button.

3. After you have entered all of the securities in this account, click **Next**.

4. Type the number of shares in the first **Total Shares** text box. Quicken will look up the total market value of each stock for you. Click the options to indicate if the security is a stock, a mutual fund, or another type of security. Use TAB to move between fields. Click **Next** to continue.

5. A summary window shows all of the information you have entered about your securities. If there is a cash balance, that displays as well. Click **Done** and skip to step 8.

6. Quicken may ask if this is a single mutual fund account. If it is, click **Yes** and then click **Next**. See the "Creating a Single Mutual Fund Account" QuickSteps later in this chapter. If this account is not a single mutual fund account, click **No** and then click **Next**.

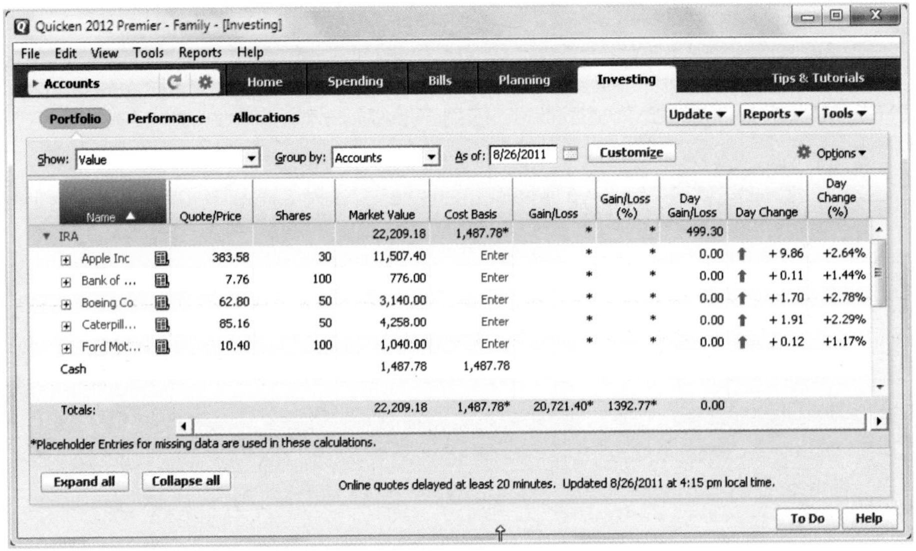

Figure 3-2: Quicken automatically updates the current price of your securities if you're online; if you enter the cost, Quicken can calculate your gain or loss.

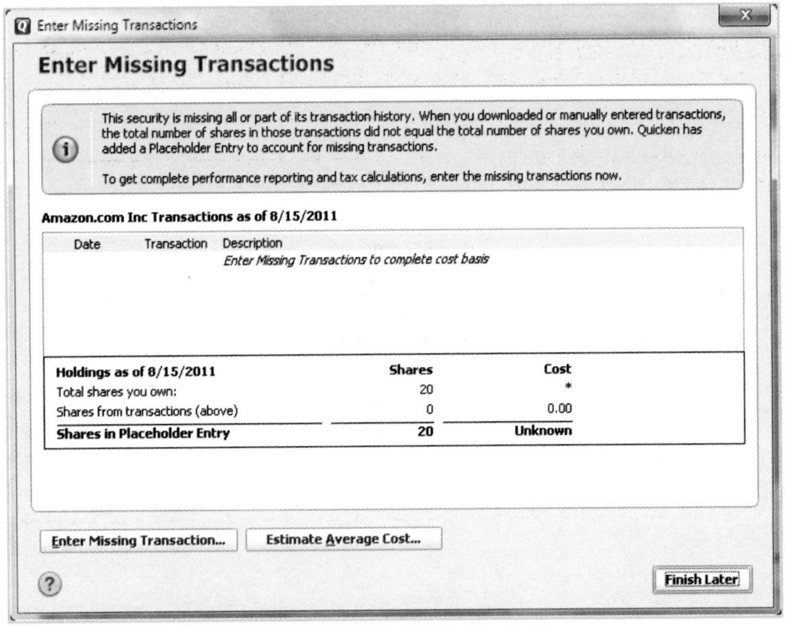

7. If you are entering an IRA/Keogh account, you need to select who owns the account and what type of IRA it is, and then click **Next**.

8. The Account Added dialog box appears. Click **Finish** and click the **Investing** tab to see the results of your work.

Your new account information appears in the Investing tab, as seen in Figure 3-2. With your Internet connection, Quicken downloaded the current prices for your securities. However, Quicken cannot calculate the gain or loss on each investment without knowing what you paid for your securities.

The amount you paid is called your *cost basis*. Quicken displays an asterisk in the Gain/Loss columns, called a *placeholder entry*, until you complete the information. You may enter this information now or later.

ENTER COSTS FOR SECURITIES

To enter the cost for your security:

1. Click the **Investing** tab, and click the account name with which you want to work. The account is displayed, as seen in Figure 3-3.

2. Click **Enter Cost** in the Inv Amt column for a security for which you want to enter the cost. The Enter Missing Transactions dialog box appears.

If your placeholder entries don't show, you may need to set the preferences to view hidden investment transactions. Click **Edit** and click **Preferences**. Then click **Investment Transactions**, and click **Show Hidden Transactions**. For a more complete display in the account register, choose **Two Line** in the List Display text box.

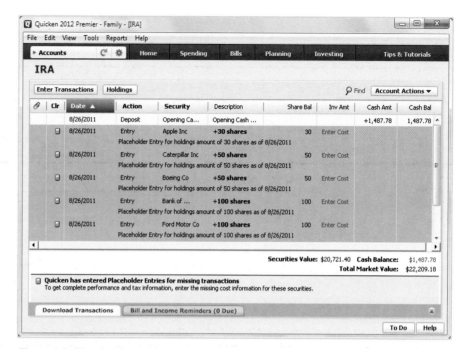

Figure 3-3: *Placeholder entries show the number of shares you own, but not what you paid for those shares.*

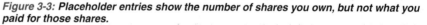

3. Click **Enter Missing Transaction**. The Buy – Shares Bought dialog box appears:

- Enter the transaction date, number of shares, the price per share you paid on that date, and the commission that you paid. Quicken will calculate the total cost. Click **Enter/Done** when finished.

  –Or–

- If you purchased the shares over time, click **Estimate Average Cost**. Enter values in either the **Cost** or the **Price/Share** field, and click **OK**. This option is not as accurate as entering each batch of shares you purchased, but it is quicker and may be enough if you don't need all the detail. You can come back and enter the individual transactions at a later date.

Enter Missing Transactions

Estimate the total cost of your **First Solar Inc** holdings. Enter the total cost for all shares you own, or the average price per share.

Use this screen if you are not ready or able to enter all missing transactions - for example, if you have a mutual fund with many dividend reinvestment transactions. When you do, Quicken can provide partial performance reporting for **First Solar Inc**, including the average annual return at the end of each year. However, Quicken will not be able to help you with the tax implications of your investments, and some performance measures will still be incomplete. For complete investments reporting, enter missing transactions (see previous screen).

As of: 8/15/2011

Holdings as of 8/15/2011	Shares	Cost	Price/Share
Total shares you own:	30	4,270.50	142.35
Shares from transactions:	0	0.00	0.00
Shares in Placeholder Entry:	**30**	**4,270.50**	**142.35**

OK   Cancel

4. Repeat steps 1 through 3 for each security you own. When you are done, click **Holdings** to see your gains and losses.

Account Overview: IRA

Holdings   ⚙ Options ▼

Show: Value   As of: 8/26/2011

Name ▲	Quote/Price	Shares	Market Value	Cost Basis	Gain/Loss	Gain/Loss (%)	Day Gain/Loss	Day Change	Day Change (%)
Apple Inc	383.58	30	11,507.40	8,063.45	3,443.95	42.71	295.80 ↑	+ 9.86	+2.64%
Bank of ...	7.76	100	776.00	1,465.95	-689.95	-47.07	11.00 ↑	+ 0.11	+1.44%
Boeing Co	62.80	50	3,140.00	3,421.45	-281.45	-8.23	85.00 ↑	+ 1.70	+2.78%
Caterpillar ...	85.16	50	4,258.00	4,482.45	-224.45	-5.01	95.50 ↑	+ 1.91	+2.29%
Ford Mot...	10.40	100	1,040.00	1,541.95	-501.95	-32.55	12.00 ↑	+ 0.12	+1.17%
Cash			1,487.78	1,487.78					
Totals:			22,209.18	20,463.03	1,746.15	8.53	499.30		

Online quotes delayed at least 20 minutes. Updated 8/26/2011 at 4:15 pm local time.

Set Up One Step Update

Quicken 2012 allows you to update all of your financial information in one step. You can download transactions from your bank, credit union, brokerage firm, and credit card company. This single-access feature allows you to schedule downloads at your convenience or whenever you use Quicken. To set up One Step Update:

1. Click the **Update** icon (the circular blue arrow) at the top of the Account Bar to display the One Step Update Settings dialog box. You can also access this dialog box from the Quicken menu: click **Tools** and click **One Step Update**.

2. Depending on how you have managed the passwords for each of your financial institutions, you may be prompted for individual passwords or for your Password Vault password.

3. Get Quotes And Investment Information, Financial Institutions, and your particular institutions should all be checked by default, which should allow you to obtain information about and control the securities you have entered. Click **Select Quotes** to open the Security List dialog box.

4. To *exclude* a security from being downloaded, click the **Download Quotes** check mark to the right of the security name to clear it.

5. To add a new security, click **New Security**. Enter the information for this new security. If necessary, use the Look Up button to find its ticker symbol. Click **Next**. Quicken uses your Internet connection to download information about this security. Review the information presented, and click **Done** to add the security to your list.

6. To edit or change a security in the list, select that security, click **Edit** to the right of the security, and make any changes to its details. When you are done making changes, click **OK**.

7. To add market indexes to your watch lists, click **Choose Market Indexes**, click the check box opposite the index you want, and click **Done** to return to the Security List dialog box.

8. You can delete securities in this dialog box only if they are not in any of your portfolios. Select the security to be deleted and click **Delete** to the right of the name.

9. When you are finished with the Security List, click **Done**. Keep One Step Update Settings open.

UPDATE YOUR PORTFOLIO ON QUICKEN.COM

The Quicken.com option on the One Step Update dialog box lets you set up and update accounts on Quicken.com so that you can track your investment accounts and Watch List from any Internet connection throughout the world. If you have created your Quicken.com account during registration, you can access it by going to www.quicken.com/investments and signing in.

To make changes to your Quicken.com portfolio:

1. From the One Step Updates dialog box, click **Select Quicken.com Data To Update** to open the Preferences dialog box with the Quicken.com Portfolio section displayed.

2. Select which of your accounts you want to view online by clicking them individually, or click **Select All** or **Clear All** to select all or none of your portfolios.

3. Click **Send My Shares** to track the value of your securities.

4. Click **Send Only My Symbols** to track only the current market-share prices of your portfolio.

5. Click **Track My Watch List On Quicken.com** to receive information about securities on your Watch List.

6. Click **OK** when you are finished working with your Quicken.com portfolio preferences.

SELECT ACCOUNTS TO UPDATE

If you chose to use One Step Update for one or more of your financial institutions, that will be displayed whenever you choose to update one or more of your accounts. You can stop using One Step Update with that institution by clicking the check box to the left of the name. For other institutions that are available for One Step Update, click **Activate For One Step Update** and follow the instructions in Chapter 2.

When you have selected the accounts to update and chosen your other settings, you are returned to the One Step Update Settings dialog box. Click **Manage My**

CAUTION

While some 401(k) plans allow you to take loans against the funds in the plan, it may not be a good idea. The interest payments on these loans are not tax-deductible, and you lose the growth you would have gotten on the amount of the loan. See your tax professional for more information.

QUICKSTEPS

CREATING A SINGLE MUTUAL FUND ACCOUNT

A single mutual fund account is an account that you buy directly from a mutual fund company. Many new investors start with this type of account, as it often requires a smaller initial investment, and one can contribute regular, small amounts. This type of fund has no cash or money market balance, as all contributions are used to purchase more shares in the fund. When you first buy a single mutual fund from a mutual fund company (or if you already own one), you can use a single mutual fund account to track it. To add this type of account, follow the first four steps in setting up an investment account as described in "Set Up an Investment Account" earlier in this chapter, selecting the appropriate account type (Standard Brokerage, IRA, etc.) and manual transaction entry.

TIP

The only reason to set up this type of account is if the financial institution you will download from demands it. Otherwise, just stick with a brokerage account.

1. Follow the instructions in "Set Up an Investment Account" earlier in this chapter. After entering a single mutual fund security and its number of shares, clicking **Next** as needed, the Summary dialog box appears showing a single mutual fund. Click **Done**.

Continued . . .

Passwords to work with the Password Vault. If you want to schedule updates, click **Schedule Updates** to establish what you want updated and how often.

Click **Update Now** to run the update, or click **Cancel** to close the One Step Update Settings dialog box.

Use the Property & Debt Tab

The Property & Debt tab contains accounts that provide a way to integrate all your other financial information into Quicken so that you can see your total financial position at any given moment. The Property and Debt accounts in this tab include

- **House** accounts are used for your main residence, vacation home, rental properties, or other real estate. You can create a liability account for each property at the same time you create the asset account.

- **Vehicle** accounts are used for all types of vehicles, including cars, trucks, motorcycles, boats, motor homes, and campers. You can create liability accounts for the loans on each vehicle at the same time you create the asset accounts.

- **Asset** accounts are used for assets other than real property, vehicles, or investments. Examples include sterling silver, antiques, baseball card collections, first-edition and rare books, and business equipment.

- **Liability** accounts are used for personal debts other than credit cards. Credit cards are, by default, included with the Banking accounts. Examples of liability accounts include personal loans and promissory notes you owe banks, loan companies, and individuals, as well as student loans. You can also link a liability with an asset, such as a home equity loan or line of credit. For more information on linking asset and liability accounts, see Chapter 6.

CREATING A SINGLE MUTUAL FUND ACCOUNT (Continued)

2. A dialog box appears asking if this is a single mutual fund account. In response to the Are You Setting Up This Type Of Account? dialog box, click **Yes**. Click **Next** to continue.

3. The Account Added dialog box appears. Click **Finish**.

This account tracks only the one mutual fund. The register displays share balances and the market value of these shares, but does not track interest, miscellaneous income, or expenses, as all dividends from the shares are usually reinvested. If your single mutual fund holder offers online services, you may download information directly into your account register. If you are unable to download transactions, or if you choose not to download, you can revise the value of this type of account from your paper statement, as described in "Enter Costs for Securities" earlier in this chapter.

Add Brokerage Account

Is this a single mutual fund account?

Some brokers keep track of your mutual funds by creating a separate account for each mutual fund you hold. These accounts

- Can contain exactly one mutual fund (and no other types of securities such as stocks or bonds).
- Do not have a cash balance (depositing money immediately purchases shares of the fund in that account).
- If you purchase another mutual fund, another account is created.

Are you setting up this type of account?
- ○ Yes
- ● No

NOTE

If the Property & Debt tab is not displayed, from the Quicken menu, click **View**, click **Tabs To Show**, and click **Property & Debt**.

Work with the Property & Debt Tab

You use the Property & Debt tab to

- Record your major assets and debts to better understand your overall financial standing
- Allow Quicken to calculate the amount due on your mortgage and other obligations
- Track the amount of interest you are paying on any specific debt and in total

Not all Quicken users need to enter information in the Property & Debt tab, but if you have a mortgage, make car payments, or have other assets and liabilities, you might want to consider adding the information to Quicken so that you can see your full financial picture.

Set Up a House Account with a Mortgage

For most people, their biggest asset is their home. There are several methods by which you can enter this asset and any associated liability.

1. Click **Add An Account**, click **House**, and click **Next**.

2. Type a name for the account or accept the default "House," or if you have more than one house account, "House 2," "House 3," and so forth, unless you type another name. Click **Next**.

3. Enter or select the date you acquired the property. You can use the small calendar icon to the right of the date of acquisition field to select the date. Press **TAB** to move to the next field.

4. Enter the purchase price, and again press **TAB**. Estimate the value of your home today. Quicken requires that you enter an amount, so use your best guess. You can change the value later. Click **Next**.

Add House (Asset) Account

Tell Quicken about the house you'd like to track.
Don't worry if you don't have all the details- you can make changes to your account later.

When did you acquire this house? 4/19/2001
Purchase Price 346,500.00
Estimate of its Current Value 450000

It's okay to enter approximate values. You will be able to change them later.

5. Choose if and how you want the liability account set up for the house:

- Click **Yes** and **I'd Like To Track The Mortgage In Quicken** if you have not already created a liability account for the mortgage.

- Click **Yes** and **I'm Already Tracking The Mortgage In Quicken** if you have entered the liability account. Choose which account is associated with this asset in the **Select Existing Account** drop-down box.

- Click **Yes** and **I Do Not Want To Track The Mortgage In Quicken** if that is your choice.

- Click **No** if you have no mortgage.

6. Click **Next** to continue.

SET UP A MORTGAGE IN QUICKEN

If you chose to track the mortgage in Quicken and you have not already set up the mortgage liability account, the Loan Setup dialog box appears with the information you entered in the last section.

1. Review the information in the Loan Setup dialog box. The Original Balance field initially displays the total you paid, so you probably want to deduct the down payment you made. Use the small calculator icon to the right of the **Original Balance** field if you want. Adjust that figure and enter the length of the loan in years.

2. The default for the compounding period is monthly, but most financial institutions use daily, so you probably need to make that change. The normal payment period is monthly, so you can probably leave that default. Click **Next**.

3. If you are unsure of the current balance and the payment amount, enter the interest rate, and click **Calculate** for both items to have Quicken compute the amount of principal and interest for each payment as well as the current balance.

4. Click **Done**. A message appears advising you that Quicken has estimated the current balance and the next payment. Click **OK** to return to the Loan Setup dialog box. You see the estimate of the current balance, the next payment amount, and the date on which it is due. You can change this later if you want.

TIP

Try using the ten-key pad on your keyboard to enter numbers (make sure the **NUMLOCK** light on the keyboard is lit; press the **NUMLOCK** key if it isn't). Using the ten-key pad is similar to using a calculator.

Loan Setup

Loan Information
- Opening Date: 4/19/2001
- Original Balance: 346,500.00
- Original Length: ___ Years
- Compounding Period: Monthly

Payment Period
- ⦿ Standard Period: Monthly
- ○ Other Period: Payments per Year

Cancel | Next

Loan Setup

Balloon Information
- ⦿ No Balloon Payment
- ○ Amortized Length: ___ Years
- ○ Calculate

Current Balance
- ⦿ Current Balance: 179,645.34 as of: 8/15/2011
- ○ Calculate

Payment
- ⦿ Payment Amount (P+I): 1,146.21 due on: 8/19/2011
- ○ Calculate   Interest Rate: 4.50%

Cancel | Back | Done

5. Click **Done**. The Set Up Loan Payment dialog box appears. If you want, change the interest rate and/or adjust the principal and interest payment.

6. Click **Edit** to include other amounts you pay with your mortgage payment, such as real estate taxes and homeowners' insurance. In the **Split Transaction** dialog box, enter the category for each portion and the amount for each category, and then click **OK**.

7. If you will be printing the check from Quicken, click **Print Check** in the Type drop-down list.

8. Click **Payment Method** to select how the payment will be entered into Quicken:

   ● Choose **Scheduled Bill** to tell Quicken how to enter the payment, from which account it is to be paid, and how many days in advance the payment should be entered.

   ● Click **Memorized Payee** to simply memorize the payee and not schedule the payment.

   ● If you have enabled this mortgage payment as a recurring online payment, click **Repeating Online Payment**.

NOTE

Some variable-rate or adjustable-rate loans change the interest rate with the next payment that is due. Others change the interest rate for all future payments.

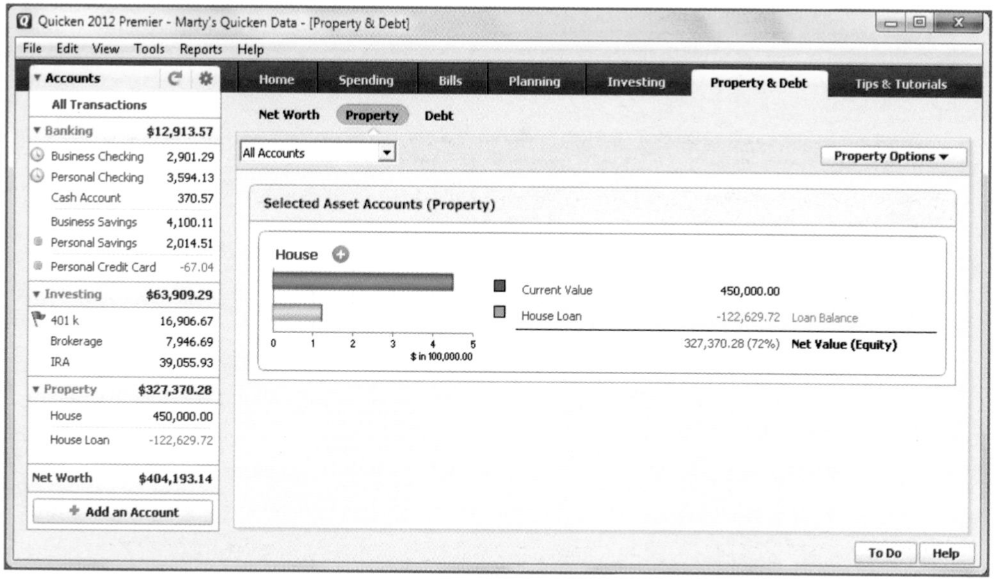

9. Click **OK** to close the Select Payment Method dialog box.

10. Click in the **Payee** field to enter the name of your mortgage lender. Adjust the next payment date, and, if desired, change the interest category.

11. Enter any memo, such as the account number, that should be included on the printed check. By default, Quicken uses "Interest Exp" as the category.

Quicken 2012 Premier - Marty's Quicken Data - [Property & Debt]							

File   Edit   View   Tools   Reports   Help

▼ Accounts   ⟳   ✿

All Transactions

▼ Banking   **$12,913.57**

Home   Spending   Bills   Planning   Investing   **Property & Debt**   Tips & Tutorials

Net Worth   **Property**   Debt

Business Checking   2,901.29
Personal Checking   3,594.13
Cash Account   370.57
Business Savings   4,100.11
Personal Savings   2,014.51
Personal Credit Card   -67.04

All Accounts ▾   Property Options ▾

Selected Asset Accounts (Property)

▼ Investing   **$63,909.29**

House   ⊕

401 k   16,906.67
Brokerage   7,946.69
IRA   39,055.93

▼ Property   **$327,370.28**

House   450,000.00
House Loan   -122,629.72

■ Current Value   450,000.00
□ House Loan   -122,629.72   Loan Balance

0 1 2 3 4 5   327,370.28 (72%)   **Net Value (Equity)**
$ in 100,000.00

Net Worth   **$404,193.14**

✚ **Add an Account**

To Do   Help

Figure 3-4: You see both your property and your debts when opening the Property & Debt tab.

12. Enter the website for the payee, if desired, so you can go to the website for information or to pay the loan.

13. Click **Address** to create an address for the payee's name you entered. If you did select Print Check as the payment type you will get a message that the payment type must be a check to have an address.

14. After you have completed setting up the loan, click **Done**.

15. At the Account Added dialog box to which you are returned, click **Finish**.

Your new asset account and its related liability account appear in the Property & Debt tab both under Property and under Debt (see Figure 3-4), as well as on the Account Bar.

Add Other Property & Debt Accounts

You can create other accounts within the Property & Debt tab. As you work with the dialog boxes, you will see similarities between the various accounts. To add a vehicle, for example:

1. Click **Add An Account** in the Account Bar, or use any of the other methods to add an account described earlier in this chapter.

2. Click **Vehicle** under Assets, and click **Next**. Type the account name, and click **Next**.

NOTE

If one of your vehicles is a motor home, consult your tax professional to see if you should consider this your primary home or a second home.

3. Type the vehicle make or manufacturer, its model, and model year, pressing **TAB** to move from field to field. Enter the date you acquired the vehicle, its purchase price, and its estimated current value, and then click **Next**.

Add Vehicle (Asset) Account

Tell Quicken about the vehicle you'd like to track.
Don't worry if you don't have all the details- you can make changes to your account later.

Vehicle Make/Manufacturer	Toyota
Vehicle Model	Prius
Vehicle Year	2008
When did you acquire this vehicle?	8/14/2008
Purchase Price	23,850.00
Estimate of its Current Value	21500

It's okay to enter approximate values. You will be able to change them later.

4. Choose if and how you want the liability account set up for the vehicle:

- Click **Yes** and **I'd Like To Track This Loan In Quicken** if you have not already created a liability account for the vehicle.

- Click **Yes** and **I'm Already Tracking The Loan In Quicken** if you have entered the liability account. Choose which account is associated with this asset in the **Select Existing Account** drop-down box.

- Click **Yes** and **I Do Not Want To Track The Loan In Quicken** if that is your choice.

- Click **No** if there is no loan on this car. Click **Next** to continue.

5. If you indicated that you wanted to create a loan, the Loan Setup dialog box appears. Follow the instructions in "Use Loan Setup" later in this chapter. Otherwise, if you chose not to track the loan, click **Done** at the next window.

Use Loan Setup

Quicken provides Loan Setup to help you set up an amortized loan. This feature can be opened automatically, as described in the previous section, or you can open it directly.

1. From the bottom of the Account Bar, click **Add An Account** and choose **Loan**.

–Or–

From the Property & Debt tab's Property section, click **Property Options** and click **Add A New Loan**.

2. Either way, the Loan Setup dialog box appears. Choose between borrowing money and lending money. Borrowing is the default.

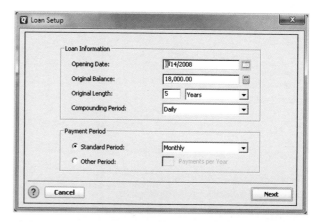

3. Enter the name of a new account, or link this loan to an existing account (with a new asset like a car, Quicken automatically sets up a new loan account for it).

4. If you have made payments on this loan, click **Yes**; otherwise, click **No**. Then click **Next**. You are asked for the initial loan information.

5. If this is a new account, you need to provide the opening date and original balance of the loan. If this is an existing account, Quicken provides the information for you, but remember to subtract your trade-in and any cash payments.

6. Enter the loan period in years, the compounding period, which often is daily, and the payment period, normally monthly. Click **Next** to continue.

NOTE

By default, Loan Setup compounds interest monthly, but most lending institutions compound it daily.

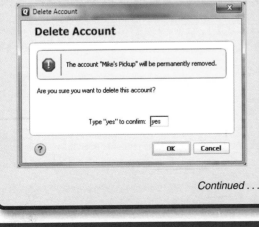

UICKSTEPS

DELETING AND HIDING ACCOUNTS

If you want to remove an account from view in Quicken, you can *delete* it, which means the account and all its related transactions are permanently removed from Quicken. Or you can *hide* it so that it is not seen in the Account Bar and not included in the totals. If you hide an account, you still have access to all of its related transactions.

DELETE AN ACCOUNT

1. Click the **Tools** menu, and click **Account List**, or press **CTRL+A**, to display the Account List. Click the account you want to delete, and click **Edit** to the right of the account name.

   –Or–

   Right-click the account in the Account Bar, and click **Edit/Delete Account**.

2. In the Account Details dialog box that appears, click **Delete Account**.

3. In the dialog box prompting you to confirm that you want to delete this account, type <u>yes</u> to verify that you want to delete the account (it does not matter if you use uppercase or lowercase letters). Click **OK** to delete this account.

Continued . . .

7. If there is a balloon payment and it is amortized, click **Amortized Length** and enter the time period. If there is a balloon payment and you want Quicken to determine it, click **Calculate**. Otherwise, leave the default **No Balloon Payment**.

8. If you know the current balance, enter it and the "as of" date. Otherwise, click **Calculate** to have Quicken calculate the amount for you.

9. If you know the amount of the next payment, enter it and the date on which the next payment is due. If you don't know the amount of the next payment, click **Calculate** and enter the interest rate for the loan, and click **Done** to have Quicken execute the calculations.

10. You are told that Quicken has calculated the next loan payment. Click **OK**. Review the current balance and loan payment information. If all is in order, click **Done** again. Alternatively, click **Back** to go back and change some of the assumptions and repeat steps 8 and 9.

DELETING AND HIDING ACCOUNTS

(Continued)

HIDE AN ACCOUNT

1. Follow the first step in "Delete an Account" earlier.

2. In the Account Details dialog box that appears, click the **Display Options** tab. Click the **Hide This Account In Quicken (Lists, Menus, Reports)** check box to hide this account everywhere in Quicken. By default, the next two options are also selected.

Account Details

General | Display Options

Hide or Show Accounts

☑ Hide this account in Quicken (lists, menus, reports)
☑ Hide this account in Account Bar
☑ Don't include this account in net worth total

3. Click the **Hide This Account In Account Bar** check box to keep the account from displaying in the Quicken Account Bar. The total of all balances in accounts that you have hidden in this manner will appear on the Account Bar as a total in "Other Accounts."

4. Click **Don't Include This Account In Net Worth Total** to keep the account's balance from being included in the totals. The account will still show in the Account Bar, but its balance will not be included in the totals.

5. Click **OK** to hide the account, and, if you started in the Account List dialog box, click **Done** to close it.

TIP

If there are bill and income reminders for the account, you must delete the reminders or update them to use another account before you can delete the account.

---

11. When the Set Up Loan Payment dialog box opens, review and make any needed changes to the loan payment information, enter the name of the payee, any memo information, and the website, if desired. The default category is the standard Interest Exp category, but you can change it to another category or create a new category. If all appears to be correct, click **Done**.

12. If you are asked if there is an associated asset with this loan and you want to enter it, click **Yes** to create the asset account; enter the asset name, acquisition date, current value, and any optional tax information; and then click **Done**. Otherwise, click **No** to finish creating the liability account.

13. If you are completing setting up an asset and loan combination, click **Finish** to end that process.

Add Other Debt Accounts

Other debt accounts are used for loans other than your house or vehicle. These types of loans can be promissory notes, student loans, loans against insurance policies, loans for medical expenses, or any other liability.

1. Click **Add An Account** in the Account Bar, or use any of the other methods described to add an account.

2. Click **Other Liability** and click **Next**. Type a name for the debt, and click **Next**.

3. Enter the starting date of the loan or the date on which you want to start keeping track of this loan. Then enter the value of the loan—that is, what you owed on that date.

4. If the debt has tax implications, click **Tax**. Consult your tax professional for information on tax implications, and, if needed, enter the recommended information. Click **OK** and then click **Next**.

Add Debt Account

Enter the ending date from your latest statement (or the date you want to start tracking this liability) and the balance of the liability

Date to start tracking | 8/15/2011 |

Liability Amount | 5,800.00 | This becomes the opening balance of your Quicken Account.

Enter Optional tax information **Tax...**

Understand Basic Transactions

A *transaction* in Quicken is something that affects the balance in an account. You enter a transaction into the *register* of the account. A register looks like a checkbook register, where you enter the activity, or transactions, regarding your accounts. Table 4-1 explains some of the terms used when talking about transactions. When using these terms, it is important to distinguish between the following:

- **Checking or savings accounts** in which you deposit your money and write checks or make withdrawals against your own funds. In essence, the bank owes you your money.

- **Credit card accounts** in which the bank extends you a line of credit, you make charges against that line, and then make payments to it. In essence, you owe the bank their money.

TERM	DEFINITION
Charge or debit	A transaction that increases the balance in a credit card account or decreases the balance in a checking account. A charge can also be something you purchased with a credit card or a fee from a financial institution.
Credit	A transaction that decreases the balance in a credit card, like a payment, or increases the balance in a checking account, like a deposit.
Deposit	A transaction that increases the balance in a checking or savings account.
Field	An area where you can make an entry, such as the date *field* or the amount *field*.
Payee	The company or person to whom you make a payment; for a deposit, it is the person from whom you get money you are depositing.
Payment	A transaction that lowers the balance in a credit card account.
Reconcile	To make what you have entered into a Quicken account agree with the statement you receive from your financial institution.
Transaction	An action that changes the balance in an account.
Transfer	To move funds from one account to another.

Table 4-1: Terms Used with Quicken Transactions

You create a transaction when you write a check, make a deposit, enter a credit card charge, or make a payment on your credit card. To keep your account register up to date, you need to enter the transaction into the account register, either manually or by downloading the information from the financial institution. You also need to reconcile your accounts on a regular basis against your financial institution's records. Quicken offers an Automatic Reconciliation feature. Chapter 7 discusses that and other methods of reconciling your accounts in more detail.

Establish Preferences for Your Registers

Before you use a register for the first time, you may want to set your preferences. Preferences are the ways in which you tell Quicken how to display and process your information.

CAUTION

The settings used for investment accounts are slightly different because they use transaction lists rather than registers.

Set Register Preferences

To set your preferences for an account:

1. Click the **Edit** menu, and then click **Preferences**.

2. Click **Register**. The Quicken Register Preferences dialog box appears, as shown in Figure 4-1.

3. Choose how you want the register fields displayed by checking or unchecking the two choices. By default, both are checked to display date first and memo first.

4. In the Transaction Entry area, click the relevant check boxes:

   - **Automatically Enter Split Data** changes the way you enter a split transaction (see "Create a Split Transaction" later in this chapter). This check box is not selected by default.

   - **Use Automatic Categorization** lets Quicken choose the category for a transaction based on Quicken's database or on the category you used before for this payee. This check box is selected by default.

   - **Automatically Place Decimal Point** sets the decimal point to two places. By default, Quicken enters zero cents when you enter a number. For example, if you type the number <u>23</u> in the Amount field, Quicken displays it as $23.00. If you choose to set the decimal point automatically, the number 23 becomes .23, or 23 cents. This check box is not selected by default.

5. In the Register Appearance area, select how you want the register to look:

   - **Gray Reconciled Transactions**, which is selected by default, displays all reconciled transactions in gray rather than in black. This feature allows you to quickly scan your register and find transactions that have not yet cleared the bank.

   - Clicking **Remember Register Filters After Quicken Closes** saves the settings you set in the filter fields shown at the top of your register.

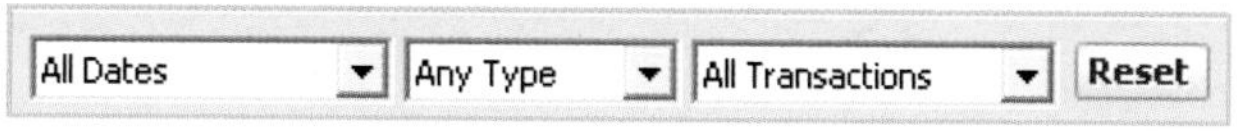

   - **Use Pop-up Registers** allows your register to display in a separate, moveable window not attached to its tab and facilitates looking at two or more registers at the same time.

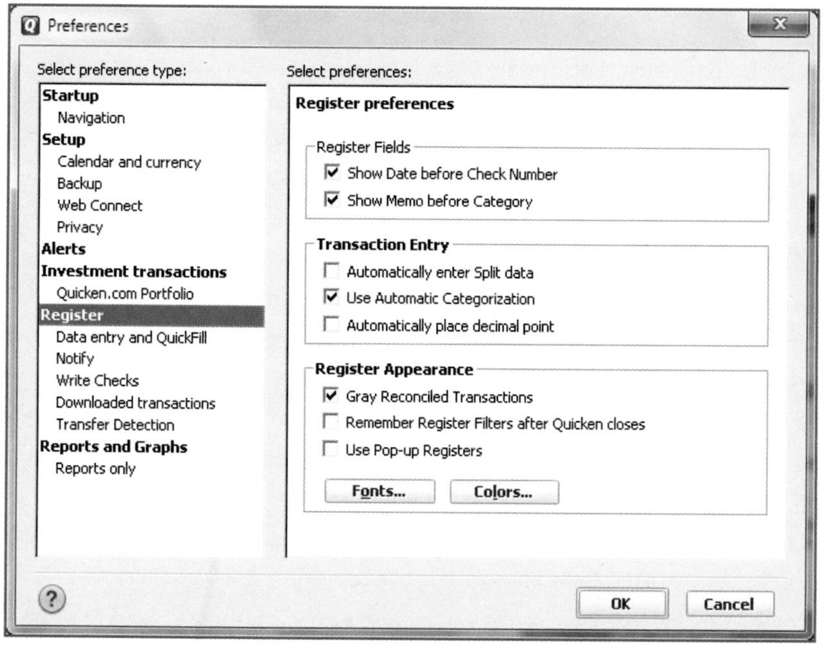

Figure 4-1: Quicken gives you several ways to customize the register to meet your needs.

NOTE

Some fonts display better than others. Look at how your choice appears in the register. If you can't read it easily, choose another font and/or size.

6. Click the **Fonts** button to see a menu of available fonts for the register. You can choose from several different fonts and sizes. Click the font and size to see in the preview box how characters in the register would look using this font. When finished, click **OK**.

Choose Register Font

Font: | Size:
Tahoma | 8

Tahoma
Technical
Tempus Sans ITC
Times New Roman

8
9
10
11

☐ Bold

Sample Text

Reset

? | OK | Cancel

Choose Register Colors

Accounts
Spending:
Savings:
Credit:
Investment:
Retirement:
Asset:
Liability:

OK
Cancel
Restore Defaults

Help

7. Click the **Colors** button to display the available colors for each register. Click the down arrow to the right of each account name to see the available choices. You can choose from seven different colors, including the default color. Click **OK** to close the dialog box.

8. Click **OK** to close the dialog box when you have selected your register preferences.

Determine QuickFill Preferences

Quicken saves you time during data entry with what Intuit calls *QuickFill* features. For example, Quicken provides drop-down lists from which you can choose categories and payees. You can choose to have a field automatically completed after typing only a few letters using Quicken's memorization of payees, transactions, and categories. You can determine how these features work in the QuickFill Preferences dialog box, shown in Figure 4-2.

1. Click the **Edit** menu, click **Preferences**, and then click **Data Entry And QuickFill**. The Data Entry And QuickFill Preferences dialog box appears. In the Data Entry area:

   a. Choose whether to use the **ENTER** key in addition to the **TAB** key to move between fields in your registers. By default, the **ENTER** key is used only to complete a transaction.

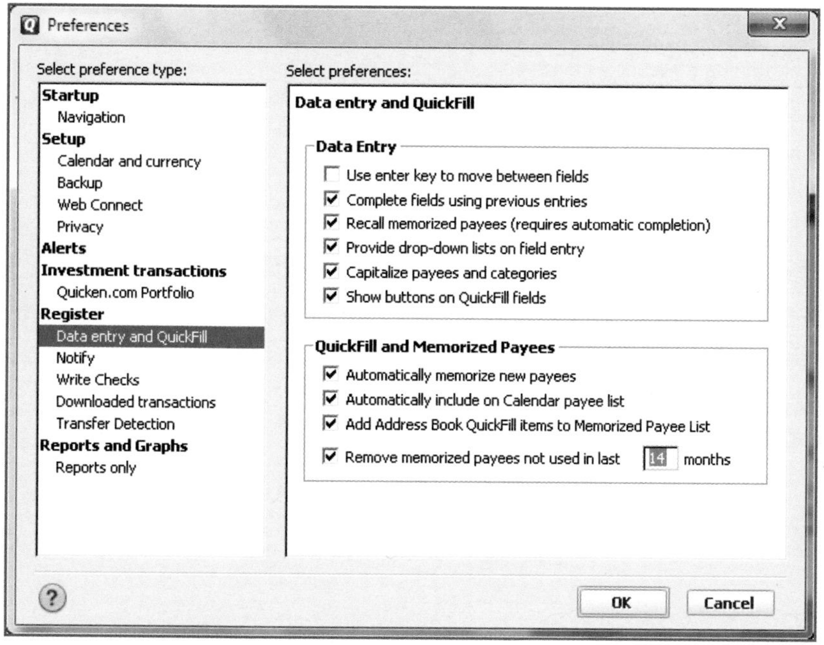

Figure 4-2: *Use QuickFill preferences to configure your registers according to the way you want to enter and view your data.*

b. Choose whether to automatically complete each field using the entry previously made for this payee. If you choose this option, which is selected by default, you can also choose whether to have Quicken recall your memorized payees.

c. Choose whether to have Quicken display a drop-down list for the number, payee, and category fields (this is selected by default).

d. Choose whether you want the leading character in the payee and category names capitalized.

e. Choose whether you want Quicken to display the buttons on QuickFill fields. If you choose to clear this check box, the buttons, such as those next to the Category field, will not display. [Other Inc ▼]

2. In the QuickFill and Memorized Payees area (all of which are selected by default):

a. Choose to automatically memorize new payees and memorize transactions to the Calendar List.

b. Choose to automatically add any Address Book QuickFill group items to the Memorized Payee List.

c. Click **Remove Memorized Payees Not Used In Last *nn* Months** to remove seldom-used payees and enter the number of months after which the payees should be removed. Fourteen months is the default.

3. Click **OK** when finished.

Set Notify Preferences

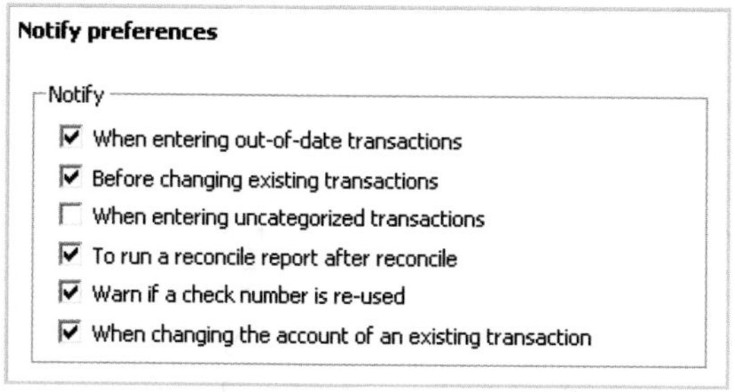

Notify preferences tell Quicken the circumstances under which you want to receive warning messages. By default, all but one of the warnings are activated.

1. Click the **Edit** menu, click **Preferences**, and then click **Notify**. The Notify Preferences dialog box appears.

2. Choose whether to get a warning message when

- Entering transactions that are not in the current year
- Changing an existing transaction

NOTE

If you choose a two-digit year, the on-screen image still shows four digits, but when you print the check, only the rightmost two digits are printed.

QUICKSTEPS

SETTING DOWNLOADED TRANSACTIONS PREFERENCES

From the Preferences dialog box, you can set preferences for transactions you download from financial institutions.

1. Click the **Edit** menu, click **Preferences**, and then click **Downloaded Transactions**. The Downloaded Transactions Preferences dialog box appears.

2. Choose if after downloading, you want to automatically record banking and, separately, investing downloaded transactions in the register to which they belong. If this automatic-entry capability is enabled, which it is by default for banking transactions, you do not have to review and approve each downloaded transaction.

3. Choose whether to apply renaming rules to downloaded transactions. Renaming rules change the name of a payee on a downloaded transaction—for example, "Grocery 198775" becomes "Corner Grocery" in your register. Renaming rules are discussed further in Chapter 5.

- Click **Automatically Create Rules When Manually Renaming** to clear the check box. This asks you if you want to create a renaming rule

Continued . . .

- Entering a transaction without a category (not selected by default)
- Not running a reconciliation report after you complete a reconciliation
- Using a check number more than once
- Changing the account of an existing transaction

3. Click **OK** when finished.

Set Preferences for Writing Checks

Quicken gives you six options from which to choose when using the program to write checks. To set those options:

1. Click the **Edit** menu, click **Preferences**, and then click **Write Checks**. The Write Checks Preferences dialog box appears.

2. Choose whether you want a four-digit year, such as 4/5/2012, or a two-digit year, such as 4/5/12, to be printed on your checks.

3. Click the **Spell Currency Units** check box to have Quicken print the currency amount on your check with the currency unit displayed, for example, "Twenty Dollars and 37 Cents" rather than "Twenty and 37/100."

4. Click the **Allow Entry Of Extra Message On Check** check box if you want to include information for the payee's records, such as your account number or the invoice number you are paying with this check.

5. Click the **Print Categories On Voucher Checks** check box if you want to include that information. A voucher check has a perforated portion that can include additional information.

6. Click the **Change Date Of Checks To Date When Printed** check box if you enter data over time and print all your checks at once.

7. Click **OK** to close the dialog box.

Work with a Register

A register in Quicken looks a lot like the paper check register you may have used in the past. It displays in the color choices you selected in your preferences setup. You can open a register by clicking the name of the register's account on the Account Bar on the left of your Quicken page. Figure 4-3 displays a register window for a checking account.

Enter a Check

To enter a check into the register:

1. If it is not already selected, click in the Date field in the empty line at the bottom of the register. By default, this is highlighted in a darker blue color. This activates the transaction line.

   When you click in the Date field, the month is selected, which you can change by typing a new number. To move to the day, press the **RIGHT ARROW** key or press forward slash (**/**), and press either the **RIGHT ARROW** key or slash again to move to the year. Change the day by pressing the plus (**+**) or minus (**−**) keys on the numeric keypad (this will not work if the computer's date setting is set to display the date with dashes instead of slashes), and change either the day or year by typing a value. You can enter the current day's date by pressing the letter **T**.

2. Accept today's date, type a date using either the numeric keys at the top of the keyboard or the ten-key pad on the right of the keyboard (with **NUMLOCK** activated), or click the small calendar to the right of the field. (If the calendar does not appear in the field, double-click to open a calendar.) In the calendar, click the date you want using the arrows in the upper-left and upper-right corners to select a different month.

8/17/201	Check...	Payee

«	**August – 2011**	»
Su	Mo	Tu	We	Th	Fr	Sa
	1	2	3	4	5	6
7	8	9	10	11	12	13
14	15	16	**17**	18	19	20
21	22	23	24	25	26	27
28	29	30	31			

Print Checks with Quicken

Quicken will print checks for you if you have special paper checks for your printer that have been tailored to work with Quicken. You can order these checks through your bank, through Quicken, or through third-party companies (do an Internet search on "Quicken checks"). Printing your checks makes them easier to read and potentially saves you time in that you can enter information directly into a check form or print checks already entered into the register. Before you start, you need to load the special paper checks into your printer.

PRINT CHECKS IN THE REGISTER

If you have transactions to print in your register with "Print" in the Num field, you can directly print them instead of entering them into the check form to be printed. When you use the form, however, the information is automatically entered into the register.

1. Click the **File** menu, and then click **Print Checks**. If you do not have transactions in your register with "Print" in the Num field, you will see a message stating that you do not have any checks to print. If you do have transactions with "Print" in the Num field, the Select Checks To Print dialog box will appear.

2. Enter the number of the first paper check in the printer if it is not already correct.

3. Choose which checks to print:

   - **All Checks** prints any checks that have not yet been printed. This includes any postdated checks you may have entered.

   - **Checks Dated Through** allows you to print unprinted checks through a date you enter or select.

Select Checks to Print

Print	Date	Payee	Category	Amount
☑	8/17/2011	Host Gator	Utilities:Internet	9.95
☑	8/17/2011	Acme Food	Food & Dining:Groceries	104.18
☑	8/17/2011	Amazon	Shopping:Books	9.76

Mark All   Clear All

Done

NOTE

Each check style shows a message "Order…checks" in blue. This is a direct link to the Quicken check-ordering website.

NOTE

Legislation enacted in 2004, often referred to as "Check 21," means that financial institutions no longer have to retain paper copies of your checks. For more information about Check 21, go to www.federalreserve.gov/paymentsystems/regulations.htm.

NOTE

If you create payments in the register with "Print" in the Num field and then click **Account Actions** and click **Write Checks** at the top of the register, the payments you created will appear in the list of checks to print in the Write Checks dialog box.

- **Selected Checks** allows you to choose which checks to print. Click **Choose** and clear the check marks for any checks you don't want to print at this time.
- Click **Mark All** to print all of the checks.
- Click **Clear All** to clear all of the listed checks, and then click in the Print column just the checks you want to print.
- Click **Done** to close the dialog box and print the checks.

4. Click the **Check Style** down arrow, and choose a style. Depending on the style you are using, click the number of checks on the first page with your style.

5. Click **Print First Check** to print the first check and see how it looks. Click **OK** if your check printed correctly. Otherwise, enter the check number of the check, and Quicken will reprint it. Make any necessary corrections to how checks are printed.

6. Click **OK** to print all the checks you selected. When the printing is completed, click **OK** if all checks printed correctly. Otherwise, enter the check number of the check on which there was a problem so that Quicken can reprint it and any following checks.

PRINT CHECKS FROM THE CHECK FORM

If you would like to see a representation of the check you will be sending, Quicken provides a form into which you can enter the information you want on the final printed check, as shown in Figure 4-4. To use the check form:

1. From the Account Bar, select the account from which you want to write checks and display its register. Click **Account Actions** and click **Write Checks**. The Write Checks dialog box appears with a blank check displayed that you can fill in.

2. Click in the **Pay To The Order Of** text box, or click the down arrow at the end of the line, to display a drop-down list of previous payees.

Write Checks: Business Checking

Write checks from: Business Checking

Pay to the order of   Date 8/17/2011
Acme Food $ 104.18

One Hundred Four and 18/100** Dollars

Bill Pay
Address
Acme Food
2145 W 34th Ave.
My Town, ST 12345

Edit Address...

WELLS FARGO

Memo Invoece 432198, 8/17/11

Category --SPLIT--   Record Check

Date	Type	Payee	Category	Amount
8/17/2011	Print	Host Gator	Utilities:Internet	9.95
8/17/2011	Print	Acme Food	--SPLIT--	104.18
8/17/2011	Print	Amazon	Shopping:Books	9.76
			Total:	123.89

New Check   Ending Balance: 4,693.92

? Order Checks Reports ▼   Print Done

Figure 4-4: The Write Checks dialog box gives you a way to visualize the checks you are preparing.

NOTE

Because the Memo field can be visible when you use window envelopes, confidential information, such as your account number, should be entered into the Message field rather than the Memo field.

3. Type as much of the payee's name as needed to select the payee you want, or click the payee you want in the drop-down list.

4. Press **TAB** to move to the Amount field. If you have sent checks to this payee previously, the most recent amount you paid will be filled in. Press **TAB** again to accept the previous amount and move to the Address field. Otherwise, enter the new amount, and then press **TAB**.

5. Type the address, if one is not already attached to the payee. If you want to edit the address, click **Address** to open the Address Book. Make any changes or additions to the address, and click **OK**.

6. Press **TAB** to move to the Memo field. Type a memo entry, if you want, and press **TAB** again to move to the Category field.

7. Begin to type the category. If there is an existing category starting with the letters you've typed, it will be filled in. Alternatively, you can click the down arrow at the end of the **Category** line, and click the category you want to use.

8. If you want to have portions of the money you are paying go to different categories, click **Split** and follow the instructions in the section "Create a Split Transaction" later in this chapter.

9. If you don't want to use the default of today's date, click in the **Date** field, and enter a new date using any of Quicken's date-entering features described in "Enter a Check" earlier in this chapter.

10. When the check looks the way you want, click **Record Check**. The new check appears on a list of checks to be printed at the bottom of the window, and the check form is once more blank.

11. When you have entered all the checks you want to print, click **Print**. The Select Checks To Print dialog box appears. To continue, see "Print Checks in the Register," and complete the steps in that section, starting with step 2.

QUICKSTEPS

ENTERING A DEPOSIT

Entering a deposit is like entering a check, except that you enter the amount in the Deposit field rather than the Payment field. To enter a deposit:

1. If it is not already selected, click in the empty **Date** field at the bottom of the Date column.

2. If you want to change the date, use one of the techniques described in "Enter a Check."

3. Press **TAB** to move to the Num field, and press **D** to have "DEP" placed in the field.

4. Press **TAB** and enter the name of the payer, or select it from the drop-down list that is displayed.

5. Press **TAB** to move to the Memo field, type any information you want, and press **TAB** again to move to the Category field. Type a category or choose one from the drop-down list.

6. Press **TAB** to move to the Deposit field, and enter an amount.

7. Press **ENTER** or click **Save** to complete the transaction.

Create a New Transaction Category

When you enter a check or a deposit, you can easily create a new category if there isn't one in the Category List that you want to use.

1. Press **TAB** to move to the Category field and automatically open the list of existing categories, or click the **Category** down arrow to open the list.

2. Click **Add Category**. The Set Up Category dialog box appears.

3. Type the name and description of the new category. Press **TAB** to move from field to field.

4. Click **Income** or **Expense** or **Subcategory Of** and its name to tell Quicken what type of category this is.

5. Press **TAB** and, if desired, type a description of the category in the Description field, maybe the types of transactions this category is meant for. Again, optionally, click the **Group** down arrow and select the group you want the category to be in.

6. Click the **Tax Reporting** tab, click **Tax Related Category**, select the type of tax-line item, and select the tax-line item if this category has tax implications.

7. Click **OK** to close the dialog box.

Perform Activities with Check Registers

Not all transactions in your register are as straightforward as a check or a deposit with one category. Some transactions require you to split categories or transfer funds from one account to another. One of the most complex is tracking the deductions on your paycheck. Quicken makes all of these transactions easy to enter. Other activities you may want to perform are locating, sorting, or filtering transactions; attaching invoice copies or other images to your transactions; and printing your check register.

Create a Split Transaction

A *split* transaction is one that has more than one assigned category. For example, a check you write to the insurance company might be for both homeowners' and automobile insurance, or a deposit might be for both the principal amount of a loan and interest. You can assign up to 250 categories for any single transaction by using the Add Lines button. To enter a split transaction:

1. Click the empty line at the bottom of your register.

2. Enter the date, check number, payee, and the total amount of the check, as described in "Enter a Check" earlier in this chapter.

3. Click the **Split** button in the transaction menu on the right of the transaction.

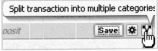

–Or–

Click the **Category** field and, if it doesn't open automatically, click the drop-down arrow to open the Category List. Click **Split** at the bottom of the list or press **CTRL+S**.

In either case, the Split Transaction dialog box appears, as shown in Figure 4-5.

4. The Category field on the first line may already be selected. If not, choose a category from the drop-down list, or type a category. Press **TAB**, type any additional information or notes in the **Memo** field, and again press **TAB**.

CHANGING, VOIDING, OR DELETING A TRANSACTION *(Continued)*

3. If you have not yet pressed **ENTER** or clicked **Save** and the transaction is still selected, you can restore it by clicking the **Edit** menu on the Quicken menu bar and clicking **Transaction**. Or, you can click **More Actions** on the transaction menu. After using either of these methods, click **Restore Transaction**.

4. Press **ENTER** or click **Save** to complete the procedure.

DELETE A TRANSACTION

When you delete a transaction, Quicken recalculates all balances and permanently removes that transaction from the register.

1. With the register containing the transaction you want to delete displayed, click the transaction.

2. Press **CTRL+D** and click **Yes** to delete the transaction.

–Or–

Click the **Edit** menu, click **Transaction**, click **Delete**, and click **Yes** to delete the transaction.

–Or–

Continued . . .

Split Transaction

Enter multiple categories to itemize this transaction; use the Memo field to record more details.

	Category	Memo	Amount
1.	Entertainment:Amusement	Concert tickets	75 00
2.	Food & Dining:Restaurants	Dinner	85 00
3.	Auto & Transport:Parking	Parking	25.00
4.			
5.			
6.			
7.			
8.			
9.			
10.			
11.			
12.			
13.			
14.			
15.			
16.			

Add Lines   Clear All   Allocate

Split Total: 185.00
Remainder: 0.00
Adjust   Transaction Total: 185.00

OK   Cancel

Figure 4-5: Splitting a transaction among multiple categories allows you to refine your accounting and better understand where your money goes.

5. The total amount of the transaction appears under Amount on the first line. Type the actual amount for the first category over that amount. Press **TAB**.

6. Quicken computes the remainder and shows it in the Amount field of the second line. Enter or select the next category, press **TAB**, enter any information you want in the Memo field, press **TAB** again, and either accept the computed amount or type a new one. Press **TAB**.

7. Repeat step 6 until you have all the categories you want. If you need to adjust any of the entries, click the amount that needs to be adjusted.

QUICKSTEPS

CHANGING, VOIDING, OR DELETING A TRANSACTION *(Continued)*

Right-click anywhere in the transaction, click **Delete** from the context menu, and click **Yes** to delete the transaction.

3. The transaction is completely deleted, and your balance is recomputed.

Note that Quicken can restore a deleted transaction only in the Quicken session in which it was deleted (that is, before you exit Quicken).

To restore a deleted transaction, click anywhere in the register, click the **Edit** menu on the Quicken menu bar, and click **Transaction**; or click **More Actions** on the transaction menu. After either step, click **Undo Delete**.

TIP

By entering deduction information from your regular paycheck, Quicken can create tax reports, help you plan for taxes, and export information to TurboTax for year-end tax reporting.

8. If the entries are correct and you have a difference, either positive or negative, from the original check amount, click **Adjust** to make the total for the transaction the sum of the split categories.

9. Click **OK** to close the Split Transaction dialog box. Instead of a single category appearing in the Category field, Quicken displays "--Split--" to remind you that there are multiple categories for this transaction.

| | | 8/20/2011 | 2227 | Tickets Unlimited | *Memo* | --Split-- | ☑☒▣ | 185 00 |

10. Hover your mouse pointer over "--Split--" in the Category field to see the amounts in each split category.

Bills & Utili		
--Split--	▯ Entertainm...	-75.00
	▯ Food & ...	-85.00
	▯ Auto & ...	-25.00

11. Click the transaction and three buttons appear next to "--Split--":

   a. Click ☑ to open the Split Transaction dialog box, where you can edit the split.

   b. Click ☒ to clear all of the split categories and amounts so that you can replace them with a single new category.

   c. Click ▣ to open the Activity dialog box, where you can see the recent transactions in the categories used in this transaction.

Track Paycheck Deductions

One of the most complex split transactions is tracking your paycheck deductions. Quicken allows you to set up your recurring paycheck so that all the deductions can be fed into separate categories. This is done through Quicken's Bill and Income Reminders.

1. Click the **Tools** menu, click **Manage Bill & Income Reminders**, click **Create New** in the menu bar at the top, and click **Income Reminder**. The Add Reminder dialog box will open.

2. Click **Paycheck Setup Wizard** at the bottom of the dialog box. The Paycheck Setup dialog box will open. To track all deductions, click **Gross Amount**, and click **Next**.

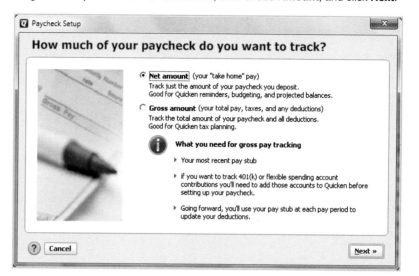

3. Click whether it is your paycheck or your spouse's, and type the name of the company from whom you are earning the paycheck. Press **TAB** to move to the Memo field. Type any additional information in this optional field, for example, if you receive two checks, one for base pay and one for commissions. Click **Next** to open the Track Paycheck dialog box shown in Figure 4-6.

4. Click the down arrow on the Account field, and select the bank account into which this income is deposited. Press **TAB**, enter or select the date, choose whether you want it automatically entered or just a reminder, and finally select the frequency on which you get paid.

5. If you change your mind and want to track your net pay only, click **Track Net Only** and jump to "Transfer Funds from One Account to Another."

6. Otherwise, click in the **Salary Amount** field to open it. Enter the gross amount of income you receive. If you do not receive the same amount each time, enter an average.

7. If you have other components of your income, such as a regular bonus or commissions, click **Add Earning**, select the category of other earnings, enter the amount, and click **OK**.

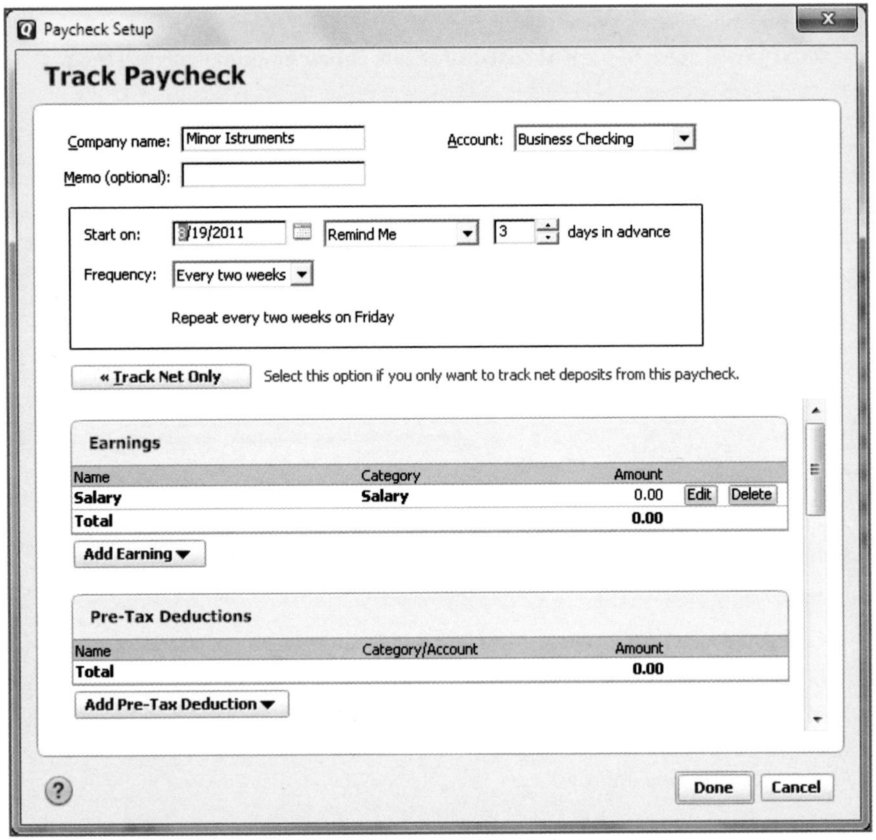

Track Paycheck

Company name: Minor Istruments   Account: Business Checking

Memo (optional):

Start on: 3/19/2011 Remind Me 3 ÷ days in advance

Frequency: Every two weeks

Repeat every two weeks on Friday

« **Track Net Only**   Select this option if you only want to track net deposits from this paycheck.

Earnings

Name	Category	Amount		
Salary	Salary	0.00	Edit	Delete
Total		0.00		

Add Earning ▼

Pre-Tax Deductions

Name	Category/Account	Amount
Total		0.00

Add Pre-Tax Deduction ▼

Done   Cancel

Figure 4-6: Quicken's Track Paycheck feature gives you the ability to follow the amounts you have deducted from your paycheck for taxes, insurance, and other items.

NOTE

If you don't already have one or more investment accounts set up in Quicken, when you select the 401(k) pre-tax deduction, Quicken will start the add account process so you can set up the account. If you have not downloaded transactions yet for the day, Quicken will first refresh the financial institution list, and then initiate the add account process.

8. If you have pre-tax deductions such as 401(k) contributions or health insurance, click **Add Pre-Tax Deduction**, select the category, select the account, enter both the contribution and employer matching amounts, if applicable, and click **OK**.

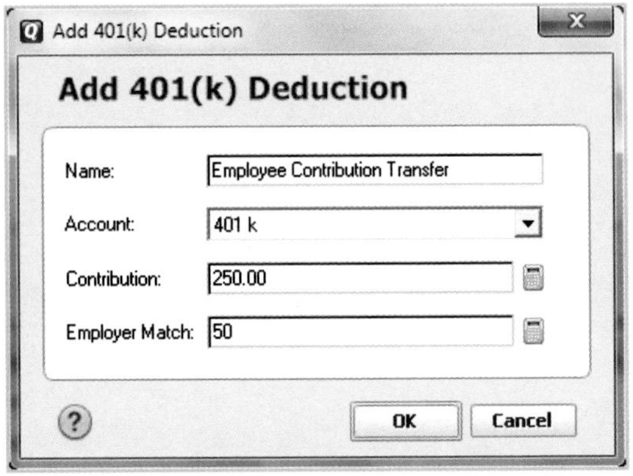

Add 401(k) Deduction

Name: Employee Contribution Transfer

Account: 401 k

Contribution: 250.00

Employer Match: 50

OK   Cancel

9. Click in the amount field next to each of the tax items that are on your pay stub, and enter the amount. If you want to make any changes to the name and category, click **Edit**, make the changes, and click **OK**.

10. Click **Add After-Tax Deduction**, such as stock purchases, correct the name if needed, select the category you want to use to collect this deduction, enter the amount, and click **OK**. Repeat this for multiple deductions.

11. If you want to split your paycheck deposit over two or more accounts, click **Add Deposit Account**, select the additional account, type any memo information you want, enter the amount of your paycheck that will go into that account, and click **OK**.

12. When you have entered all of the paycheck information you want to track, click **Done** to close the Track Paycheck dialog box.

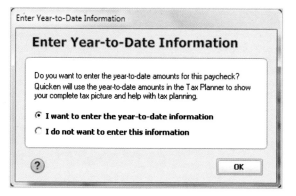

Enter Year-to-Date Information

Do you want to enter the year-to-date amounts for this paycheck? Quicken will use the year-to-date amounts in the Tax Planner to show your complete tax picture and help with tax planning.

○ I want to enter the year-to-date information

○ I do not want to enter this information

13. You will be asked if you want to enter year-to-date information. If you choose the default to enter that data, click **OK**, click in each of the **Year To Date** amount fields, type the desired amount, and, after entering all you want, click **Enter** to close the dialog box. Otherwise, click **I Do Not Want To Enter This Information**, and click **OK**.

Transfer Funds from One Account to Another

You can easily record the transfer of funds from one account to another in Quicken. The quickest way is to open the register of the account the money is from. Then:

1. Click **Account Actions** at the top of a register, and then click **Transfer Money**. The Transfer Money Within Quicken dialog box appears.

Transfer Money Within Quicken

Transfer date	8/21/2011
Amount	
From account	Business Checking
To account	
Payee/Description	Transfer Money (optional)

OK   Cancel

2. If you want to use a date other than today's date, enter or select it, and type the amount of the transfer.

3. If you want to use a From Account other than the account you were in, click the **From Account** down arrow and choose the account you want to use.

4. Click the **To Account** down arrow, and select the account into which you are transferring the funds.

5. Press **TAB** if you want a different payee other than the recommended "Transfer Money". If you want to do that, type that description or edit the current text.

6. Click **OK** to make the transfer and close the dialog box. You should see the transaction in the receiving register.

8/21/2011	TXFR	Transfer Money		[Personal Checkin	1,500 00

Locate Transactions

There are several ways to find a transaction within Quicken.

1. Click **Find** 🔎 Find at the top of any register.

   –Or–

   Click the **Edit** menu on the Quicken menu bar, and click **Find/Replace**.

   –Or–

   Press **CTRL+F**.

Quicken Find

Quicken Find

Find | Any Field ▾ | Contains ▾ | 3/22/2011 | Find | Find All
☑ Search Backwards

? Close

2. Click the **Find** down arrow to open a list of fields on which to search. Click the field you want to search on.

3. Click the next down arrow to open a list of expressions or types of comparisons to use in the search. Click the expression you want to use.

Any Field ▾
Any Field
Amount
Category
Check number
Cleared status
Date
Memo
Payee
Tag

Exact ▾
Contains
Exact
Starts with
Ends with
Greater
Greater or equal
Less
Less or equal

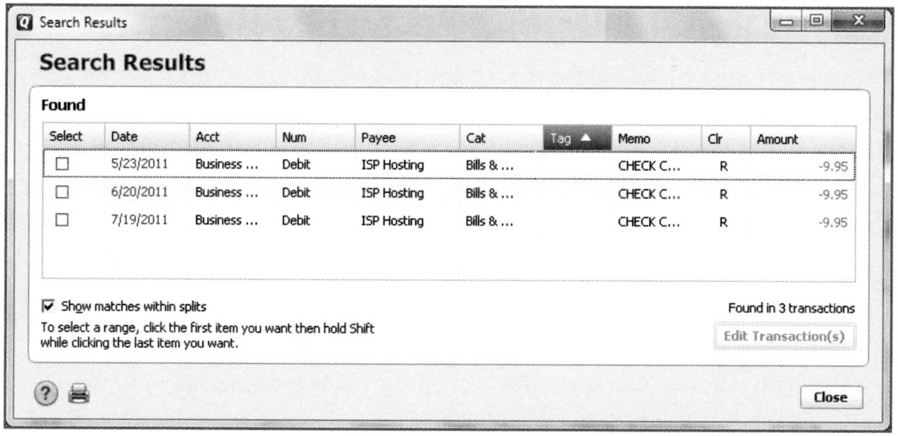

Search Results

Found

Select	Date	Acct	Num	Payee	Cat	Tag ▲	Memo	Clr	Amount
☐	5/23/2011	Business ...	Debit	ISP Hosting	Bills & ...		CHECK C...	R	-9.95
☐	6/20/2011	Business ...	Debit	ISP Hosting	Bills & ...		CHECK C...	R	-9.95
☐	7/19/2011	Business ...	Debit	ISP Hosting	Bills & ...		CHECK C...	R	-9.95

☑ Show matches within splits

To select a range, click the first item you want then hold Shift while clicking the last item you want.

Found in 3 transactions

Edit Transaction(s)

Close

Figure 4-7: Quicken's ability to search transactions allows you to find, for example, all the transactions to a given payee or all transactions over a certain amount.

4. Click in the text box, and type what you want to find.

5. Click **Find** to select the most recent transaction that matches your criteria. You may see a dialog box asking if you want to continue your search from the end of the register. If so, click **Yes**.

–Or–

Click **Find All** to open the Search Results dialog box showing all the transactions that match your criteria. Figure 4-7 shows all the transactions containing the word "ISP Hosting" in the Payee field.

TIP

You can right-click any field in a transaction to bring up a context menu. Click **Find** to open the Quicken Find dialog box.

NOTE

Filtering just selects the transactions to be viewed and does not sort them. You must do the sorting separately.

Filter Transactions for More Information

Quicken can filter the transactions displayed in a register so that only the ones you are interested in are shown. This can help you quickly locate specific information.

1. At the top of the register, click the leftmost down arrow to display the date-related filter options, or click **Custom** to enter or select a specific date range.

All Dates ▼
All Dates
This Month
Last Month
Last 30 Days
Last 60 Days
Last 90 Days
Last 12 Months
This Quarter
Last Quarter
This Year
Last Year
Custom...

2. Click the transaction type filter (the middle down arrow) to choose between payments and deposits.

3. Click the transaction status filter (the right down arrow) to choose among uncategorized, unreconciled, cleared, uncleared, and flagged transactions.

After selecting the filters, your register will display the results.

SORTING TRANSACTIONS

You can sort your transactions by any of the columns in your register except the Balance column. Depending on your choices in Preferences, Quicken can keep the sorted column as you have set it or go back to its default of sorting by date.

- Click the column heading to sort by that column. A small triangle appears by the name to indicate that it is the sort column. **Date ▲**

- Click **Date** to sort first by date and then by check number. The oldest date is displayed at the top.

- Click **Check Number** to sort by check number. This sorts the checks numerically first and then words, such as "ATM" or "Deposit," (A to Z), with the smallest check number at the top. If you click **Check Number** again, you get the reverse order.

- Click **Payee** to show payees displayed alphabetically, with "a" at the top.

- Click **Payment** to sort by payments, with the smallest payment amount at the bottom of the list.

- Click **Clr** to show all reconciled transactions first, and then cleared transactions, and finally any unreconciled transactions.

- Click **Deposit** to show the deposits in descending order, with the largest deposits at the top.

- Click **Account Actions** and then click **Sorting Options** at the top of the register to see all the sorting options: Attachments, Category, Check #, Cleared, Date, Deposit, Flags, Memo, Payee, Payment, and Status. In addition, you can sort by Order Entered or by Date/Order Entered.

Attach Digital Images to a Transaction

If you use Quicken 2012 Deluxe, Premier, Home & Business, or Rental Property Manager, Quicken works with your scanner, Windows Explorer, and the Clipboard in Windows so that you can attach digital images to each transaction in your register. You can attach any type of file that can be viewed in Microsoft Internet Explorer, such as .jpg, .gif, .txt, .html, .pdf, and .png. These attachments are then stored in the same file as your Quicken data. A digital attachment can be a picture of your new snowboard, a receipt for a donation, or any other item you may want to scan or download and keep with your transaction for tax or warranty purposes. You must first bring these items into Quicken and then attach them to a transaction.

ATTACH IMAGES TO TRANSACTIONS

1. Click the **Add An Attachment** icon (the small paper clip with a plus sign to the left of the date) on the left of a selected transaction. The Transaction Attachments dialog box will open.

2. Click the **Attach New** down arrow, and click the **Check, Receipt/Bill, Invoice, Warranty**, or **Other** option, depending on the type of attachment you want to use.

3. Depending on how you intend to acquire the attachment, select one of the following:

   a. Click **File** to attach an image already in your computer. In the Select Attachment File dialog box that appears, locate your file, and click **Open**. Your image appears on the screen with its default name, such as "Receipt/Bill" or "Warranty."

   b. Click **Scanner** to see the Select Source dialog box. Select the scanner you wish to use to scan the item. Follow the directions for your scanner. The image will appear in the Transaction Attachments window.

   c. Click **Clipboard** to attach an item you have copied to your Clipboard. The item appears in the Transaction Attachments window. For more information on using the Clipboard in Windows, see the "Using the Windows Clipboard" QuickSteps later in this chapter.

4. When you have finished, the attachment appears in the window. Click **Done** when you have finished attaching documents.

5. A small attachment icon (a paper clip) appears to the left of the transaction's date.

NOTE

Include alerts as part of the Main View of your Home tab by customizing the Main View, as discussed in Chapter 1.

Alerts		⚙ Options ▾
Date	Message	
8/21/2011	Payment: Personal Checking has scheduled bills or deposits due soon.	
8/19/2011	Payment: Business Checking has scheduled bills or deposits due soon.	

Show all alerts **Set Up Alerts**

NOTE

To read any notes, click the small flag to the left of the transaction date. Click the attachment icon to see the attachments.

ADD A FOLLOW-UP FLAG OR NOTE TO A TRANSACTION

1. Click the **Add A Flag** icon for the transaction, which will cause the Transaction Notes And Flags dialog box to appear.

   a. Type any notes you want as part of this transaction.

   b. Click **Flag This Transaction** if you need to mark the transaction. Choose the color of the flag from the drop-down list.

   c. Click the **Alert For Follow-Up On** option, and enter a date to have this transaction appear on your Alert List in the Quicken Home tab.

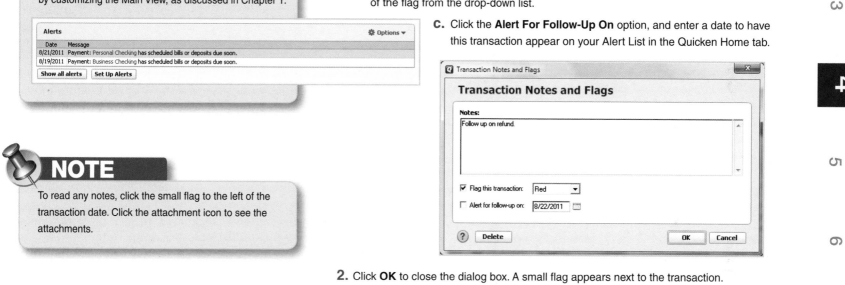

2. Click **OK** to close the dialog box. A small flag appears next to the transaction.

Set Up Your Printer and Print a Register

As you continue to work with Quicken, you may want to print a register. Before you do, you may need to set up your printer to print reports or graphs.

QUICKSTEPS

USING THE WINDOWS CLIPBOARD

Microsoft Windows XP, Vista, and Windows 7, as well as older Windows operating systems, have some handy keyboard shortcuts to capture on-screen images and place them on the Windows Clipboard. An example of an on-screen image might be a scanned deposit slip from your bank's website. To capture this image directly from your screen:

1. Press the **PRINT SCREEN** button, usually located on the upper-right area of your keyboard, to capture the entire screen shown on your monitor.

   –Or–

   Hold down the **ALT** button, usually located on either side of the **SPACEBAR**, and press the **PRINT SCREEN** button to capture a copy of the active window.

   Either action will put the image on the Windows Clipboard.

2. Use the **Clipboard** button in the Transaction Attachment view to attach your captured image to a transaction.

NOTE

Only you can decide whether you need a printed copy of your check register. If you back up your information on a regular basis, you may never need one. You might consider printing one at year-end and filing it with your tax information.

SET UP YOUR PRINTER

1. Click the **File** menu, click **Printer Setup**, and click **For Reports/Graphs**. The Printer Setup For Reports And Graphs dialog box appears.

2. Click the **Printer** down arrow to show a list of your printers, and click the one you want to set up.

3. Click in each of the margin text boxes you want to change, and type the new margin.

4. Click **Heading Font** to change the font, font style, and size. Click the name of the font, the style, and the size from their respective lists; and then click **OK**.

5. Click **Body Font** and repeat step 4. The choices you make will be used with all of the reports or graphs you print on this printer.

6. Click **OK** to close the Printer Setup dialog box.

PRINT A REGISTER

1. With the register you want to print open, use the register filters to display the transactions you want to print.

2. Press **CTRL+P** to open the Print dialog box, make any needed changes, and click **Print**.

CHECK REGISTERS	CREDIT CARD REGISTERS
Date: The date of the transaction.	**Date**: The date of the transaction.
Check Number: The check number or an alphabetic description of the transaction. There is a drop-down list to assist you in choosing.	**Reference #**: Is not displayed by default since there is no transaction number or drop-down list.
Payee/Memo/Category: The person or organization paid and its category. Drop-down lists are available for payees and categories.	**Payee/Memo/Category**: The person or organization paid and its category. Drop-down lists are available for payees and categories.
Payment: The amount of the check or charge. There is a calculator available if you need it.	**Charge**: The amount of the charge or fee. There is a calculator available if you need it.
Clr: Whether a transaction has appeared on a statement from your financial institution and has been cleared.	**Clr**: Whether a transaction has appeared on a statement from your financial institution and has been cleared.
Deposit: The amount that has been deposited into this account. A calculator is available if you need it.	**Payment**: The amount you have paid on this credit card. A calculator is available if you need it.
Balance: The amount of money you have in this account after entering all of your deposits and checks.	**Balance**: The amount of money you owe on this credit card after entering all of your charges and payments.

Table 4-2: Differences Between Checking and Credit Card Registers

TIP

A credit card payment is easily made in one of your checking account registers. Simply identify the credit card you want paid in the Category field of the check using one of the "Transfer To/From" categories. When you go back into the credit card register, the amount of the payment and the checking account from which it was paid appear on the next transaction line.

Use Other Banking Registers

When you first open the register for a credit card account, its appearance is much like a check register. However, there are a few differences that you should recognize, as described in Table 4-2.

ENTER A CREDIT CARD CHARGE, FINANCE CHARGE, OR CREDIT

If you are familiar with entering checks into your checking account register, the process is similar in your credit card register.

1. Click the credit card account in the Account Bar to open that card's register. The empty transaction line at the bottom of the register should be selected, as shown in Figure 4-8.

2. If it isn't already selected and you want to change the date, click in the **Date** column, and use the date-picking techniques described in step 2 of "Enter a Check" earlier in this chapter.

3. Press **TAB** or click in the **Payee** field, and enter the name of the business.

4. Press **TAB** or click in the **Memo** field, and enter any identifying information, such as Dinner with Megg and Cooper or School clothes for Sally.

5. Press **TAB** or click in the **Category** field, and select from the drop-down list or type the category.

6. Press **TAB** or click in the **Charge** field, and enter the amount of the charge.

7. Click **Save** or press **ENTER** to complete the transaction.

WORK WITH A CASH ACCOUNT REGISTER

Creating an account to track your cash spending can be useful. It is a great learning tool for young people to track where they spend their money. You can enter data each time money is spent or add information in bulk at the end

Figure 4-8: Credit card registers have many similarities to check registers.

of each week or month. Many people who use this type of account enter only whole-dollar amounts. Use the same procedures described in "Enter a Check" earlier in this chapter.

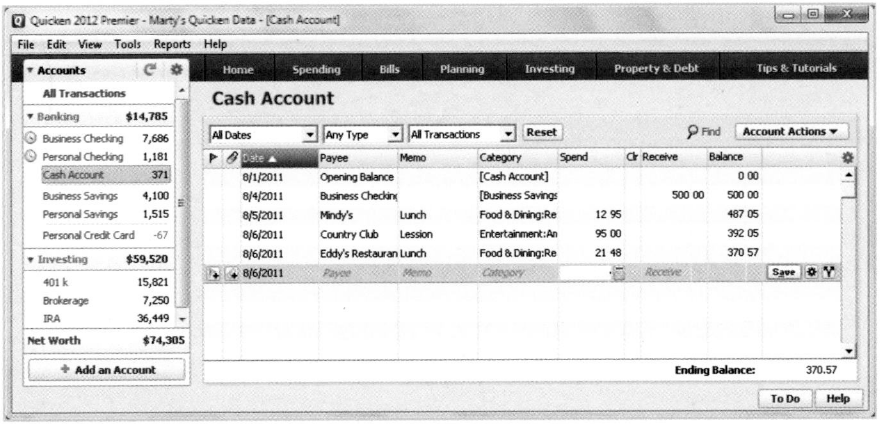

1. Create a cash account, as described in Chapter 2. Open that account's register, and, if it isn't already selected, click in the empty transaction line.

2. If needed, change the date, press **TAB**, and type a payee to identify the transaction.

3. Press **TAB**, enter a memo, if desired, press **TAB** again, and select a category.

4. Press **TAB**, enter the amount spent in the Spend column or click in the Receive field and enter the amount received.

5. Click **Save** or press **ENTER** to complete the transaction.

Chapter 5

Taking Control with Quicken

After using Quicken to enter your day-to-day transactions, you may want to step up to the next level and start using more of the features Quicken provides to help you save time as you manage your finances. In this chapter you will learn how to automate Quicken, memorize payees, schedule transactions, make more use of the Calendar, automate transactions or schedule your bills online, create reports, and produce useful graphs.

Memorize Your Entries

When you set your preferences (see Chapter 4), you told Quicken how to use QuickFill to make data entry faster and whether to automatically update new payees. You might recall that one choice was to automatically memorize new payees and then recall them when you next entered them. Whether or not you chose to have Quicken do this, you can also memorize transactions and payees manually.

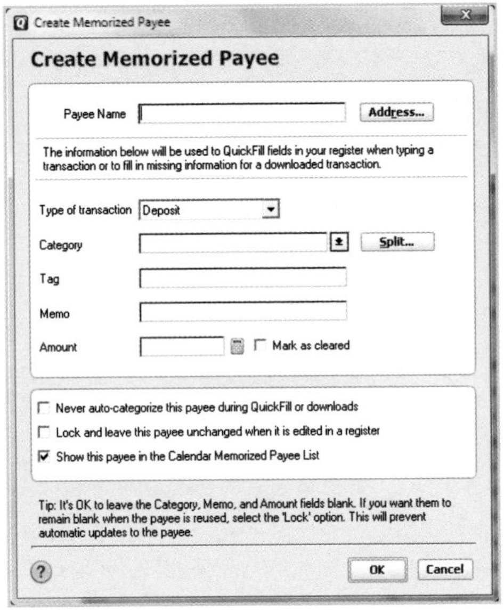

Create a Memorized Payee

Memorizing saves you valuable data-entry time. Use the Memorized Payee List, shown in Figure 5-1, to create a memorization.

1. Click **Tools** and click **Memorized Payee List** to display the list.

   –Or–

   Press **CTRL+T**.

2. Click **New Payee** on the bottom of the Memorized Payee List. The Create Memorized Payee dialog box appears.

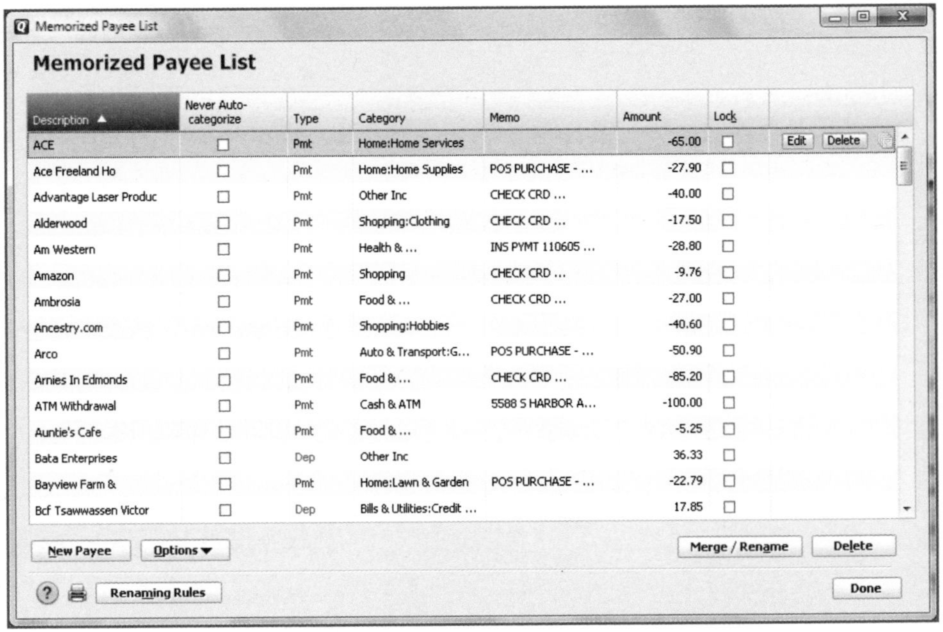

Figure 5-1: *The Memorized Payee List lets you create, edit, use, rename, and delete your memorized payees.*

NOTE

The Address button in the Create Memorized Payee dialog box opens the Edit Address Book Record only when you select Payment or Print Check as the transaction type *before* you click the Address button.

3. Type the name of the payee in the Payee Name field. Press **TAB** to go to the Address button if you print checks to the payee. Press **ENTER**, fill out the address and any other information you want to record, and click **OK**.

4. Press **TAB** and click the **Type Of Transaction** down arrow to choose the transaction type.

5. Press **TAB**, click the **Category** down arrow, and choose a category from the list or type one in the Category text box.

6. Press **TAB** to move to the Split button, and press **ENTER** to open the Split dialog box if this is a transaction with several categories. If you choose to split the transaction into two or more categories, *-Split-* will appear in the Category field. Click **OK** to close the Split Transaction dialog box.

7. Press **TAB**, type a tag if you want one, press **TAB** again, and type any memo text you want to appear on the payment.

8. Press **TAB** to move to the Amount field, and type one if you pay the same amount each time. If you entered a split transaction, the total amount of the splits will automatically appear in the Amount field. If you want, you can have the transaction automatically marked as cleared in the register, but most people want to wait until they see it in their bank statement, either printed or online.

9. Choose by clicking the relevant check box if you don't want the payee auto-categorized during QuickFill or downloads, if you want to leave the payee unchanged when it's edited in a register, and if you want to hide this payee in the Calendar Memorized Payee List.

10. To save the memorized payee and close the dialog box, click **OK**.

Change Memorized Payees

You can work with the Memorized Payee List in several ways. As you look at the list shown in Figure 5-1, you see a number of buttons on the bottom of the list. Some of the things you can do with the Memorized Payee List include the following (if your Memorized Payee List isn't already displayed, press **CTRL+T**):

- You can click **New Payee** using the button at the bottom to create a new memorized transaction.

- Click **Options** to determine whether to show the Locked and Calendar status columns. Click the options to display those items on the list.

Options ▼

✓ Show Locked status column in list

Show Calendar status column in list

- Select any payee on the list, and click **Edit** on the right side of the item to make changes to existing information.
- Select any payee and click **Delete** on the right side of the item to delete that payee. A dialog box appears prompting you to confirm this action. Click **OK**.
- Select any payee and click **Payee Report**, the stack of paper icon on the right side of the item, to generate a report of the transactions using that payee. A report window opens displaying the results. Use it as you would any report (see "Use Reports and Graphs" later in this chapter), and click **Done** when you are finished.
- Click the **Print** icon to open the Windows Print dialog box to print your Memorized Payee List.
- Click the **Help** icon to open the Quicken Help dialog box.
- Click **Merge/Rename** to merge this payee with another one. See "Merge and Rename Payees" later in this chapter.
- Select a payee and click the lock check box on the right, if you choose to show it in Options, to lock a payee's transaction.
- Right-click a payee to open the context menu. Most of the options have been discussed already. Click **Use** to use the memorized payee as the next transaction in your current register. Click **Never Auto-Categorize This Payee** to force the entry of a category each time you use this payee.

| Edit |
| Delete |
| Use |
| Lock |
| Never Auto-categorize this Payee |
| ✓ Show on Calendar |
| New Payee |
| Report |

Use Renaming Rules for Downloaded Transactions

When banks assign a payee name to a transaction, they may not use the name you want in your check register. Quicken allows you to establish renaming rules so that the payees in these transactions can be cleaned up and be more concise. You can add renaming rules from the Memorized Payee List, the Tools menu, or the Quicken Preferences dialog box.

ADD RENAMING RULES FROM THE MEMORIZED PAYEE LIST

1. Click **Tools** and click **Memorized Payee List**.

   –Or–

   Press **CTRL+T**.

   In either case, the Memorized Payee List appears.

2. Click the name of one or more payees that you want to rename. To choose multiple names and rename them with the same name, press and hold down **SHIFT** while clicking the first and last names in a contiguous sequence, or press and hold down the **CTRL** key while clicking individual names.

3. Click **Merge/Rename** at the bottom of the window. The Merge And Rename Payees dialog box appears. Type the name you want to use in the New Name field. If you want only the current payee to be renamed and do *not* want all future downloaded transactions to use the new name, clear that check box and click **OK**. If you did not clear the check box, the Edit Renaming Rule dialog box appears.

4. Make any changes to the rule, and, if needed, click **Add New Item** to add any names that should be renamed using this renaming rule. Click **OK** to close the Edit Renaming Rule dialog box.

5. From the Memorized Payee List, click **Renaming Rules** and see the next section, "Work with Renaming Rules from the Tools Menu," for a discussion of the Renaming Rules dialog box that opens.

6. Click **Done** to close the Renaming Rules dialog box, and then click **Done** again to close the Memorized Payee List.

WORK WITH RENAMING RULES FROM THE TOOLS MENU

Quicken Preferences allows you to add a renaming rule when you don't have a current memorized name to work with. To add a renaming rule from the Tools menu:

1. Click the **Tools** menu, and then click **Renaming Rules**. The Renaming Rules dialog box appears.

2. Click **New**. The Create Renaming Rule dialog box appears. Enter the new payee name and the name or names that should be renamed to the new name. Then click **OK** to return to the Renaming Rules dialog box.

3. If you do *not* want Quicken to use renaming rules, click to clear the Apply Renaming Rules To Downloaded Transactions check box. (It is selected by default.)

4. If you do not want Quicken to automatically create new rules when manually renaming payees, click to clear the check box on the left of that option as well.

5. Click **Done** to close the Renaming Rules dialog box.

MERGE AND RENAME PAYEES

If you have more than one name for a specific payee, such as Cooper Store, Cooper's, and Coopers, you can merge these payees and still save all the detailed transaction information. To merge payees:

1. Press **CTRL+T** to open the Memorized Payee List.

2. To choose multiple names, press and hold down **SHIFT** while clicking the first and last names in a contiguous sequence, and/or press and hold down the **CTRL** key while clicking individual names.

3. Click **Merge/Rename** to open the Merge And Rename Payees dialog box.

4. In the **New Name** text box, type the name you want to use.

5. Click **OK**. The Edit Renaming Rules dialog box appears. Quicken shows each of the names you have selected to ensure you really want to include that name, as you saw earlier in this chapter.

6. Click **Remove** to remove any of the names from this new name.

7. Click **Add New Item** to include additional items that may not have appeared on your Memorized Payee List.

8. Click **OK** when you have entered all the names you want to merge.

9. You are returned to the Memorized Payee List, and only the newly created name appears on it.

10. Click **Done** to close the Memorized Payee List.

Distribute a Split Transaction

You create a split transaction to distribute the total transaction over several categories or even several accounts. You can do that in three ways:

- Splitting using fixed dollar amounts in each category, as described in Chapter 4

- Distributing using a percentage in some or all of the categories to direct Quicken to calculate an amount rather than using the specific dollar amount for each category

- Allocating amounts among several categories using either an even distribution or proportional to amounts in the categories' amount fields

To create a split transaction:

1. Open the account register that will contain the transaction. Enter the date, number or reference, payee, and total amount as you normally would.

2. Click **Split** in the Transaction toolbar on the right of the transaction.

    –Or–

    Click in the **Category** field, and click **Split**.

    –Or–

    Press **CTRL+S**.

    In all cases, the Split Transaction dialog box appears.

3. Click the **Category** down arrow, and select a category. Press **TAB**, enter a memo or description if you choose, and press **TAB** again.

Split Transaction

Enter multiple categories to itemize this transaction; use the Memo field to record more details.

	Category	Memo	Amount
1.	Travel:Hotel	Room	150 00
2.	Auto & Transport:Gas & Fuel		15%
3.			Next Edit ▼
4.			
5.			
6.			
7.			
8.			
9.			
16.			

Split Total: 200.00
Remainder: 0.00
Transaction Total: 200.00

Add Lines   **Clear All**   Allocate   Adjust

OK   **Cancel**

Figure 5-2: The Split Transaction dialog box allows you to assign multiple categories to one transaction by either dollar amount or percentages.

Allocate empty split line

The value of the empty split line is: **$48.00**

How would you like to divide this amount between the other split lines?

○ Distribute proportionally between all other split lines

◉ Distribute evenly: $16.00 to all other split lines

OK   Cancel

4. If you want to use percentages, in the Amount field, which initially contains the total amount, replace that by typing a percentage as a number followed by the percent (%) sign and pressing **TAB**. Quicken automatically calculates the dollar amount for the category by multiplying the total amount of the transaction by the percentage and then displays the balance on the next line. (This does not work if you happen to choose a payee that has a split already memorized.)

For example, if the check is for $200.00 and you type <u>75%</u> on the first line and press **TAB**, the amount displayed on the first line will be $150.00 and $50.00 will be displayed on the second line. You can leave the second line as is or put a percentage smaller than 25% there to leave a balance on the third line, as you can see in Figure 5-2. (Remember to enter the category and possibly a memo for each split line.)

5. Click **OK** to apply the split and close the window. Click **Save** or press **ENTER** to save the transaction.

6. If you want to allocate evenly over several categories, enter the several categories, enter <u>1</u> (or any number other than zero) in the Amount field of each, and click **Allocate** at the bottom of the dialog box to open the Allocate Empty Split Line dialog box. Click **Distribute Evenly** and click **OK**.

7. If you want to allocate proportionally over several categories, enter the several categories, enter a set of numbers in the amount fields (for example, enter <u>50</u>, <u>20</u>, and <u>30</u> to put 50% in the first field, 20% in the second, and 30% in the third), and click **Allocate**, as you see in Figure 5-3. Click **Distribute Proportionally** and click **OK**.

8. If you desire to memorize the new split transaction, right-click the transaction, and then click **Memorize Payee** (or press **CTRL+M**). A dialog box asks if you want to memorize the split payees as percentages. If so, click **Yes**. Then click **OK** to complete the memorization.

Quicken 2012

Memorize split payees as percentages?

Yes   No

LOCKING A MEMORIZED PAYEE

If you choose to automatically memorize new payees in Quicken Preferences, each time you use a memorized payee, the transaction amount associated with that payee is updated. You can lock a memorized payee transaction so that the transaction amount won't change if you enter a transaction with a different amount for that payee. For example, let's say you send your son in college, Cooper Collegiate, an allowance of $150 per month for spending money and have locked that transaction. If you send him a birthday check for $250, the locked transaction will not change. If you do not lock it, the new memorized payee amount will be $250. To lock a transaction that is already in the Memorized Payee List:

1. Click **Tools** and click **Memorized Payee List**. If you don't see the Lock column, click **Options** at the bottom of the window, and click **Show Locked Status Column**.

2. Select the transaction you want to lock, and click the **Lock** check box on the right of the payee entry.

3. Click **Done** to close the list.

You can unlock a transaction in the same way. When a transaction is unlocked and your preferences are set to automatically memorize new payees, the next time you enter a transaction for this payee, the new amount is memorized.

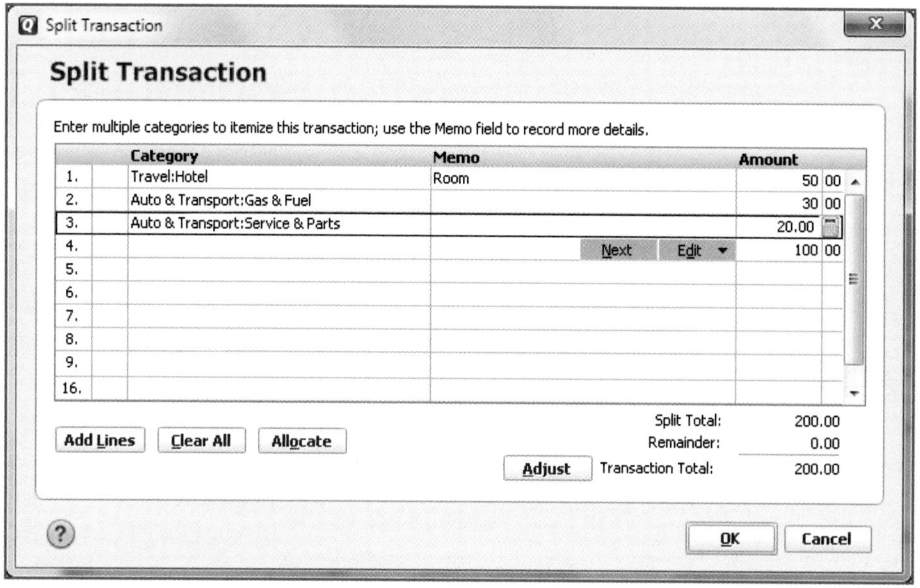

Split Transaction

Enter multiple categories to itemize this transaction; use the Memo field to record more details.

	Category	Memo	Amount
1.	Travel:Hotel	Room	50 00
2.	Auto & Transport:Gas & Fuel		30 00
3.	Auto & Transport:Service & Parts		20.00
4.		Next Edit ▼	100 00
5.			
6.			
7.			
8.			
9.			
16.			

Split Total: 200.00
Remainder: 0.00
Transaction Total: 200.00

Add Lines   **Clear All**   **Allocate**   **Adjust**

OK   **Cancel**

Figure 5-3: The Allocate button allows you to either evenly or proportionally distribute an amount over several categories.

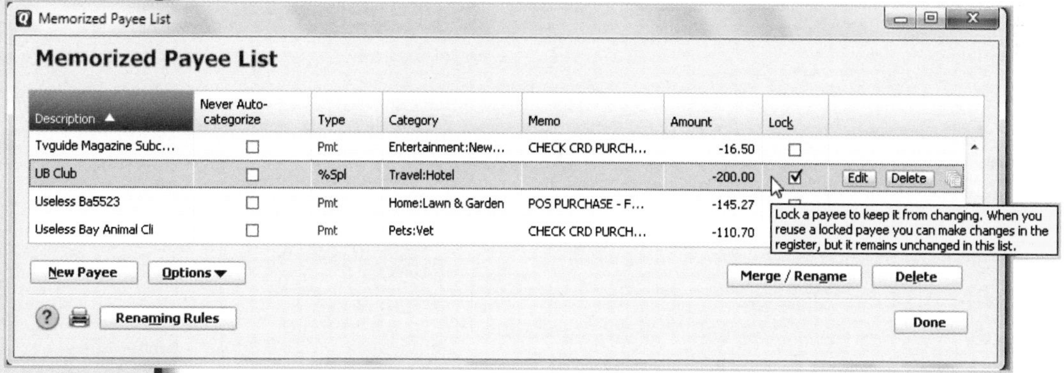

Memorized Payee List

Description ▲	Never Auto-categorize	Type	Category	Memo	Amount	Lock
Tvguide Magazine Subc...	☐	Pmt	Entertainment:New...	CHECK CRD PURCH...	-16.50	☐
UB Club	☐	%Spl	Travel:Hotel		-200.00	☑ Edit Delete
Useless Ba5523	☐	Pmt	Home:Lawn & Garden	POS PURCHASE - F...	-145.27	
Useless Bay Animal Cli	☐	Pmt	Pets:Vet	CHECK CRD PURCH...	-110.70	

Lock a payee to keep it from changing. When you reuse a locked payee you can make changes in the register, but it remains unchanged in this list.

New Payee   **Options ▼**   **Merge / Rename**   **Delete**

Renaming Rules   **Done**

Create Bill Reminders and Scheduled Transactions

Most of us have bills we pay every month. Your list may seem endless, with utility bills, rent or mortgage payments, property tax payments, and so on. Quicken's Bill And Income Reminders feature helps you automate the process. You can select and schedule all recurring transactions so that you don't accidentally overlook a regular payment. Quicken can even enter them automatically. You can set up reminders or record transactions several days earlier than they are actually due to remind yourself to put money in the bank to cover them. You can set up your paycheck using Quicken Paycheck Setup (see Chapter 4) to keep track of your gross wages and deductions to help with tax planning. (See Chapters 9 and 10 for information on taxes and budgeting.) You can even enter the scheduled transactions 30, 60, or 90 days in advance to do cash-flow forecasting in your account register (that is my personal preference).

Understand Scheduled Transactions

Quicken has two types of scheduled transactions: recurring transactions, such as insurance or mortgage payments, and one-time transactions, such as the balance due on the new deck you're having built. You can also create a scheduled transaction to be paid later online. Other scheduled transactions can include the following:

- Income:
  - Miscellaneous income
  - Paychecks
  - Alimony or child support payments
  - Social Security or retirement checks
- Payments:
  - Mortgage or rent payments
  - Car payments
  - Health and other insurance payments

- Taxes
- Membership dues
- Utility payments

Schedule a Transaction

You can schedule payments and deposits at any time.

1. Click the **Bills** tab, and click **Manage Reminders** on the top-right corner to open the Bill And Income Reminders dialog box.

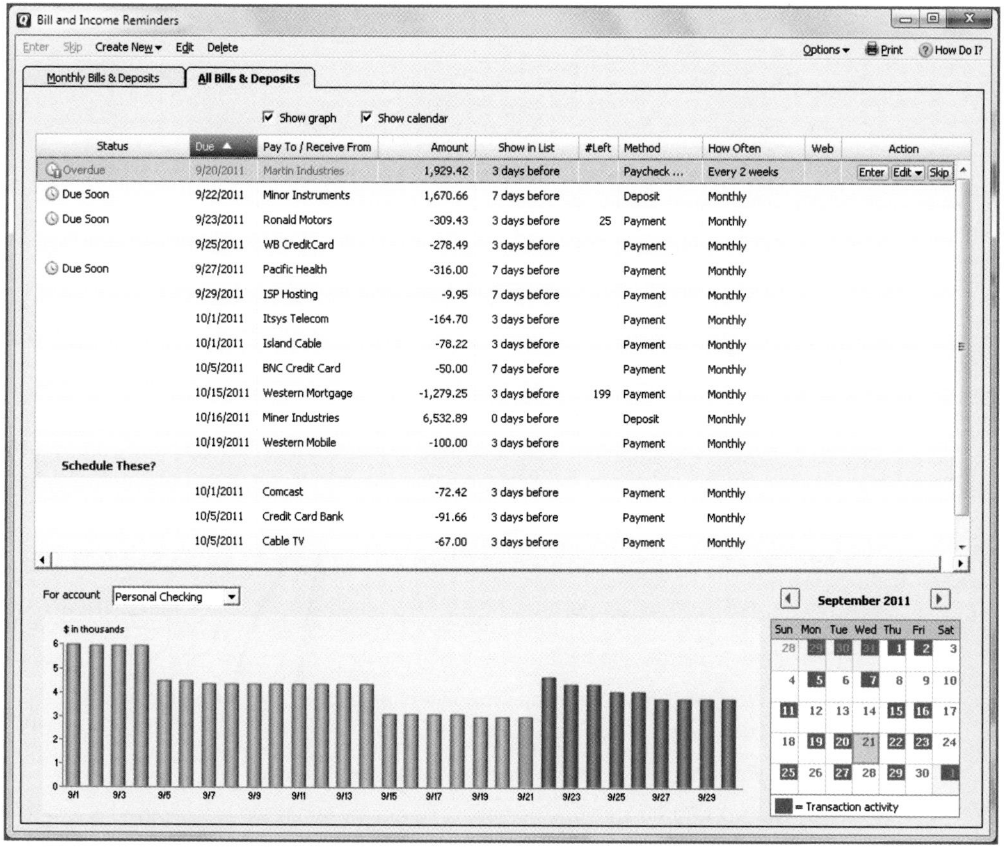

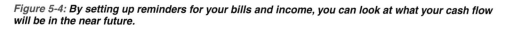

Figure 5-4: *By setting up reminders for your bills and income, you can look at what your cash flow will be in the near future.*

–Or–

Press **CTRL+J**.

–Or–

Click **Tools** and click **Manage Bill & Income Reminders**.

In all cases, the Bill And Income Reminders dialog box appears, as you can see in Figure 5-4.

2. In the top menu bar, click **Create New** and click **Bill Reminder** to open the Add Reminder dialog box.

3. Enter, or select from the drop-down list, the name of the payee, and choose the type of transaction:

- Click **Bill Reminder** if the transaction you want to schedule pays a bill.
- Click **Income Reminder** to schedule funds coming into your accounts.
- Click **Transfer Reminder** to schedule a transfer from one account to another.

SCHEDULE A BILL OR PAYMENT

If you want to schedule funds going out of your accounts:

1. In the Add Reminder dialog box, choose **Bill Reminder** and click **Next**.

2. Press **TAB** and enter or select from the calendar the date on which the bill is next due.

3. If you want to change the frequency, click **Change** opposite Due Next On, make any needed changes to the **Start Date**, and click the **How Often** down arrow. Select how often this transaction occurs. The default is **Monthly**, but you have other choices, as shown in Table 5-1.

4. Leaving the default, **With No End Date**, selected makes the transaction occur forever. Click the down arrow and then:

- Click **No End Date** to keep the scheduled transaction in your Reminders List forever.
- Click **End On** to enter the date of the last payment.
- Click **End After** to enter the number of payments remaining to this payee.

  Click **OK** to close this dialog box.

FREQUENCY FOR SCHEDULED TRANSACTIONS	EXPLANATION
Weekly	Use this if the transaction occurs every week. Quicken uses the starting date of the transaction to determine which day of the week it will occur, but you can change that. Weekly defaults to every week, but you can make it every 2 weeks, or every *n* weeks from 1 to 231.
Monthly	This is the default setting, since most recurring transactions happen monthly. You can designate a specific date or a specific day, such as the third Tuesday of each month. The default is every month, but you can select any number of months up to 231.
Twice A Month	You tell Quicken on which two days each month to schedule this transaction.
Quarterly	Use this if you have something that occurs every three months, such as estimated income tax payments. The four calendar periods will be specified for you based on your starting dates. If you want more flexibility, use Monthly, every 3 months.
Yearly	This option is for annual payments. You can set a specific date, such as August.
Twice A Year	This option allows you to choose two days per year on which to schedule the transaction. Auto insurance and property tax payments are often paid twice each year.
Only Once	This is for transactions that will only happen once, such as an upcoming balloon or final payment.
To Pay Estimated Taxes	You can schedule four equal payments on 4/15, 6/15, 9/15, and 1/15.

Table 5-1: Choices for the Frequency of Scheduled Transactions

NOTE

The Optional Settings area is expanded or not when you first enter the dialog box, depending on how you last left it. Immediately after installing Quicken, if you look at the Add Reminder dialog box the Optional Settings area will be closed.

5. Click in **Amount Due** and enter or change the amount. Click the **From Account** down arrow to open a list of accounts, and select the one from which you want to pay this bill.

6. Click in the **Add Category, Tag, Or Memo** fields to enter or change the category, split a category, enter a tag, or enter a memo. If you do that, click **OK** to close the dialog box.

7. If they are not already displayed, click the **Optional Settings** right-pointing arrow to display several additional settings:

- If you want Quicken to remind you of the bill other than three days in advance, click **Change** opposite that question and either type the number of days in advance you want in the **Remind Me** field or use the spinner to select a number. Alternatively, you can automatically enter the transaction in the register a number of days in advance if it is automatically taken from your account, and you can choose to count only business days. Click **OK** when you are finished.

- If you want to go to an organization's website to pay a bill on a recurring basis, click **Add** opposite Related Web Site, enter the website's address (URL), and click **OK**.
- If you want Quicken to estimate an amount for a payment that varies, click **Change** opposite Estimate Amount For Me. In the dialog box that opens click the down arrow in the middle drop-down list and choose:

- **Fixed Amount** if you want to use the same amount for each payment.
- **Previous Payments** if you want Quicken to enter an amount based on what you've paid the last few times. You can change the number of payments from which Quicken estimates by using the spinner or entering a number.
- **Time Of Year** if this is a seasonal payment and you want Quicken to find the amount based on periodic payments in the last year.
- Click **OK** when you have completed estimating a variable payment.
- Click **Sync To Outlook** if you want this bill to appear in your Outlook Calendar.
- Click **Print Check With Quicken** if you want to do that with this bill.

8. Click **Done** when you have completed entering all the information you want for a bill reminder.

SCHEDULE A DEPOSIT

To schedule a receipt of funds into your accounts:

1. Click **Create New**, click **Income Reminder**, and in the Add Reminder dialog box that opens, opposite **From**, type or select the organization from which you are getting the income, and click **Income Reminder** if it isn't already selected.

2. Click **Next**. Press TAB and enter or select from the calendar the date on which the income is next due.

3. If you want to change the frequency, click **Change**, make any needed changes to the **Start Date**, and click the **How Often** down arrow. Select how often this transaction occurs. The default is **Monthly**, but you have other choices, as shown in Table 5-1. Select the end date, and click **OK**.

4. Click in the **Amount Due** field, and enter or change the amount.

5. Click the **To Account** down arrow to open a list of accounts, and select the one to which you want to deposit this income.

6. Click in the **Add Category, Tag Or Memo** field to select or change the category, split a category, enter a tag, or enter a memo. If you do that, click **OK** to close the dialog box.

7. Click the **Optional Settings** right-pointing arrow to display several optional settings. Follow the instructions in step 7 of "Schedule a Bill or Payment" earlier in this chapter.

8. Click **Done** to return to the Bill And Income Reminders dialog box.

SCHEDULE A TRANSFER

To schedule a transfer between your accounts:

1. Click **Create New**, click **Transfer Reminder**, and in the Add Transfer Reminder dialog box that opens, type a description, click **Transfer Reminder**, and click **Next**.

2. Press **TAB** and enter or select from the calendar the date on which the transfer is to be made.

3. If you want to change the frequency, click **Change**, make any needed changes to the **Start Date**, and click the **How Often** down arrow. Select how often this transaction occurs. The default is **Monthly**, but you have other choices, as shown in Table 5-1. Select the end date, and click **OK**.

4. Click in the **Amount Due** field, and type the amount to be transferred.

5. Click the **From Account** down arrow, and select the account from which the funds will be transferred. All of your accounts that are not hidden in Quicken are available on this list.

6. Click the **To Account** down arrow, and select the account into which the transfer will be made.

7. Click in the **Add Tag Or Memo** field to enter a tag or enter a memo. If you do that, click OK to close the dialog box.

8. Click the **Optional Settings** right-pointing arrow to display several optional settings. Follow the instructions in step 7 of "Schedule a Bill or Payment" earlier in this chapter.

9. Click **Done** to return to the Bill And Income Reminders dialog box.

Add Transfer Reminder

Add Transfer Reminder

Description: Monthly Savings

Due Next On: 9/21/2011   21st of every month (change)

Amount due: 500.00

From account: Personal Checking

To account: Personal Savings

Details

Add tag or memo

▶ Optional Settings

Cancel   Back   Done

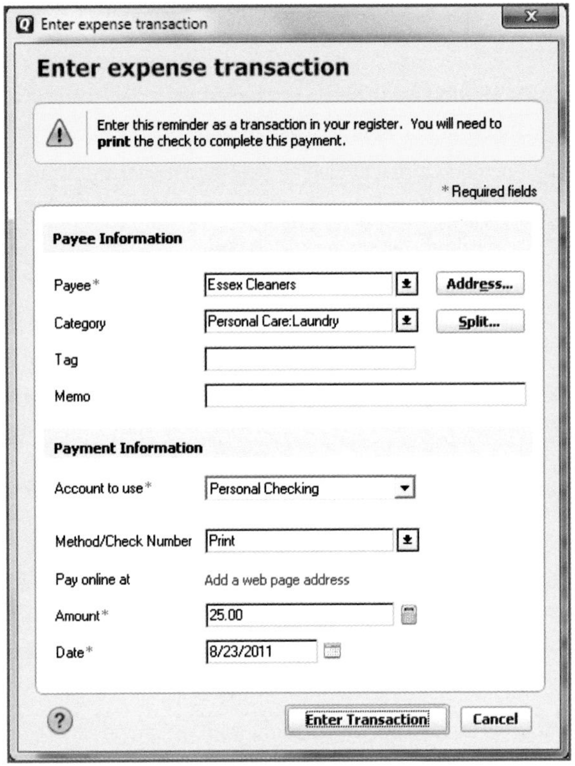

Figure 5-5: *The Enter Transaction dialog box reminds you to both enter a transaction into your register and physically complete the transaction.*

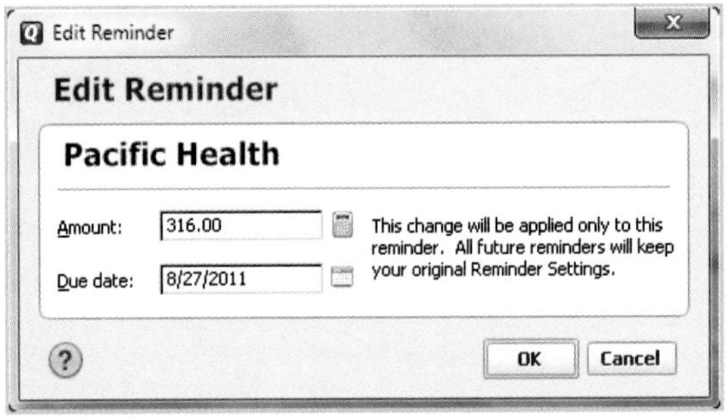

CREATE A SCHEDULED TRANSACTION FROM A REGISTER

You can create a scheduled transaction directly from a transaction in a register.

1. With a register open, right-click the transaction you want to schedule to display a context menu.

2. Click **Schedule Bill Or Deposit**. The Add Reminder dialog box appears, as described in "Schedule a Transaction" earlier in this chapter.

Work with Scheduled Transactions

The Bill And Income Reminders dialog box has several ways you can work with each scheduled transaction.

1. Click **Tools** and click **Manage Bill & Income Reminders** to open the Bill And Income Reminders dialog box.

2. Select a reminder to work with it, and click **Enter** on either the menu bar or the Reminder toolbar to open the Enter Transaction dialog box, as seen in Figure 5-5.

3. Verify the information that appears. If you want to enter this transaction into the referenced account, click **Enter Transaction** (or **Enter/Done** depending on the reminder type). Remember that just because you enter a transaction into a Quicken register, no payments or deposits have physically been made until you make them! Otherwise, click **Cancel** to return to the Bill And Income Reminders dialog box.

4. Select a reminder and click **Skip** on either the menu bar or the Reminder toolbar to remove this instance of the reminder. Initially, a dialog box opens asking if you are sure you want to skip the reminder. Click **Skip** again to do so, or click **Don't Skip** to not. You can click the **Don't Show Me This Again** check box if you don't want to be prompted about being sure when you skip a reminder.

5. To change a reminder you have two choices to edit: only the current reminder, or this and all future reminders.

   ● With a reminder selected, if you click **Edit** on the top menu bar it will open the Edit Reminder dialog box you saw earlier in "Schedule a Transaction," and any change you make will change all future reminders.

   ● If you click **Edit** in the Reminders List to the right of a reminder, you can choose between **Only This Instance**, which opens the Edit Reminder dialog box where you can change only the amount and the due date, or **This And All Future Reminders**, which opens the Edit Reminder dialog box you saw earlier in "Schedule a Transaction."

6. To delete a reminder, select it, and click **Delete** on the menu bar. A warning message appears telling you that you are about to delete a scheduled bill or deposit. Click **OK** if that is your desire, or click **Cancel** to stop the deletion.

SORT BILL AND INCOME REMINDERS

When working in the Bill And Income Reminders dialog box, you can sort in three ways. From the menu bar, click **Options** and then:

- Click **Sort By Payee** to sort alphabetically on the name of the payee.

- Click **Sort By Amount** to sort on the amount of the payment or deposit, lowest to highest.

- Click **Sort By Next Date** to return to the default setting. This option sorts in chronological order.

PRINT SCHEDULED TRANSACTIONS

Once you have scheduled all of your transactions in Quicken, you can create a printed list if you wish.

1. Click **Print** on the right of the Bill And Income Reminders menu bar.

2. A Windows Print dialog box appears. Enter the number of copies, the location of the printer, and so on.

Print	
Printer: \\WIN7\HP Photosmart 2600 series on USB00 ▾ **Properties**	Orientation: Portrait / Landscape
This printer prints to paper.	
Export to: Text file ▾	
☐ Print in color ☐ Print in draft mode ☐ Fit to one page wide	Print Range: All / Pages: From: To: Number of copies: 1
Printer Setup Preview	Print Cancel

3. Click **Print** to print the list.

TIP

You can also sort these three ways by clicking the corresponding column headings.

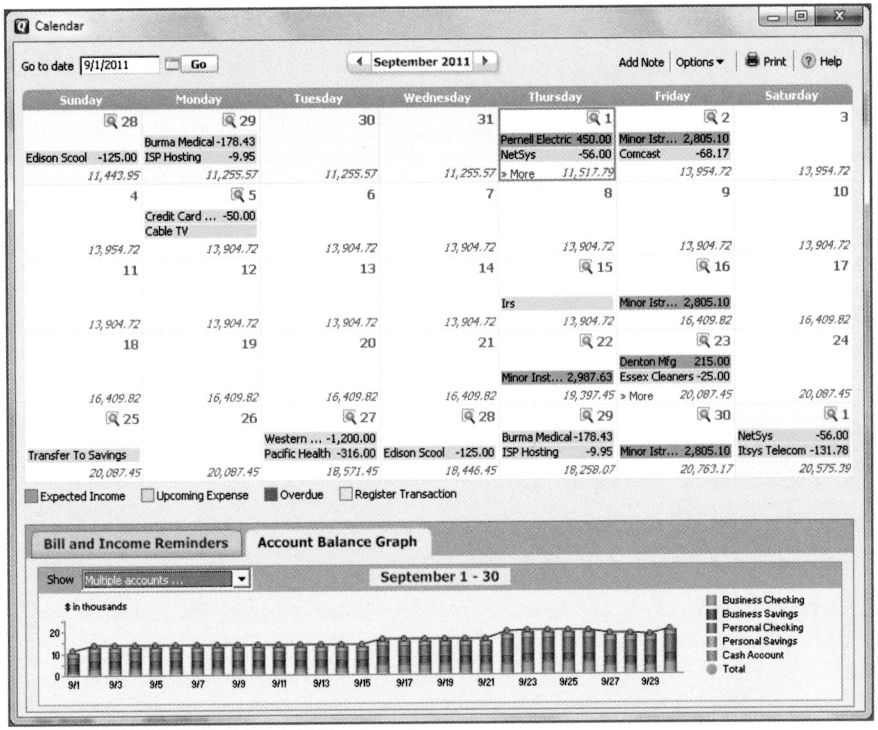

Figure 5-6: ***Quicken's Calendar helps you organize your financial transactions.***

Use the Calendar

Sometimes, it's helpful to see events on a calendar to reinforce them in your mind. The Calendar in Quicken lets you see at a glance your financial events for each month, as shown in Figure 5-6.

1. Press **CTRL+K**.

   –Or–

   Click the **Tools** menu, and then click **Calendar**.

   In both instances, the Calendar window opens.

2. Click the arrows to the left and right of the month on the menu bar to move between months. The current month is displayed by default.

3. In the **Go To Date** text box, type a date or click the calendar icon on the menu bar to open a small calendar from which you can select any specific date you want to view. Use the right and left arrows to go to other months. Click **Go** to display that date in the large calendar.

IDENTIFY THE COLOR CODES USED ON YOUR CALENDAR

Quicken color-codes information on your Calendar to make it easier to quickly spot specific types of transactions (see Figure 5-6 earlier in this chapter):

- Deposits or payments that have been recorded in your account register are displayed in black text on a grey background.
- Scheduled transactions that are overdue display with a red background.
- Income items scheduled in the future display on a green background.
- Payment items scheduled in the future display on an orange background.

TIP

You can also use a variety of keyboard shortcuts on the Calendar to select a date: T for today, M for first day of the month, H for last day of the month, and so on. See the help entry on keyboard shortcuts for a more complete list.

WORK WITH SPECIFIC DATES

Transactions
Note

Add expense...
Add income...
Add reminder...

Previous month
Next month
Calendar accounts

To work with a specific date:

1. Right-click the date on the Calendar to display a context menu.

2. Click **Transactions** on the context menu or just double-click a calendar date to display the Transactions Due (or On): *this date* dialog box.

Transactions due: 9/1/2011

Payee	Method	Amount
Pernell Electric	<Sched>	450.00
NetSys	<Sched>	-56.00
Itsys Telecom	<Sched>	-131.78

Enter   Edit   Skip   Schedule

Add ▼   Close

a. Click **Add** and click **Add Expense**, **Add Income**, or **Add Reminder**; or click those options on the context menu opened in step 1. With both Add Expense and Add Income, the Enter Expense Transaction or Enter Income Transaction dialog box is displayed, in which you can enter a single transaction for the selected date. Add Reminder opens the Add Reminder dialog box that you saw and that was described in "Schedule a Transaction" earlier in this chapter. In either case, fill in the applicable fields, clicking **Next** as needed, and clicking either **Enter Transaction** or **Done** when you are finished.

Enter expense transaction

* Required fields

Payee Information

Payee*
Category
Tag
Memo

Address...
Split...

Payment Information

Account to use*
Method/Check Number
Amount*
Date*   8/29/2011

Enter Transaction   Cancel

b. If you selected a transaction in the calendar that has already been entered, you can click **Go To Register** to review the transaction there.

c. If you selected a transaction that has not been entered, you can click **Enter** to open the Enter Income Reminder or Enter Bill Reminder dialog box. Click Enter Transaction to add that transaction to the register.

d. Select a transaction and click **Edit** to edit that transaction. The dialog box that opens depends on the type of transaction and whether it has been entered in the register. For scheduled transactions, the Edit Bill/Income/Transfer Reminder dialog box will open, as discussed in "Schedule a Transaction" earlier in this chapter, where the dialog box was called "Add Bill/Income/Transfer Reminder." If the transaction has already been entered in a register, the Edit Register Transaction will open and allow you to change any of the register fields.

NOTE

You can also add a note to a specific date by clicking that date on the calendar and selecting **Add Note** on the Calendar menu bar. The default is today's date. To delete a note from a specific date, right-click the date on the Calendar, click **Note**, and then click **Delete Note**.

Add Note

Insurance needs to be renewed.

Delete Note   Note Color   Yellow

(?)   OK   Cancel

CAUTION

Each date can hold only one note; however, you can combine several reminders into one note.

---

e. If the transaction has not been scheduled, click **Schedule** to open the Add Reminder dialog box. Follow the instructions in "Schedule a Transaction" earlier in this chapter.

f. If you have not scheduled a selected transaction for Online Bill Pay and sent the information to your bank, you may have the option to delete it by clicking **Delete**. The deletion warning message will appear. Click **OK** to delete the transaction, or click **Cancel** to close the warning box without deleting the transaction.

g. If you have not yet entered a reminder into a register, you can click **Skip** to not enter the current instance of the transaction but leave it as a reminder for the next period. You are asked if you are sure you want to skip it. If so, click **Skip** again; if not, click **Don't Skip**.

h. If the Transactions Due (or On): *this date* dialog box didn't automatically close, click **Close** to do that.

3. With a date selected, click **Note** on the context menu to add a reminder note to the date. The Add Note dialog appears.

   a. Type the note you want on that date.

   b. Select the color of the note from the drop-down box if you want a color other than the default one of yellow.

   c. Click **OK** to close the dialog box.

4. Click **Previous Month** or **Next Month** on the date's context menu to see this account's Calendar for the previous or next month. This is the same as clicking the left- and right-pointing arrows on the month at the top of the calendar.

5. Click **Calendar Accounts** on the context menu to select the accounts to include on this Calendar:

   a. Click **Mark All** to have scheduled transactions for all accounts display on the Calendar.

   b. Click **Clear All** to clear all selected accounts.

   c. Click to check or uncheck the names of the accounts you would like displayed or not displayed on the Calendar.

QUICKSTEPS

SHOWING TRANSACTIONS ON YOUR CALENDAR

When you are using your Calendar, you can easily add memorized transactions to any date on it. From your Calendar:

1. Click **Options** and click **Show Memorized Payee List** to display the list of memorized items displayed on the right side of your Calendar.

2. Drag any item on the list to the date on which you want the transaction to take place. The Enter Expense/Income Transaction dialog box appears. You may click **Enter Transaction** to add the transaction on a specific date.

3	<new transaction>
	Ace Freeland Ho -27.90
	ACE -65.00
	Advantage Lase... -40.00
12,754.72	Alderwood -17.50
	Am Western -28.80
10	Amazon -9.76
	Ambrosia -27.00
12,704.72	Ancestry.com -40.60
17	Arco -50.90

3. The transaction now appears on your Calendar and in your register on the date you chose, assuming the transaction is for an account you have selected to show on the Calendar.

---

d. Click **OK** to close the Calendar Accounts dialog box.

USE THE CALENDAR OPTIONS

The Options menu on the Calendar toolbar allows you to tailor the Calendar to meet your needs:

- Click **Show Recorded Transactions In Calendar** to display all of the transactions for each date.

- Click **Show Bill And Income Reminders In Calendar** to display upcoming expenses or income that you have scheduled.

- Click **Show Daily Balances In Calendar** to display the total balance each day for all of the accounts you have selected.

- Click **Show Snapshots Below Calendar** to display the Bill and Income Reminders and the Account Balance graph below the Calendar.

- Click **Show Memorized Payee List** to display a list of your memorized transactions, which you can drag onto specific dates on your Calendar. See the "Showing Transactions on Your Calendar" QuickSteps for further information.

- Click **Edit Memorized Payee List** to display the Memorized Payee List so that you can make necessary changes.

- Click **Select Calendar Accounts** to open the Calendar Accounts dialog box to choose which accounts to be included in your Calendar.

Use Reports and Graphs

After you have been working with Quicken for a while, it may be easier to see information in a report or graph format rather than viewing the various registers and lists. You can create reports directly from registers, use one of the many standard reports included with Quicken, customize an existing report in a number of ways, and memorize the reports you use regularly. You can print reports and graphs, and you can copy or transfer the data on a report to other programs, such as Microsoft Excel or TurboTax. By setting your preferences, you can change how reports use color and display information, and you can set the default date range for your reports. In this chapter we discuss some of the standard reports and graphs available. In later chapters we discuss ways you can customize and change reports, and you'll learn about reports you can create regarding your investments, taxes, and net worth.

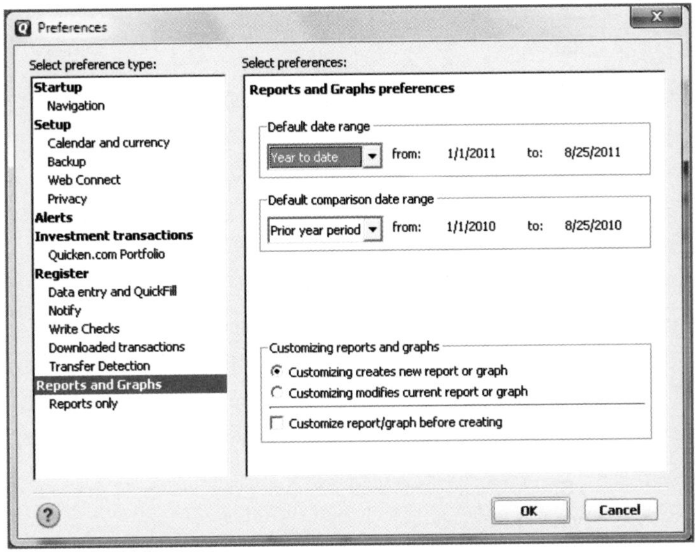

Set Report Preferences

You can determine how each report displays your data from two different locations in Quicken: the Preferences menu and from within the Reports Action Bar in the various tabs. To set how your reports display:

1. Click **Edit**, click **Preferences**, and click **Reports And Graphs**. The Quicken Preferences Reports And Graphs Preferences dialog appears, as seen in Figure 5-7:

- Click the **Default Date Range** down arrow to choose the range you will most often use when running reports. Year To Date is selected by default.

- Click the **Default Comparison Date Range** down arrow to choose the range that you will compare the current data to when creating a report. Prior Year Period is selected by default.

- In the Customizing Reports And Graphs area, click **Customizing Creates New Report Or Graph** or **Customizing Modifies Current Report Or Graph**. Customizing Creates New Report Or Graph is selected by default. You can also click **Customize Report/Graph Before Creating** to customize reports or graphs before creating them.

Figure 5-7: Use Quicken Preferences to set the default report and graph displays.

2. Click **Reports Only** to view the options for how reports will display information. For the display of both accounts and categories:

Select preference type:	Select preferences:
Startup	**Report only preferences**
Navigation	
Setup	┌─ Account display ─┐
Calendar and currency	○ Description
Backup	● Name
Web Connect	○ Both
Privacy	
Alerts	┌─ Category display ─┐
Investment transactions	○ Description
Quicken.com Portfolio	● Name
Register	○ Both
Data entry and QuickFill	
Notify	☑ Use color in report
Write Checks	☑ QuickZoom to investment forms
Downloaded transactions	☐ Remind me to save reports
Transfer Detection	
Reports and Graphs	Decimal places for prices and shares: ☐ 3 (0-6)
Reports only	

- Click **Description** to include each account's or category's description in your reports.
- Click **Name** (selected by default) to include the name of an account or category.
- Click **Both** to include the name and description in each report.

3. For other display options:
   - Clear the **Use Color In Report** check box if you want to print your report in black and white.
   - Click **QuickZoom To Investment Forms** to see what information makes up each line of data on an investment report. With QuickZoom To Investment Forms on, double-clicking takes you to the transaction's Enter Transaction form—for example, if the transaction is a buy, you'll see the transaction in the Buy – Shares Bought screen. With QuickZoom To Investment Forms off, double-clicking takes you to the transaction in the investment transaction list.
   - Click the **Remind Me To Save Reports** check box if you want Quicken to remind you to save any reports you have created.
   - Type a number in the **Decimal Places For Prices And Shares** field if it is different from the default choice of 3.

4. Click **OK** to close the Quicken Preferences dialog box.

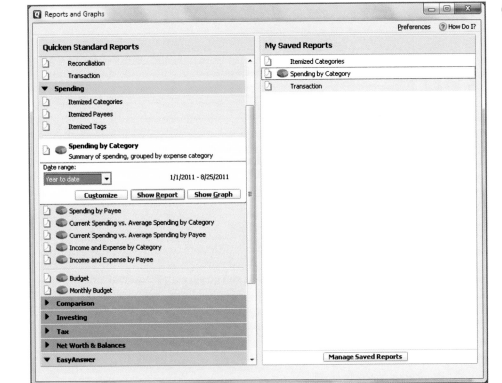

Figure 5-8: *Quicken's standard reports help you create detailed information about your finances.*

Create a Standard Report

To create a standard report in Quicken:

1. Click the **Reports** menu, and then click **Reports & Graphs Center** to display the Reports And Graphs window (see Figure 5-8).

2. Click the small triangle icon in the area, such as Spending And Comparison, from which you want the report created. The standard reports available in this area are displayed in the window.

3. Click the report you want to create. Choose the date range if it is different from the default range you set under Preferences.

4. Click **Customize** to open the Customize dialog box for this report (see Chapter 6 for more information).

5. Click **Show Report** to see the report. The report will be displayed on the screen, as you can see in Figure 5-9.

6. Click the **Printer** icon on the toolbar to open the Print dialog box and print the report.

7. Click the **Disk** icon on the toolbar to save the report. Close the report window and the Reports And Graphs window.

CREATING A MINI-REPORT

Quicken's standard reports are designed to give you broad information about your accounts and activities. However, sometimes you might only want to find out how much you have paid to one payee to date or how much money you have spent eating out during the last three months. You can create a mini-report from any register regarding a payee or a category.

1. Open a register that has either the category or the payee on which you want your mini-report.

2. Click in either the **Payee** or the **Category** field.

3. Click the mini-report icon (it looks like an orange square with one corner folded down) 🗋 . You will see a small report on your screen displaying the last few transactions for this category or payee. The time period for the mini-report will vary based on the amount of matching transactions. If there are many recent transactions, the time period will be the last 30 days. If there are only a few transactions, the time period could be the last three years.

	close ✕
Itsys Telecom	
Last 90 days ▼ (All accounts)	
Date	**Amount**
8/1/2011	-184.86
7/5/2011	-130.91
6/23/2011	-79.58
6/21/2011	-142.00
6/16/2011	-148.29
6/6/2011	-136.69
Total:	-822.33
Average:	-137.05
Monthly Average:	-274.11

Show Report

Continued . . .

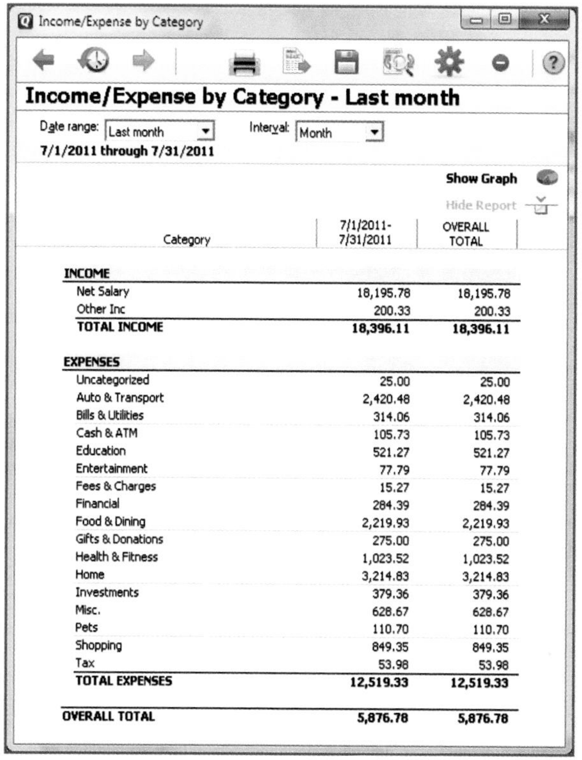

Figure 5-9: *A great power of Quicken is that you can see where you are spending money.*

Category	7/1/2011-7/31/2011	OVERALL TOTAL
INCOME		
Net Salary	18,195.78	18,195.78
Other Inc	200.33	200.33
TOTAL INCOME	**18,396.11**	**18,396.11**
EXPENSES		
Uncategorized	25.00	25.00
Auto & Transport	2,420.48	2,420.48
Bills & Utilities	314.06	314.06
Cash & ATM	105.73	105.73
Education	521.27	521.27
Entertainment	77.79	77.79
Fees & Charges	15.27	15.27
Financial	284.39	284.39
Food & Dining	2,219.93	2,219.93
Gifts & Donations	275.00	275.00
Health & Fitness	1,023.52	1,023.52
Home	3,214.83	3,214.83
Investments	379.36	379.36
Misc.	628.67	628.67
Pets	110.70	110.70
Shopping	849.35	849.35
Tax	53.98	53.98
TOTAL EXPENSES	**12,519.33**	**12,519.33**
OVERALL TOTAL	**5,876.78**	**5,876.78**

Income/Expense by Category

Income/Expense by Category - Last month

Date range: Last month   Interval: Month

7/1/2011 through 7/31/2011

Show Graph
Hide Report

Create a Standard Graph

Quicken supplies you with several standard graphs for each report area, some of which can be customized. On the Standard Reports List, if there is a standard graph associated with a report, you will see both a report and a graph icon by the report name. To create a graph:

1. Click the **Reports** menu, and then click **Reports & Graphs Center** to display the Reports And Graphs window.

2. Choose a report that has a small graph icon to its left, as seen in Figure 5-9.

QUICKSTEPS

CREATING A MINI-REPORT (Continued)

4. Click **Show Report** to see a full report. However, Show Report defaults to the last 12 months, no matter what the time period for the mini-report was, so you may end up with no transactions in the full report. This can be confusing if you have transactions in the mini-report but get no transactions in the full report.

5. In the Transaction report window, a standard report appears about this payee or category. From this window, you can:

   ● Change the date range from the default settings.

   ● Determine how the report calculates subtotals.

   ● Edit one or more transactions in the report.

   ● Click **Close** to close the Transaction report window.

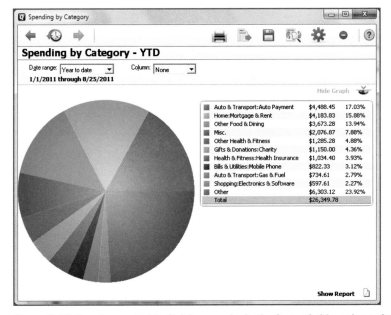

Figure 5-10: Graphs created in Quicken can be in the form of either pies or bars.

3. Click the graph you want, and click **Show Graph**. The standard graph will appear, as shown in Figure 5-10.

4. If you want to customize the graph, click **Customize**. (Customizing graphs is discussed further in Chapter 6.)

5. Click the **Printer** icon on the toolbar if you want to print the graph.

6. Click **Close** to close the graph.

How to...

- Link an Asset to a Liability Account
- Adjust the Value of an Asset
- Linking Multiple Liability Accounts to One Asset Account
- Understanding Depreciation
- Adjust the Interest Rate on a Loan
- Handle Other Loan Functions
- Making Additional Principal Payments
- Set Up Alerts
- Deleting an Alert
- Customize an Existing Report
- Save a Customized Report
- Recalling a Saved Report
- Add a Report to the Quicken Toolbar
- Create a Net Worth Report
- Use the Refinance and Loan Calculators

Chapter 6

Tracking Your Assets and Liabilities

In the last chapter you learned how to memorize and schedule transactions and were introduced to reports and graphs. In this chapter you use those skills as you work with property and debt transactions in the Property & Debt tab. This chapter will teach you how to link your assets with the related liabilities, enter information that affects the value of your assets, track your loans, and record other liabilities or payments. You'll find out how to customize reports, set alerts, and display your net worth. You will also learn to use the Quicken Refinance Calculator and the Quicken Loan Calculator.

LOAN TYPE	DESCRIPTION
Mortgage	A long-term loan, secured by real property, such as your house. A mortgage can have a *fixed* or an *adjustable* interest rate. Fixed rate means the amount of interest you pay is set at the beginning and stays at that rate for the life of the mortgage. Adjustable rate means that the rate of interest is adjusted at regular intervals throughout the life of the mortgage. Adjustable-rate mortgages are sometimes called variable-rate or floating-rate mortgages.
Home Equity	This type of loan is secured by the equity in your house. It is sometimes called a *second mortgage.* In some cases, the interest you pay on this type of loan may be tax-deductible. Consult with your tax professional for more information. Home equity loans can also have either a fixed or variable interest rate.
Reverse Mortgage	This type of loan allows homeowners with no mortgage to borrow against the equity in their home. The homeowner is paid regular monthly payments, and the loan is paid off when the home is sold. A reverse mortgage is often used by people on a fixed income to provide additional income, such as during retirement.
Vehicle Loan	This type of loan uses a vehicle—such as a boat, automobile, or recreational vehicle—as the *collateral* for the loan. Collateral is property used as security for a loan. The interest is normally not tax-deductible, but check with your tax professional to be sure.
Personal Loan	A loan that usually requires no collateral, and interest is often charged at a higher rate than with the other types of loans.

Table 6-1: **Types of Loans You Can Track in Quicken**

Work with Asset and Liability Accounts

During Quicken setup (see Chapter 1), you may have set up your house and its accompanying mortgage accounts. It is a good idea to track the asset value in one account and the liability, or amount you owe, in another. While you may not have an asset account for every liability account, review your accounts now to ensure that you include all of the assets you want to watch. Quicken can track any loan type you may have, as described in Table 6-1.

For most of us, our biggest asset is our home, so much of the information in the following section is focused on that. However, you can make adjustments to any asset in the same way as described here.

Link an Asset to a Liability Account

If you have created your mortgage account but not the asset account, create the asset account now and then link them. If you have not yet created your house or mortgage account, do it now, following the directions in Chapter 3. If you have created both accounts but not yet linked them, you can do so quickly.

NOTE

The account-linking feature is available in Quicken Deluxe, Premier, Home & Business, and Rental Property Manager versions.

1. Click the **Tools** menu, and click **Account List**.

   –Or–

   Press **CTRL+A** to see the Account List.

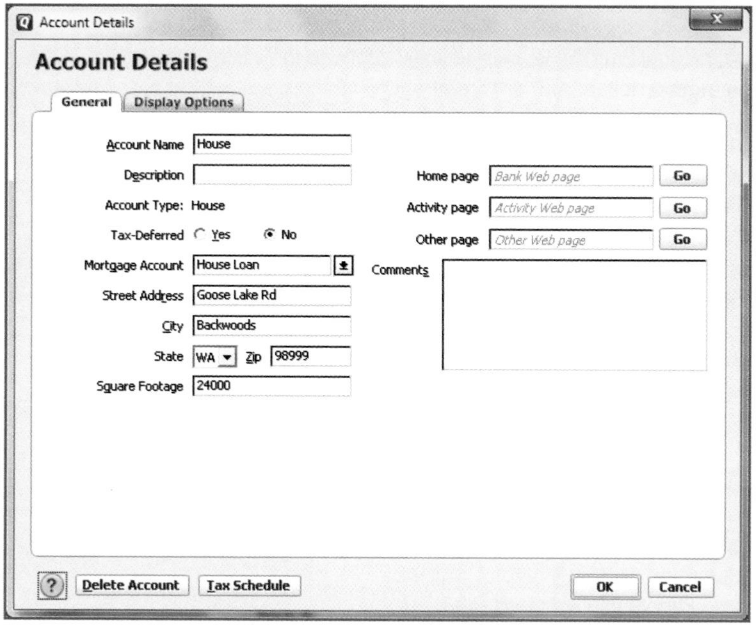

Account Details
Account Details
General
Display Options
Account Name
House
Description
Account Type: House
Tax-Deferred
Yes
No
Mortgage Account
House Loan
Street Address
Goose Lake Rd
City
Backwoods
State
WA
Zip
98999
Square Footage
24000
Home page
Bank Web page
Go
Activity page
Activity Web page
Go
Other page
Other Web page
Go
Comments
Delete Account
Tax Schedule
OK
Cancel

Figure 6-1: ***The Account Details dialog box can be used to link an asset account with a liability account, as well as to enter other information.***

TIP

You can also set up a link between an asset and a loan in the Property & Debt tab's Property view by clicking the small green circle with a white plus sign icon next to the asset account name.

NOTE

Although the cost of the garage affects the cost basis, it doesn't necessarily change the value of your home. While you paid $25,000 for the garage, someone buying your home may not be willing to pay $25,000 more to buy it.

2. Click **Edit** in the asset account with which you want to work. The Account Details dialog box appears, as shown in Figure 6-1.
3. Click the **Mortgage Account** down arrow to see a list of liability accounts. If the asset is not a house, the list will be called Linked Liability Account or, if the asset is a vehicle, Vehicle Loan Account.

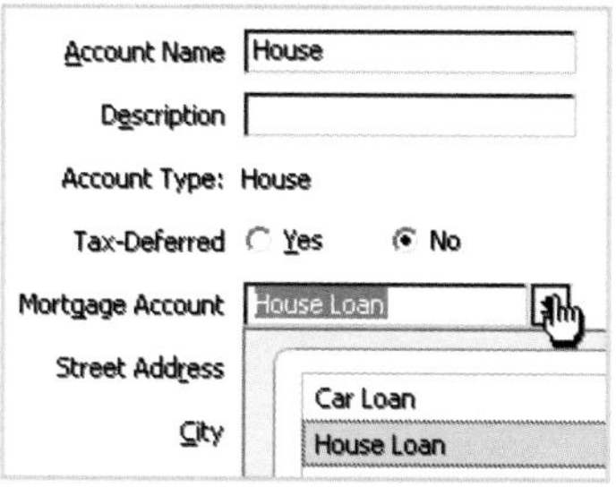

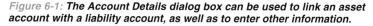

Account Name
House
Description
Account Type: House
Tax-Deferred
Yes
No
Mortgage Account
House Loan
Street Address
City
Car Loan
House Loan

4. Click the relevant liability account, and click **OK**.

Adjust the Value of an Asset

As time passes, you will probably add improvements to your home, thereby increasing its value. Furthermore, in many areas, real-estate market values fluctuate over time. You may want to record this information in your Asset Account register.

RECORD IMPROVEMENTS

An improvement such as remodeling a bathroom or adding a garage is called a *capital improvement* and adds to the value of your home. For example, if you purchased your home for $180,000 and added a garage for $25,000, the adjusted basis, or cost, of your home is $205,000. For additional information on how capital improvements may affect you, consult your tax professional. To record an improvement in your Asset Account register:

1. Open the account from which you want to pay for the improvement, for example, **Checking**.
2. Enter the transaction in the normal manner.
3. In the Category field, select **Transfers**, and select the name of the asset account.

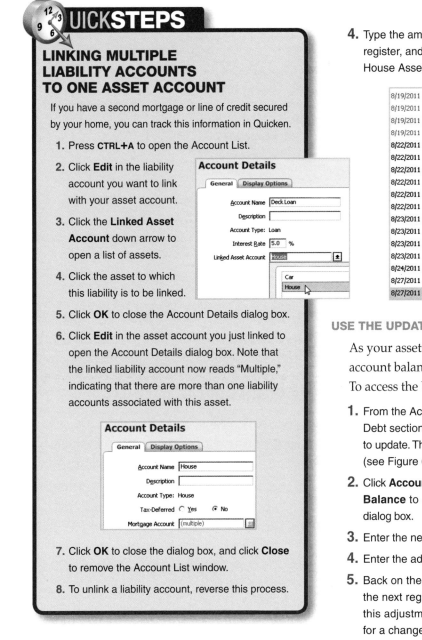

QUICKSTEPS

LINKING MULTIPLE LIABILITY ACCOUNTS TO ONE ASSET ACCOUNT

If you have a second mortgage or line of credit secured by your home, you can track this information in Quicken.

1. Press **CTRL+A** to open the Account List.

2. Click **Edit** in the liability account you want to link with your asset account.

3. Click the **Linked Asset Account** down arrow to open a list of assets.

4. Click the asset to which this liability is to be linked.

5. Click **OK** to close the Account Details dialog box.

6. Click **Edit** in the asset account you just linked to open the Account Details dialog box. Note that the linked liability account now reads "Multiple," indicating that there are more than one liability accounts associated with this asset.

7. Click **OK** to close the dialog box, and click **Close** to remove the Account List window.

8. To unlink a liability account, reverse this process.

4. Type the amount and press **ENTER**. The transaction appears in the Checking Account register, and the improvement is automatically added to the value of the house in the House Asset register.

USE THE UPDATE BALANCE DIALOG BOX

As your assets increase and decrease in value, you may want to adjust the account balances to ensure your financial net worth shows properly in Quicken. To access the Update Balance dialog box:

1. From the Account Bar, in the Property & Debt section, click the account you want to update. The account register displays (see Figure 6-2).

2. Click **Account Actions** and then click **Update Balance** to open the Update Balance dialog box.

3. Enter the new total value of the asset in the Update Balance field.

4. Enter the adjustment date if it is different from today's date, and click **OK**.

5. Back on the property account register, where your updated information appears on the next register line, click the **Category** down arrow to open a list of categories for this adjustment. Quicken uses the default of no category, which may make sense for a change in valuation that does not affect any other account.

CAUTION

With any transaction that may have significant tax implications, consult your tax professional for the best way to handle the transaction for your particular situation.

NOTE

Many people use their annual property-tax valuation statement as the way to determine their home's market value. You can also use home valuation websites such as www.zillow.com or www.realestateabc.com.

Figure 6-2: *The account register for a property is similar to registers for other types of accounts.*

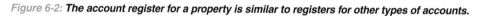

Date ▲	Payee	Memo	Category	Decrease	Clr	Increase	Balance
8/3/1998	Opening Balance		[House]			169,900 00	169,900 00
8/26/2007	Balance Adjustment		[House]		R	280,100 00	450,000 00
8/27/2011	Balance Adjustment		[House]	100,000 00	R		350,000 00

Consult your tax professional for a recommendation if needed. Personal net worth statements often show the market value of assets, as opposed to business balance sheets, which, by business accounting standards, show the historical cost of an asset.

Work with Loans

Whether you used the initial process to set up your loans or manually entered the information regarding your debts (other than credit cards), you may have to change interest rates or otherwise work with your loan information on occasion.

UNDERSTANDING DEPRECIATION

If you rent out an asset, gain income from it, or use an asset in business, your tax advisor may want you to depreciate that asset. *Depreciation* is the amount that the value of property or an asset declines because of general wear and tear, heavy use, or it is outdated. There are several instances when you may want to track depreciation in Quicken:

- You rent out part of your home.
- One or more of your assets is a rental property.
- You rent out your motor home or houseboat.
- Part or all of your home or other asset is used for your business.

In all cases, consult your tax professional for advice on whether depreciation should be recorded in your situation. You should understand both the type of depreciation used—since there are a number of different types—and the amount to enter every year or month. Once you know the amount to be entered, you can schedule this transaction, as described in Chapter 5.

Adjust the Interest Rate on a Loan

From time to time, your lender may adjust interest rates on loans. The rate change may take effect at some future date, or it may be effective immediately with the next payment.

CHANGE THE INTEREST RATE IN THE FUTURE

To adjust your loan when the change takes effect with future payments:

1. From the Tools menu, click **Loan Details**.

   –Or–

   Press **CTRL+SHIFT+H** to open the View Loans dialog box.

2. Click **Choose Loan** at the bottom of the dialog box to display a list of all your loans. Click the loan whose rate you want to change.

3. Click **Rate Changes**. The Loan Rate Changes dialog box appears.

Insert an Interest Rate Change

Effective Date: 8/27/2011

Interest Rate:

Regular Payment:

OK   Cancel

4. Click **New** to open the Insert An Interest Rate Change dialog box.

5. Type or select a date in the Effective Date field. Press **TAB** to move to the next field.

6. Type the new interest rate in the Interest Rate field. Press **TAB**, and Quicken calculates the new payment amount without changing the length of the loan.

7. Click **OK** to close the Insert An Interest Rate Change dialog box, and click **Close** to close the Loan Rate Changes dialog box. Finally, click **Done** to close the View Loans dialog box. The Current Interest Rate field will change after the date of the interest rate change.

CHANGE THE INTEREST RATE FOR THE NEXT PAYMENT

If a new interest rate is effective with the next payment:

1. Open the View Loans dialog box, and select your loan, as described in the first two steps of "Change the Interest Rate in the Future."

2. Click **Edit Payment** to open the Edit Loan Payment dialog box.

CAUTION

If you have set up a liability account without setting up an amortized loan, this liability will not be visible in the View Loans dialog box.

TIP

In the Insert An Interest Rate Change dialog box, you can also enter the amount of your new payment instead of letting Quicken calculate it.

Edit Loan Payment

Edit Loan Payment

*Required fields

Payment

Current Interest Rate: * 4.50%

Principal and Interest: 861.68

Other amounts in payment: 470.00   Edit...

Full Payment: 1,331.68

Transaction

Type: Print Check   Payment **Method**...

Payee: * Western Mortgage

Memo:

Next Payment Date: * 9/3/2011

Category for Interest: Interest Exp

Loan Web Site: Go

Address...   **Pay Now...**

OK   Cancel

3. Type the new rate in the Current Interest Rate field.

Quicken calculates the principal and interest payment for you using the next payment date as the effective date of the change without changing the length of the loan. However, if you change the payment amount (Principal And Interest field), Quicken changes the loan's length to accommodate the new payment.

4. Click **OK** to close the Edit Loan Payment dialog box, and click **Done** to close the View Loans dialog box.

Handle Other Loan Functions

In addition to changing the interest rate, you may need to handle other loan functions, including changing the loan balance, making additional principal payments (including tax and insurance payments), handling interest-only or balloon payments, and printing a loan summary.

CHANGE LOAN BALANCES

Periodically, you may get statements from your lender showing the current balance of a loan or the balance as of a specific date. If you want to change the loan balance in Quicken to match the lender's record:

1. In the Account Bar, click the debt with which you want to work. Click **Account Actions** and then click **Loan Details**.

–Or–

Press **CTRL+SHIFT+H** to display the View Loans dialog box.

In all cases, the View Loans dialog appears.

2. You should be viewing the loan you clicked in step 1, but if not, click **Choose Loan** and click the loan with which you want to work.

3. Click **Edit Loan** to open the Edit Loan dialog box.

4. Click **Next** in the lower-right corner.

5. Type the balance shown by the lender in the Current Balance field, and, if necessary, change the date in the As Of field.

6. Click **Done** to close the dialog box, and click **Done** again to close the View Loans dialog box.

Edit Loan

Balloon Information
- ● No Balloon Payment
- ○ Amortized Length: [ ] Years
- ○ Calculate

Current Balance
Current Balance: [169,128.29]   as of: [9/13/2011]

Payment
- ● Payment Amount (P+I): [1,279.25]   due on: [9/15/2011]
- ○ Calculate   Interest Rate: [5.50%]

Cancel   Back   Done

INCLUDE TAX AND INSURANCE PAYMENTS

Many mortgages, and some home equity loans, include other amounts with each payment, such as property taxes, *PMI* (private mortgage insurance), or homeowners' insurance. The property taxes and insurance payments are then paid by the lender directly to the taxing authority and insurance company. If these amounts are changed, you should reflect that information in your loan payment.

1. Press **CTRL+SHIFT+H** to open the View Loans dialog box.

2. Click **Choose Loan**, click the loan with which you want to work, and click **OK**.

3. Click **Edit Payment** to open the Edit Loan Payment dialog box.

4. Click **Edit** to open the Split Transaction window.

5. Fill in the **Category** and **Amount** fields for each of the fees included in your payment:

   a. You may want to use the standard Quicken category of Insurance:Home Insurance for the insurance portion of your payment.

   b. Quicken's standard category for property taxes is Taxes:Property.

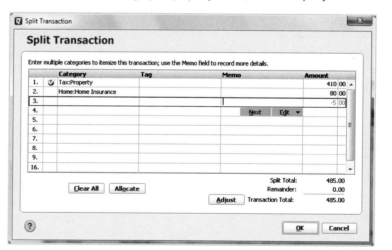

6. If you are making a change in the amount of a tax or insurance payment, creating a change in the total payment, the amount of the change will appear in the next line. Click **Adjust** opposite Transaction Total to adjust the total for the change in payments.

7. Click **OK** to close the Split Transaction window, click **OK** once more to close the Edit Loan Payment dialog box, and click **Done** to close the View Loans dialog box.

TIP

Some lenders send periodic escrow account statements. If you have entered the escrow amounts of insurance and taxes as split transactions, you can easily compare your records to that of the lender's.

While not the safest type of loans, some mortgages are interest-only, with the full amount of the loan payable at the end of the loan's term (the balloon payment). In this way, consumers have a lower monthly payment in the short term and can make principal payments whenever they choose or refinance the loan or sell the property at the end of the interest-only term.

In an interest-only balloon payment loan, the amortized length is the length of the loan, and the payment is the amount of interest per month. For example, a $10,000 ten-year, 5 percent interest-only loan with a balloon payment at the end would have an amortized length of ten years and a payment of $41.67 ($10,000 × 0.05 / 12). This gives you 120 payments of $41.67, all of which is interest, with the balance of $10,000 due at the end of ten years.

To enter a new loan of this type:

1. Press **CTRL+SHIFT+H** and click **New Loan**. The Loan Setup wizard starts.

2. Click **Borrow Money**, type an account name, tell Quicken if payments have been made on this loan by clicking **Yes** or **No**, and click **Next**.

3. Enter the date of the loan, the original balance, loan length, compounding period, and payment period:

   - Click **Standard Period** if you make regular payments—usually monthly. If you will be making payments other than monthly, use the drop-down list to choose the interval at which you will be making the payments.

   - Click **Other Period** if you will not be making regular, periodic payments. Enter the number of payments per year you will be making.

4. Click **Next**. You are asked if this loan includes a balloon payment at the end. If so, enter the number of years over which the loan is to be amortized in the Amortized Length field. If you are not sure of the amortized length, click **Calculate** and Quicken will compute the amortization period based on the amount of the payments and the interest rate.

5. If you answered "Yes" in step 2, that payments have been made on this loan, enter the current balance and as-of date, or have Quicken calculate the current balance for you.

6. Enter the payment amount if you know it, the due date, and interest rate as a percent (you don't need to include the percent sign), or have Quicken calculate the payment amount for you.

MAKING ADDITIONAL PRINCIPAL PAYMENTS

Making additional principal payments can reduce the amount of interest you pay over the term of a loan. To record these additional payments:

1. Press **CTRL+SHIFT+H** to open the View Loans window.

2. Click **Choose Loan** and click the loan with which you want to work.

3. Click **Make Payment**. The Loan Payment Type dialog box appears. Click **Extra Loan Payment** and click **OK** to open the Make Extra Payment dialog box.

4. Click the **Account To Use** down arrow, and select the account you want.

5. Click the **Type Of Transaction** down arrow, and choose how you want to make the payment.

6. Type a value in the **Amount** field. If you did not select Print Check or Online Payment in the Type Of Transaction drop-down list, click the **Number** down arrow, and select how you will reference the payment.

Continued . . .

7. Click **Done**. Quicken may display a message stating that it has calculated either the amortization period or the payment. The first Summary dialog box will appear showing you the calculated amounts. Confirm the information it contains, and click **Done** to display the Set Up Loan Payment dialog box.

8. Enter the payee information in the Set Up Loan Payment dialog box, and click **Done**. Click either **Yes** or **No** when asked if you want to create an asset account for this loan. If you click **Yes**, you will be led through the asset setup. If you click **No**, you will see a summary of your loan. Click **Done** to close the View Loans dialog box.

PRINT A LOAN SUMMARY

The View Loans dialog box allows you to print a summary of each loan and the payment schedule, and view a graph that shows the progress of the loan repayment. To access this dialog box:

1. Press **CTRL+SHIFT+H** to open the View Loans dialog box. Click **Choose Loan** and select the loan you want to print.

2. Click the **Payment Schedule** tab to see the payment schedule in the dialog box, although this is not necessary to just print the payment schedule.

3. Click the **Print** icon at the bottom-left area of the dialog box to open the Print dialog box.

4. Click **Preview** to see how the report will look when it is printed. Figure 6-3 shows an example of this report.

5. Click **Print** to print the report, or click **Close** to close the Print Preview dialog box. Click **Done** to close the View Loans dialog box.

MAKING ADDITIONAL PRINCIPAL PAYMENTS *(Continued)*

7. If you want to include your account number or other information on the check, enter it into the **Memo** field.

Make Extra Payment

Account to use:	Type of Transaction:
Business Checking	Print Check

Payee	Date:
Edna & Jeff Day Address...	8/27/2011

Category:	Amount:
[Cottage Loan] Split...	2,000.00

Memo:

Number: Print

OK   Cancel

8. Click **OK** to close the dialog box, and click **Done** to close the View Loans dialog box.

The transaction is entered in the relevant checking account and is reflected as an additional principal payment in the Liability Account register.

Note that you can also make regular extra principal payments by adding the extra principal amount to your regular payment. In the View Loans dialog box for the loan, click **Edit Payment** and opposite Other Amounts In Payment, click **Edit**. Select a category (this should be the liability account in the Transfers section of the Category field drop-down list), enter an amount, and click **OK**.

Print Preview -- Page 1 of 3

Print   Prev Page   Next Page   Zoom Out

Loan Schedule for Account "Cottage Loan"

Pmt	Date	Principal	Interest	Balance
Bal	5/6/2004	Opening Bal		125,000.00
Bal	8/27/2011	51,152.54		73,847.46
	8/27/2011	50.00		73,797.46
	8/29/2011	2,000.00		71,797.46

Projected Payments

	9/6/2011	Rate - 4.0%	New Pmt -	925.01
1	9/6/2011	685.30	239.71	71,112.16
2	10/6/2011	687.59	237.42	70,424.57
3	11/6/2011	689.88	235.13	69,734.69
4	12/6/2011	692.19	232.82	69,042.50
5	1/6/2012	694.50	230.51	68,348.00
6	2/6/2012	696.82	228.19	67,651.18
7	3/6/2012	699.14	225.87	66,952.04
8	4/6/2012	701.48	223.53	66,250.56
9	5/6/2012	703.82	221.19	65,546.74
89	1/6/2019	918.90	6.11	912.43
90	2/6/2019	912.43	3.05	0.00

Opening Date:	5/6/2004
Loan Amount:	125,000.00
Payment Amount:	925.01
Current Interest Rate:	4.0%
Original Length:	15 Years
Payment Frequency:	Monthly
Compounding Period:	Daily
Balloon Amount:	915.48

Payee:	Edna & Jeff Day
Current Balance:	73,797.46
Remaining Pmts:	90
Final Pmt Date:	2/6/2019

*Figure 6-3: **Printing a loan schedule report shows not only the payment schedule, but also a summary of the loan itself.***

VIEW A PAYMENT GRAPH

The payment graph allows you to see the history of your loan, interest, and future balance displayed in a line graph. While you cannot print this directly, it is a useful tool. To see the payment graph:

1. Press **CTRL+SHIFT+H** to open the View Loans dialog box. Click **Choose Loan** and select the loan you want to view.

2. Click the **Payment Graph** tab to view it. The colored legend on the bottom of the graph shows what each line means.

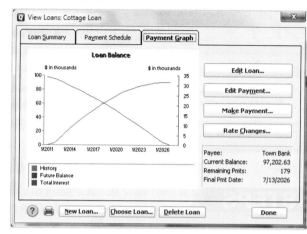

3. Click **Done** to close the View Loans dialog box.

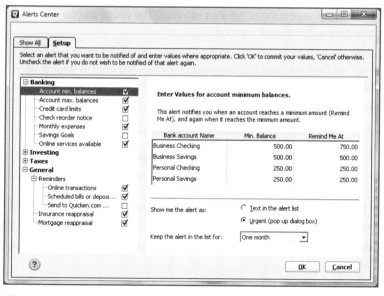

Figure 6-4: Alerts help you manage your finances.

Understand Alerts

One of the most powerful features in Quicken Premier, Home & Business, and Rental Property Manager editions is the ability to set up *alerts,* or reminders. Not all alerts are available in Quicken Deluxe or Quicken Starter edition. Alerts remind you to download transactions, pay bills, know when your credit card balance is nearing its limit, know when an account is near its minimum balance, or know when your auto insurance is approaching its renewal date, among other things. With Quicken.com, you can create a Watch List for securities you want to track. Chapter 7 discusses investments and securities in further detail. There are four major categories of alerts:

● **Banking alerts** let you monitor minimum and maximum balances, credit card limits, monthly expenses, and savings goals, as shown in Figure 6-4. You can even check your financial institutions for new services they offer.

2. Click the **Customize** icon ⚙ to open the Customize Transaction dialog box.

   a. Click the **Date Range** down arrow, and choose from a list of preset periods.

   b. Click **Custom Dates** from the Date Range list to set your own date range.

3. The Display tab allows you to tell Quicken how to lay out the report.

   a. Click in the **Title** field, and type a new title.

   b. Click the **Subtotal By** down arrow, and choose to subtotal by one of several time periods or by category, tag, payee, account, or tax schedule.

   c. Click the **Sort By** down arrow, and choose how you want your data sorted.

   d. Click the **Organization** down arrow, and choose whether the report is organized with income at the top and expenses at the bottom or with income items interspersed with expense items to show the cash flow at any period.

   e. Click **Cents (No Rounding)** if you want to see transactions to the nearest penny, or clear this check box to round items to the nearest dollar.

   f. Click **Totals Only** if you want only the summary categories displayed. Clear this check box if you want all transactions displayed.

   g. Click **Show Splits** if you want to show how split transactions were categorized.

   h. Assure that the columns you want displayed are checked in the Show Columns area by clicking the check boxes to turn them on or off. To reselect all the columns, click **Reset Columns**.

4. Click the **Accounts** tab to choose the accounts included in the report. You can choose to use all accounts or specific Banking, Investing, or Property & Debt accounts.

Date	Custom dates ▼			From: 6/1/2011 📅 To: 8/28/2011 📅

| Display | Accounts | Categories | Payees | Securities | Advanced |

	Account	Type	
All Accounts	☑ Business Checking	Bank	**Select All**
Banking	☑ Business Savings	Bank	
Investing	☑ Personal Checking	Bank	**Clear All**
Property and Debt	☑ Personal Savings	Bank	
	☑ Cash Account	Cash	
	☑ Car	Asset	
	☑ Cottage	Asset	
	☑ House	Asset	
	☑ Personal Credit Card	Credit	
	☑ Car Loan	Liab	
	☑ Cottage Loan	Liab	

☐ Show (hidden accounts)

a. Click **Select All** to choose all accounts.

b. Click **Clear All** to clear all accounts and select the ones you want to use. This is the quickest way to select only one or two accounts.

c. Click **Show (Hidden Accounts)** to include accounts that normally aren't displayed in Quicken.

5. Click the **Categories** tab to select the categories included in your report.

a. Click **Select All** to choose all categories.

b. Click **Clear All** to clear all categories and select the ones you want to use.

c. Click **Expand All** if you want details about subcategories included, or click **Collapse All** if you want only the main category information to be displayed.

d. Enter information into the Category, Payee, or Memo Contains fields if you want to include only those transactions that contain specific information in the Category and/or Memo fields. (If you have created any tags in your Quicken file, you will see a Tag tab in the report customization dialog box.)

Date	Custom dates ▼		From: 6/1/2011 📅 To: 8/28/2011 📅

| Display | Accounts | Categories | Payees | Securities | Advanced |

Select Categories
Type category name to search list:

Category	Type	
☑ Not Categorized		**Select All**
☑ Bonus	Inc	
☑ Div Income	Inc	**Clear All**
☑ Interest Inc	Inc	
☑ Net Salary	Inc	
☑ Net Salary Spouse	Inc	**Expand All**
☑ Other Inc	Inc	**Collapse All**

☑ Show (hidden categories)

Matching
Payee:

Category

Memo contains:

NOTE

It may be confusing why you can enter a payee in the Customize Transaction Category tab or enter a category in the Payee tab of the Customize Transaction dialog box. The answer is that the Category tab allows you to select all the categories in the report and to select a single payee in those categories. Step 6 of the "Customize an Existing Report" section of this chapter allows you to select all the payees in the report and to select a single category for those payees. In most instances, the payee is left blank in the Category tab and the category is left blank in the Payee tab so that you can create a report with both multiple categories and multiple payees.

TIP

Expand the date range if your payee name does not appear and you are sure you have paid this payee. If the payee name does not appear, review the list again. You may have misspelled the name the first time you entered it.

6. Click the **Payees** tab to select the payees to include in the report. Type a payee name, or choose one from the list. Click **Select All** to select all the payees, or click **Clear All** to clear the payee check boxes and select the ones you want.

7. Click the **Securities** tab to choose the securities included in the report.

8. Click **Show (Hidden Securities)** to include in your report securities you normally do not display, or clear the check box if you do not want them included.

9. Click the **Advanced** tab to further refine your report.

a. Click the **Amounts** down arrow, and click a criterion for selecting the amounts you want to include.

b. If you choose a criterion other than All, enter an amount to use with the criterion.

c. Click **Include Unrealized Gains** if you have set up investment accounts and want to include paper gains and losses in your report (see Chapter 8 for more information).

TIP

A "paper" gain or loss is an unrealized gain or loss that you might have realized if you had sold the security at today's price. The word "paper" comes from getting today's price from the newspaper.

d. Click **Tax-Related Transactions Only** to include only those transactions that relate to income tax.

e. Click the **Transaction Types** down arrow, and choose **All Transactions** (selected by default), **Payments**, **Deposits**, or **Unprinted Checks**.

f. Clear the check boxes in the Status area to limit your report to transactions that have not cleared, newly cleared (means cleared but not reconciled), and/or reconciled.

10. Click **OK** (or click **Show Report** if you have displayed the Customize dialog box before displaying the report) to display the report after you have finished customizing it.

11. If you wish, click the **Print** icon 🖶 on the toolbar to print the report (we'll save it next). Make changes as desired in the Print dialog, and then click the Print button to print your report.

Save a Customized Report

After you have created your custom report, you can save it to your My Saved Reports folder, recall it, revise it, and resave it with either a new name or as a replacement for the original saved report.

To save a customized report when you first create it:

1. Click the **Save** icon on the toolbar to open the Save Report dialog box. 💾

2. Type a name in the Report Name field to identify this report, press **TAB**, and type a description if you want. The description will appear in your list of saved reports under the title of the report.

3. Click the **Save In** down arrow, and click the folder in which you want your report stored. If you do not create a separate folder, the report will be displayed on the right side of the Report & Graph window under My Saved Reports.

4. Click **Save Report History** if you want to save all versions of this report. By default, Quicken does not save this history.

5. Click **OK** to save the report, and click **Close** to close the report window.

Save Report

Save Report

Report name: Inc/Exp Transaction by Category
Description:
Save in: My Saved Reports
☐ Save report history

My Saved Reports contents:
Spending by Category
Itemized Categories
Transaction

OK   Cancel

RECALLING A SAVED REPORT

Once you have customized and saved a report, you can easily retrieve it.

1. Click the **Reports** menu, and click **My Saved Reports & Graphs**. A list of your saved reports will appear. (If there are too many saved reports to display, you will see More Saved Reports & Graphs at the bottom of the reports list.)

2. Click the name of the report you want to view. If anything impacting the report data has changed since you saved the report—for example, new categories have been added to your Quicken file—you will be prompted to view the report as you originally saved it or to use the customize dialog to add the new items.

3. Click **Close** to close the report.

Add a Report to the Quicken Toolbar

If you choose to display the Quicken Toolbar, you can save your reports or your report folders to it. To save a report to the Quicken Toolbar:

1. Click **View** and click **Show Toolbar** to display the Quicken Toolbar.

2. Click the **Reports** menu, click **My Saved Reports & Graphs**, and click **Add Reports To Toolbar** at the bottom of the submenu. The Manage Toolbar Reports dialog box appears.

Manage Toolbar Reports

Select the items you want to display in the Quicken toolbar.

In Toolbar	My Saved Reports
☑	Inc/Exp Transaction by Category
☐	Itemized Categories
☐	Spending by Category
☐	Transaction

OK   Cancel

---

3. If you are using your own folders for your custom reports, click the small arrow to the left of each folder's check box to display the reports in that folder.

4. Click the check box of the reports (or folders) you want to appear on the Quicken Toolbar.

5. After you have made your selections, click **OK** to close the dialog box.

6. Your selections appear on the Quicken Toolbar.

Spending by Category

Net Worth

Net Worth - As of 8/28/2011

Date range: Custom dates... Interval: None

(Includes unrealized gains)

As of 8/28/2011

Show Graph

Hide Report

Account	8/28/2011 Balance
ASSETS	
Cash and Bank Accounts	
Business Checking	1,651.29
Business Savings	4,100.11
Personal Checking	1,278.13
Personal Savings	2,014.51
Cash Account	370.57
TOTAL Cash and Bank Accounts	**9,414.61**
Other Assets	
Car	20,000.00
Cottage	123,000.00
House	355,000.00
TOTAL Other Assets	**498,000.00**
Investments	
401 k	16,906.67
Brokerage	7,946.69
IRA	39,055.93
TOTAL Investments	**63,909.29**
TOTAL ASSETS	**571,323.90**
LIABILITIES	
Credit Cards	
Personal Credit Card	67.04
TOTAL Credit Cards	**67.04**
Other Liabilities	
Car Loan	8,555.42
Cottage Loan	95,202.63
Deck Loan	5,000.00
House Loan	123,178.23
TOTAL Other Liabilities	**231,936.28**
TOTAL LIABILITIES	**232,003.32**
OVERALL TOTAL	**339,320.58**

Figure 6-5: **A Net Worth report shows all of your assets minus all of your liabilities for a "net" financial "worth."**

NOTE

If you have your preferences set to Customize Report/Graph Before Creating, you will see the customize screen before the report is displayed.

Create a Net Worth Report

Your *net worth* is the difference between the value of what you own (your assets) and what you owe (your liabilities). From time to time, you may want to print a report of your net worth, and Quicken makes this easy to do. An example of a Net Worth report is shown in Figure 6-5.

1. Click the **Reports** menu, click **Net Worth & Balances**, and click **Net Worth**.

2. Since your net worth is as of a particular date, the Date Range and Interval fields have limited usefulness. The As Of date is the important element. By default, it is today's date. If you want to change it, click the **Date Range** down arrow, click **Custom Date**, set the **To** date to the one you want, and click **OK**.

3. Click **Customize** to change other items within the report, as described in "Customize an Existing Report" earlier in this chapter. Click **OK** to save your customizations and return to the report.

4. If a graph is displayed in addition to the tabular report and you don't want the graph, click **Hide Graph**.

5. Click the **Print** icon on the Report toolbar to print your report.

6. Click the **Save** icon to open the Save Report dialog box, as described in "Save a Customized Report."

7. Click **Close** to return to the main Quicken window.

Use the Refinance and Loan Calculators

As you continue to work with your assets and debts, you may want some answers to financial questions about your mortgage or other debt. The Refinance and Loan Calculators can help you make informed decisions.

USE THE REFINANCE CALCULATOR

With the Refinance Calculator, you can easily see how much you would save or gain by refinancing your current mortgage. To use the Refinance Calculator:

1. In the Property & Debt tab's Debt view, click **Loan And Debt Options**, and click **Refinance Calculator**. The Refinance Calculator dialog box appears.

2. Click in the **Monthly Payment (Total)** text box, and enter your current payment, including any escrow amounts.

Refinance Calculator

Existing Mortgage

Monthly Payment(total):	1,670.00
Impound/escrow amount:	0.00
Monthly principal/interest paid:	1,670.00

Proposed Mortgage

Principal Amount:	167,500.00
Years:	15
Interest Rate:	4.000%
Mortgage Closing Costs:	1,200.00
Mortgage Points:	0.500

Calculate

Break Even Analysis

Total Closing Costs:	2,037.50
Monthly principal/interest paid:	1,238.98
Monthly savings:	431.02
Months to break even:	**4.73**

Done

3. Click in the **Impound/Escrow Amount** text box, and enter the escrow portion of the payment you entered in step 1.

4. In the Proposed Mortgage section, enter the principal amount, the years of payments, and the new interest rate. The new monthly principal and interest amount will be calculated, as well as the monthly savings over your current monthly payment.

5. Enter any closing costs and points in the appropriate fields, and Quicken will calculate the total closing costs, as well as how many months it will take you to break even if you decide to refinance.

6. Click **Done** to close the Refinance Calculator.

WORK WITH THE LOAN CALCULATOR

Whether you are considering borrowing money or loaning it to someone else, the Quicken Loan Calculator is a handy tool. To work with the Loan Calculator:

1. In the Property & Debt tab's Debt view, click **Loan And Debt Options**, and click **Loan Calculator**. The Loan Calculator dialog box appears.

2. You can use the Loan Calculator to determine either the amount of each loan payment or the total principal. To calculate the loan payment amount:

   a. In the Calculate section, click **Payment Per Period**.

   b. Enter the annual interest rate in the relevant field. In the Number Of Years field, enter the number of years for the loan, and click **Periods Per Year** to enter the number of payments to be made each year.

   c. Click **Compounding Period** to indicate how the interest will be calculated. If the compounding period is something other than monthly, choose it from the drop-down list.

   d. Click **Loan Amount** and enter the total dollar amount of the proposed loan.

   e. Click **Calculate**, and Quicken will display the amount of each payment.

To calculate the total loan amount by entering the payment amount:

1. In the Calculate section, click **Loan Amount**.

   a. Enter the annual interest rate, number of years, periods per year, and compounding period, as described previously.

   b. Enter the payment per period, and click **Calculate**. Quicken will display the total loan amount.

c. Click **View Schedule** to open the Approximate Future Payment Schedule dialog box.

d. Click **Print** to open a Windows Print dialog box to print the schedule.

e. Click **Close** to close the Approximate Future Payment Schedule dialog box and return to the Loan Calculator dialog box.

2. Click **Done** to close the Loan Calculator.

Chapter 7

Keeping Your Records Up to Date

What does it mean to reconcile an account? Why should you do it? *Reconciling* is the process of verifying that what is in your Quicken register is the same as what the bank or other financial institution shows in their records. Reconciling, or *balancing,* your checking and other accounts ensures that you have entered any fees and charges, that all deposits have been credited to your account (banks do make errors), and that your records accurately reflect what has happened during the period since you last balanced your account. This chapter will discuss how to reconcile and update checking and savings accounts, credit card statements, and investment accounts from paper statements as well as from online ones.

NOTE

The first time you reconcile a Quicken account, Quicken uses the starting account balance as the opening balance. After you have used Quicken once to reconcile the account, Quicken uses the ending balance from the last time you reconciled as the opening balance. If you later change a reconciled transaction, the reconciled opening balance may not be equal to the last reconciliation's ending balance.

Reconcile Checking and Savings Accounts

You are probably familiar with the checking and savings account statements sent by your bank. They show the balance at the beginning of the month, all of the transactions for the account that occurred since the last statement, any fees charged to your account, and the bank's balance for the account at the end of the month. This section will show you how to reconcile your Quicken checking and savings accounts with your bank's paper statements and online information. It will also discuss how to deal with items that appear on the bank statement that aren't recorded in Quicken, what to do if the account doesn't balance the first time, and how to find discrepancies.

Reconcile Quicken with Your Bank's Paper Statement

One of the great features of Quicken is its ability to quickly reconcile or balance your bank's statement to your Quicken account. You may reconcile bank accounts to a paper statement, whether they have been enabled for online services or you enter your transactions manually.

RECONCILE AN ONLINE-ENABLED ACCOUNT TO A PAPER STATEMENT

To reconcile an account that has online services with the bank's paper statement:

1. Click the name of the account you want to reconcile in the Account Bar to open its register.

2. Click **Account Actions** and, from the menu, click **Reconcile**. You are prompted to download the latest transactions.

𝒫 Find	**Account Actions ▼**	
Transactions		
⚡ Update Now	Ctrl+Alt+U	
🔍 Edit Account Details	Ctrl+Shift+E	
✎ Write Checks	Ctrl+W	
⊘ Reconcile	Ctrl+R	
🏦 Transfer Money	Ctrl+Shift+T	
Reporting		

Your account may be out of date.

Would you like to download your latest activity before reconciling?

◉ Download transactions for this account

○ Reconcile without downloading

[OK] [Cancel]

3. If you want to do that, accept the default **Download Transactions For This Account** and click **OK**. This will stop the reconciliation process. The One Step Update dialog box appears. Enter your password and click **Update Now**. After the update, restart the reconciliation at step 2. If the account uses Web Connect rather than Direct Connect, you will be prompted with a screen to log in to your bank's website.

4. To continue reconciling with the paper statement, click **Reconcile Without Downloading** and click **OK**.

5. The Reconcile Online Account dialog box appears with Use Paper Statement selected. Type the date of the paper statement in the Ending Statement Date text box.

Reconcile: Personal Checking

◉ **Use Paper Statement**

Statement Ending Date: [   ]

Opening Balance: [1,680.98]

Ending Balance: [   ]

○ **Use Online Balance**

Balance as of 8/29/2011: **385.21**

☐ Auto reconcile downloaded transactions

Your one-click financial solution WELLS FARGO wellsfargo.com

[OK] [Cancel]

6. Confirm the amount in the Opening Balance field. If the statement opening balance is not what Quicken shows, type the statement amount. Press **TAB** to continue.

7. Type the amount from your bank statement in the Ending Balance field, and click **OK** to close the dialog box and open the Reconcile window. All of the transactions you have entered into this Quicken account that you have not yet reconciled to the statement appear in this window, an example of which is shown in Figure 7-1.

8. Check **Clr** (for "cleared") by each deposit and check that appears on the bank statement. After you have selected all the cleared checks and deposits, the difference shown in the bottom-right corner of the window should be zero. If it does, you're done reconciling. If you don't have a zero difference, see "Make Corrections in the Reconcile Window" next in this chapter.

TIP

If most of the transactions have cleared, click **Mark All** and then click the transactions that haven't cleared to deselect them.

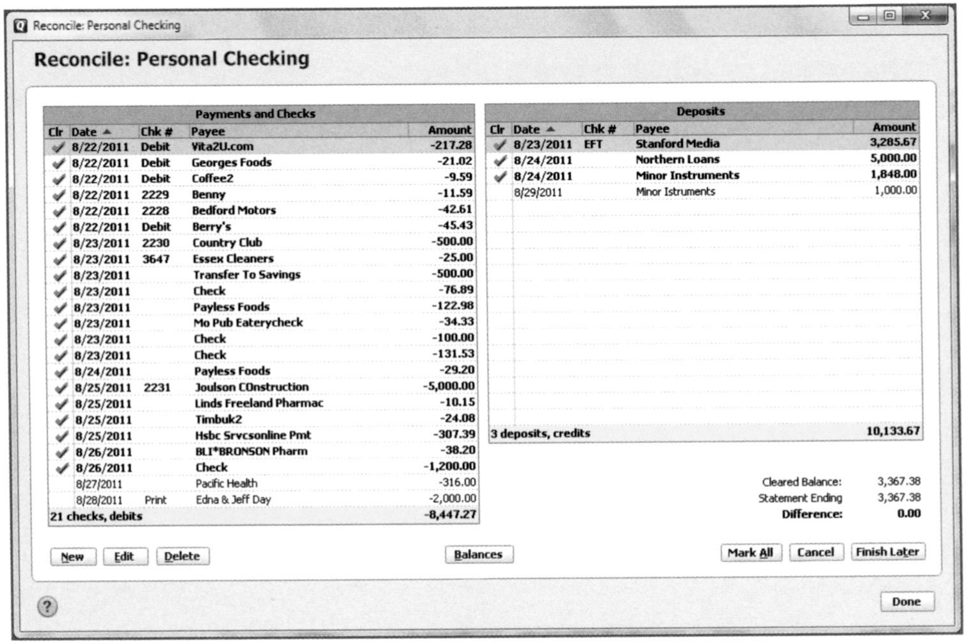

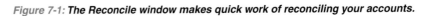

Figure 7-1: *The Reconcile window makes quick work of reconciling your accounts.*

9. Click **Done** to open the Reconciliation Complete dialog box.

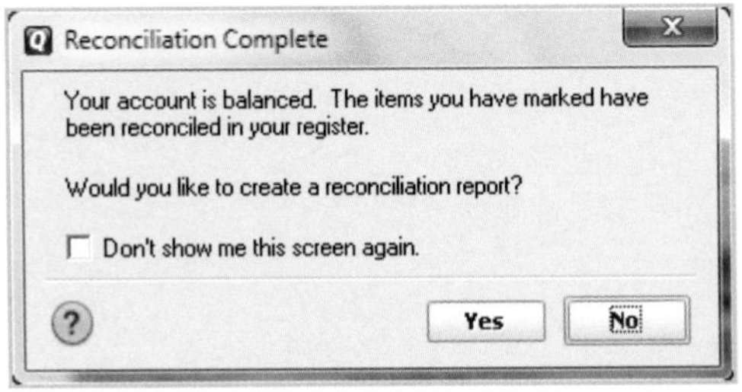

Reconciliation Complete

Your account is balanced. The items you have marked have been reconciled in your register.

Would you like to create a reconciliation report?

☐ Don't show me this screen again.

[Yes] [No]

Reconciliation Report Setup

Report Title (optional) Personal Chkng Reconcil.

Show to bank balance as of 8/30/2011

Include ○ All Transactions
         ◉ Summary and Uncleared

☐ Show Savings Goal Transactions

[OK] [Cancel]

10. Click **Yes** to create a Reconciliation Report and display the Reconciliation Report Setup dialog box, or click **No** if you don't want to create one. If you do not want to be asked this question again, click **Don't Show Me This Screen Again**.

11. If you are creating a Reconciliation Report, type a title in the Report Title field if you choose. If you leave this field blank, Quicken uses the default title "Reconciliation Report."

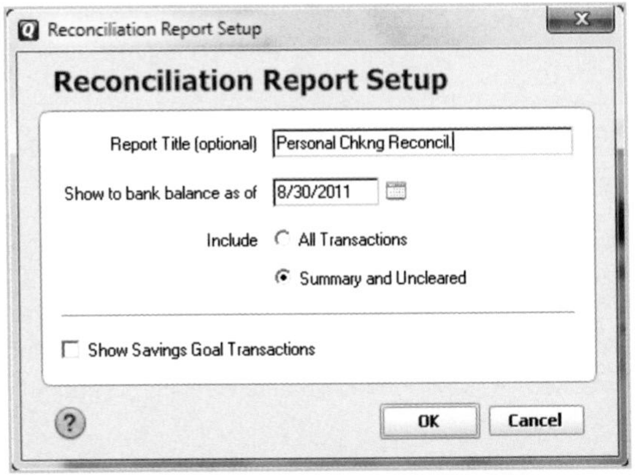

12. Change the date in the Show Reconciliation To Bank Balance As Of field if you want it to be the statement date instead of today's date.

13. Click **All Transactions** to create a report that includes all transactions through today, or click **Summary And Uncleared** to include only a summary of the cleared transactions through the bank's statement date and details about uncleared items through today. This choice creates a shorter, more concise report.

14. If you have established savings goals and want to include them in the report, click the **Show Savings Goal Transactions** check box. Chapter 9 discusses savings goals and other financial-planning matters in more detail.

15. Click **OK** to open a print dialog box. Click **Preview** to see how the report will appear when printed. From the Preview window, click **Print**.

16. If you have not chosen to see a preview of your report, from the Print dialog box, click **Print** to print the report.

RECONCILE AN ONLINE-ENABLED ACCOUNT TO THE ONLINE BALANCE

You may choose to reconcile your accounts to the balance shown by your bank. Before you reconcile online, however, ensure that all of your transactions have been downloaded and that you have reviewed and accepted them. When you update your Quicken register, the transactions can be automatically reconciled (see the QuickSteps "Activating Automatic Reconciliation"). There are two methods for reconciling online:

- You can update several times during a month and then reconcile to the paper statement at the end of the month.

- You can reconcile each time you download transactions.

Whichever method you use, stick to it.

To perform the online reconciliation after you have downloaded and accepted all of the transactions:

1. Click the name of the account you want to reconcile in the Account Bar to open its register.

2. Click **Account Actions** and, from the menu, click **Reconcile**. You are prompted to download the latest transactions.

CAUTION

Working back and forth between reconciling online and with a paper statement can be confusing. Transactions that appear on your paper bank statement may not appear in the Reconcile window, since Quicken has already reconciled them.

NOTE

If the account is a credit card account, the Make Credit Card Payment dialog box displays rather than the Reconciliation Complete dialog box.

3. If you have not yet downloaded the latest transactions and you want to stop the reconciliation process to download these transactions, click **Download Transactions To This Account**. The One Step Update dialog box appears. Enter your password and click **Update Now**. After the update, restart the reconciliation.

4. To continue reconciling with the online bank balance, click **Reconcile Without Downloading**.

5. Click **Use Online Balance**. If you choose to automatically reconcile the account after you compare the transactions to the ones in your register, click the **Auto Reconcile** check box.

Reconcile: Personal Checking

Reconcile: Personal Checking

Reconcile: Personal Checking

○ **Use Paper Statement**

Statement Ending Date: [   ]

Opening Balance: [3,367.38]

Ending Balance: [   ]

● **Use Online Balance**

Balance as of 8/29/2011:   **385.21**

☑ Auto reconcile downloaded transactions

Your one-click financial solution   WELLS FARGO

wellsfargo.com

⊙   OK   Cancel

6. Click **OK** to close the dialog box and open the Reconcile window. All of the transactions you have entered into this Quicken account that you have not yet marked as having been cleared by the bank appear in this window, which is similar to Figure 7-1.

7. The difference should be zero. Click **Done** to open the Reconciliation Complete dialog box, and proceed as described in steps 10 through 16 in "Reconcile an Online-Enabled Account to a Paper Statement" earlier in this chapter.

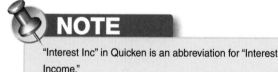

Reconcile Details

Reconcile Details

*Required fields

The last statement ending date: N/A

Enter the following from your bank statement

Opening Balance:* 2,187.38

Ending Balance:* 3,199.72

New Statement Ending Date:* 8/30/2011

Categorize your interest and bank charges, if any

Service Charge: 3.00   Date: 8/30/2011

Category: Fees & Charges:Bank Fee

Interest Earned: 1.31   Date: 8/30/2011

Category: Interest Inc

OK   Cancel

NOTE

"Interest Inc" in Quicken is an abbreviation for "Interest Income."

NOTE

If you have turned off the Reconciliation Report message, you can still obtain a Reconciliation Report. Click the **Reports** menu, click **Banking**, and click **Reconciliation** to open the Reconciliation Report Setup dialog box.

RECONCILE A MANUAL ACCOUNT TO A PAPER STATEMENT

If you have chosen to enter your transactions manually, or if your financial institution does not provide any online services, reconcile the account as follows:

1. Click the name of the account you want to reconcile in the Account Bar to open its register.

2. Click **Account Actions** and, from the menu, click **Reconcile**. The Reconcile Details dialog box appears.

3. Confirm the amount in the Opening Balance field. If the statement opening balance is not what Quicken shows, type the statement amount. Press **TAB** to continue.

4. Type the amount from your bank statement in the Ending Balance field, and press **TAB**.

5. Enter the ending date shown on your paper bank statement in the New Statement Ending Date field. Press **TAB** to continue.

6. Enter any service charge shown on the bank statement in the Service Charge field, and enter the date on which it was charged. Press **TAB**.

7. Click the **Category** field to enter or select the category for the service charge. By default, Quicken uses Fees & Charges:Bank Fee. Press **TAB**.

8. Enter the amount of interest shown on the statement in the Interest Earned field and the date the bank credited the account, and press **TAB**.

9. Enter or select the category for the interest in the Interest Earned field. By default, Quicken uses Interest Inc as the category.

10. Click **OK** to close the dialog box and open the Reconcile window. All of the transactions you have entered into this Quicken account that have not yet been marked as having been cleared by the bank appear in this window, as seen in Figure 7-1.

11. Continue as described in steps 8 through 16 in "Reconcile an Online-Enabled Account to a Paper Statement" earlier in this chapter.

Make Corrections in the Reconcile Window

If your transactions do not immediately balance, you can make corrections in the Reconcile window to eventually reconcile the account.

1. Click **New** to enter a transaction into the register that appears on the bank statement but that has not been entered into the register. This could be a charge for new checks or money withdrawn using a cash machine or a debit card. See "Deal with Unrecorded Items" next in this chapter. Click the minimized **Reconcile: *Account Name*** button at the bottom-left of the window to get back to the Reconcile window.

2. Select a transaction and click **Edit** to make changes to that transaction in the register. This is great for fixing transpositions or penny errors. Click the minimized **Reconcile: Account Name** link to get back to the Reconcile window.

3. Select a transaction and click **Delete** to permanently remove a transaction from the register. Click **Yes** to confirm the deletion.

4. Click **Balances** to go back to the Reconcile Details dialog box to make changes to the opening or ending balance. Click **OK** when you are done.

5. Back in the Reconcile ledger dialog box (Figure 7-1), click the column headings to change how Quicken sorts the transactions in this window.

6. Click the **Help** icon to display a Help window.

7. Click **Mark All** to mark all of the transactions displayed in the window. If Mark All has already been selected, Clear All is displayed to perform the reverse operation.

8. Click **Cancel** to stop the reconciliation. This opens a dialog box that asks if you want to save your work or close the window without saving it.

   - Click **Yes** to close the window without saving your work.

   - Click **Finish Later** to save what you have done so far. When you return to the register, you will notice that any transactions you have selected now display a "c" in the Clr column. When you have finished the reconciliation, the "c" turns into an "R," and, if your preferences are set to their defaults, the transaction text will be grey or dimmed.

   - Click **Done** to complete the reconciliation and open the Reconciliation Complete dialog box.

Deal with Unrecorded Items

Items may appear on your bank statement that do not appear in Quicken. Some examples can be automatic withdrawals, such as payments for your safety deposit box, or withdrawals from the cash machine you forgot to record. To enter an item from the Reconcile window:

1. Click **New** in the bottom-left corner of the Reconcile Window to open the account register.

2. Enter the date on which the transaction occurred. The default is today's date, but you probably want to use the actual transaction date.

3. Enter the type of transaction in the Check # field, and then fill in the Payee, Memo, Category, and Payment or Deposit fields (credit card fields are slightly different).

4. Click **Enter** and then click the minimized **Reconcile: *Account Name*** link to return to the Reconcile window. `Reconcile: Business Check... X`

FIND STATEMENT DISCREPANCIES

Several things need to be considered when trying to find a discrepancy between a bank statement and your Quicken account register:

- Ensure you are working with the right account. It's easy to click the wrong name if you have several accounts.

- Verify that the "Checks, Debits" total amount and the "Deposits, Credits" total amount displayed at the bottom of the Reconcile window match the total amounts shown on the bank statement.

- Check the Difference amount in the lower-right corner of the window. If the difference is evenly divisible by nine, you may have transposed an entry. For example, if the difference is $0.63, you may have entered a check into Quicken as $29.18 and written the actual check for $29.81.

- If the difference is not a transposition, you may have neglected to enter a transaction, or you entered a deposit as a check or vice versa. If the difference does not equal a check amount on either your bank statement or your register, look in both for a transaction equaling half the amount of the difference. You may have entered a deposit as a payment or vice versa.

- Determine if the difference is positive or negative. If the difference is negative, the bank shows more money than your register does. The bank may have a deposit you haven't entered, or you may have cleared checks the bank hasn't received. If the difference is positive, the bank shows less money than your register does. You may have neglected to enter a fee or an automatic withdrawal in your register.

- Watch for pennies. If your handwriting is not clearly legible, the automated machinery used by the bank for clearing checks may not read the amount correctly—for example, it might mistake an eight as a three.

- Take a time out. If you've been looking at your account for some time and can't locate the discrepancy, walk away for a few minutes. Often, when you come back after a break, the difference seems to appear as if by magic.

TIP

Using Quicken's Scheduled Transactions feature can ensure that all of your transactions are entered into your check register.

TIP

When you pay your credit card or other bills, take the envelopes directly to the post office rather than leaving them in the mailbox. This ensures that anyone stealing mail from the boxes cannot get your information.

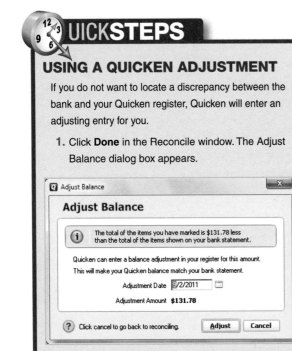

QUICKSTEPS

USING A QUICKEN ADJUSTMENT

If you do not want to locate a discrepancy between the bank and your Quicken register, Quicken will enter an adjusting entry for you.

1. Click **Done** in the Reconcile window. The Adjust Balance dialog box appears.

Adjust Balance

> The total of the items you have marked is $131.78 less than the total of the items shown on your bank statement.
>
> Quicken can enter a balance adjustment in your register for this amount. This will make your Quicken balance match your bank statement.
>
> Adjustment Date 5/2/2011
>
> Adjustment Amount **$131.78**
>
> Click cancel to go back to reconciling.   **Adjust**   Cancel

2. Click in the **Adjustment Date** field, and enter the date of the adjustment. This can be the date of the paper statement or today's date, whichever makes more sense to you.

3. Click **Adjust**.

4. A Reconciliation Complete dialog box appears. Click **Yes** if you want to create a Reconciliation Report; click **No** if you do not. If you click No, the dialog box closes and you are returned to the register.

5. In your register, locate the balance adjustment that Quicken just created, and, if you want, change the category by clicking in the **Category** field and entering a new one. Click **Save** to save the change.

Reconcile Credit Card Statements

Reconciling your credit card statement is similar to reconciling your checking or savings account statement, especially if you enter your credit card purchases as you make them. If you wait until the credit card statement arrives to enter the charges and categorize them, however, the process takes a bit longer.

RECONCILE A PAPER CREDIT CARD STATEMENT

To reconcile your manual (not online-enabled) credit card account to a paper statement:

1. From the Account Bar, click the account with which you want to work.

2. Click **Account Actions** and click **Reconcile** to open the Reconcile dialog box.

3. Enter the total from the statement in the Charges, Cash Advances field.

4. Click in the **Payments, Credits** field, and enter the total from the statement.

5. Click in the **Ending Balance** field, and enter the balance due on the statement.

6. Click in the **New Statement Ending Date** field, and enter the ending date of the statement.

7. Click in the **Finance Charges** field, and enter the amount of finance charges, if any. Click in the **Date** field, and change the date of the charges from the default of today's date if needed.

8. Click in the **Category** field, and either choose a category from the drop-down list or type the category for the finance charges.

Reconcile: WIB Credit Card

*Required fields

The last statement ending date: N/A

Enter the following from your statement.

Charges, Cash Advances: *   142.91
(other than finance charges)

Payments, Credits: *   0.00

Ending Balance: *   144.47

New Statement Ending Date: *   9/1/2011

Enter and categorize your interest charges, if any.

Finance Charges: 1.56   Date: 9/1/2011

Category: Interest Exp

OK   Cancel

9. Click **OK**. The Reconcile window opens.

10. Proceed as described in "Reconcile Quicken with Your Bank's Paper Statement" earlier in the chapter.

11. If zero appears in the Difference field, click **Done** to open the Make Credit Card Payment dialog box. You are asked if you want to make a payment on the balance now. If so:

> **Make Credit Card Payment**
>
> Do you want to make a payment now?
> You have an outstanding balance of $144.47
>
> If you would like to pay some or all of this amount, select a bank account below and click Yes.
>
> Bank Account: Business Checking
>
> Payment Method
> ⦿ Printed Check
> ○ Hand Written Check
>
> ☐ Don't show me this screen again.
>
> ⑦   Yes   No

a. Click the **Bank Account** down arrow to choose the account from which to make the payment.

b. Choose the method of preparing the check, and click **Yes**.

- If you click **Printed Check**, a check facsimile opens for you to fill in. The default category is the credit card account.
- If you click **Hand Written Check**, the check is entered into the register and pauses for you to enter the check number.
- If you click **No**, the window closes and you are returned to the register.

RECONCILE A CREDIT CARD ACCOUNT ONLINE

As with reconciling bank accounts, if your credit card company offers it, downloading and reconciling transactions directly into your credit card register is the most efficient way to reconcile your account. However, if you want to keep track of your spending by category, you must remember to enter the category for each downloaded transaction, although if your transactions are to the same establishment for the same purpose, the category will carry over from transaction to transaction. The process for performing an online reconciliation of your credit card account is the same as that described in "Reconcile an Online-Enabled Account to a Paper Statement" and "Reconcile an Online-Enabled Account to the

QUICKSTEPS

ACTIVATING AUTOMATIC RECONCILIATION

When you have activated the downloading of transactions for an online-enabled bank account, you can use a Quicken feature that makes reconciling automatic each time you download.

1. Open the register of the account you want to use.

2. Click **Account Actions** and click **Reconcile**.

3. Click **Use Online Balance**.

4. Click **Auto Reconcile Downloaded Transactions**.

The setting takes effect after the next time you go online. Quicken will automatically reconcile the downloaded transactions after you have accepted them. If the balances do not match, Quicken displays a Statement History dialog box to help you find the problem.

NOTE

Some institutions offer an "e-bills" feature that will allow you to receive your bill electronically. Check with your institution to see if they have this service.

Online Balance" earlier in the chapter. If you choose to reconcile your paper credit card statement manually, follow the directions described in "Reconcile a Manual Account to a Paper Statement," also in this chapter.

MAKE CREDIT CARD STATEMENT ADJUSTMENTS

Sometimes, you just don't want to take the time to find all the discrepancies in a credit card register. Perhaps you've just started entering transactions and some of the beginning balances aren't right. Quicken can help you fix these problems.

1. When you have completed the reconciliation as far as you want, click **Done** in the Reconcile window. The Adjusting Register To Agree With Statement dialog box appears. This can have up to three entries for differences in the opening balance, payments, and charges.

2. In the Opening Balance Difference text box, if there is one in your dialog box, click in the **Category** field, and change the category from the default "Misc" if you choose.

3. In the Register Missing One Or More Payments area, if there is one in your dialog box, click in the **Category** field, and change the category from the default "Misc" if you choose.

4. In the Register Missing One Or More Charges area, if there is one in your dialog box, click in the **Category** field, and change the category.

5. Click **Adjust** to have the entries recorded in the credit card account register.

FINDING AND RESOLVING CREDIT CARD ERRORS

Using Quicken to reconcile your credit card statements may help you find errors in your account. To ensure there are no errors on your statement and that your account is protected:

- Check each item on the statement as soon as you get it.

- Ensure that each charge is the amount you expected.

- Know the date on which your statement usually arrives. Set an alert in Quicken to remember that date. If your statement has not arrived, call the credit card company to advise them the statement has not been delivered.

- If the credit card company provides online access to your account, go online and download your transactions on a regular basis and ensure that each charge to your account is valid.

RESOLVE CREDIT CARD ERRORS

If you do find an error, or if you have a dispute with a seller, take the following steps:

- Call the seller that charged you to see if the issue can be resolved between the two of you. Document the call; the name of the seller's agent; and the date, time, and nature of the problem.

- Call the credit card company to tell them of the problem. Document the call as to date, time, and the name of the person with whom you spoke.

Continued . . .

6. If you want to apportion each entry between several categories, make no changes to the categories in the Adjusting Register To Agree With Statement dialog box. When you return to the register, locate each adjustment and select the first one with which you want to work.

- Click **Split** to open the Split Transaction window, and assign the categories you choose.

- Select the other adjustments you want to change, and assign categories to them.

Reconcile Investment Accounts

You use the same process to reconcile an investment account as you do with a checking account, except you have to balance to both a cash balance and a share balance. If your financial institution offers it, the easiest way to reconcile each account is to sign up for their download services. That way, you can download each transaction directly from your broker and use Quicken's Compare To Portfolio feature to monitor the account.

Reconcile an Investment Account to a Paper Statement

The process of reconciling an investment account is the same as described in "Reconcile a Manual Account to a Paper Statement" earlier in the chapter. To reconcile an investment account to a paper statement:

1. Select the account you want to reconcile. If the investment account has a linked cash account, you will need to perform the reconciliation in the linked cash account. Click **Account Actions** and click **Reconcile**. The Reconcile window appears.

2. Click in the **Starting Cash Balance** field, and enter the beginning balance amount from your paper statement.

QUICKSTEPS

FINDING AND RESOLVING CREDIT CARD ERRORS *(Continued)*

- Write a letter to the credit card company explaining the same information. The Fair Credit Billing Act requires that you notify your credit card company in writing. Make sure it is addressed to the correct address for billing inquiries. This address is usually listed on the back of your credit card. Include any supporting information. For further protection, send this letter via certified mail and ask for a return receipt as proof. This verifies both that you sent the letter within 60 days of the statement date and that your credit card company received the letter.
- Your credit card company must respond to your dispute letter, in writing, within 30 days. The credit card company then has two billing cycles or 90 days—whichever is less—to determine if the charge was in error. They are required to notify you in writing of their determination. If the charge was correct but there is still a dispute, write the credit card company again. They are not allowed to charge interest or require payment until the issue has been resolved.

3. Click in the **Ending Cash Balance** field, and enter the ending cash balance from your paper statement. (Note this is a cash balance, not an account balance.)
4. Click in the **Statement Ending Date** field to type the date of the statement.
5. Click **OK**. The Reconcile window opens. This is similar to the Reconcile window for your checking account; however, instead of showing checks and deposits, it shows increases and decreases to the account.
6. Click each transaction to note that it has cleared.
7. Click **Done** to complete the reconciliation. The Reconciliation Complete dialog box appears.
8. Click **Yes** to create a reconciliation report. Click **No** to close the dialog box and return to the investment account transaction list.

Reconcile Share Balances

You may want to update your share balances prior to reconciliation. To do that, you need to add share purchases and sales.

1. Select the account you want to reconcile. Click **Enter Transactions** to open the Buy - Shares Bought dialog box, which is displayed in Figure 7-2.

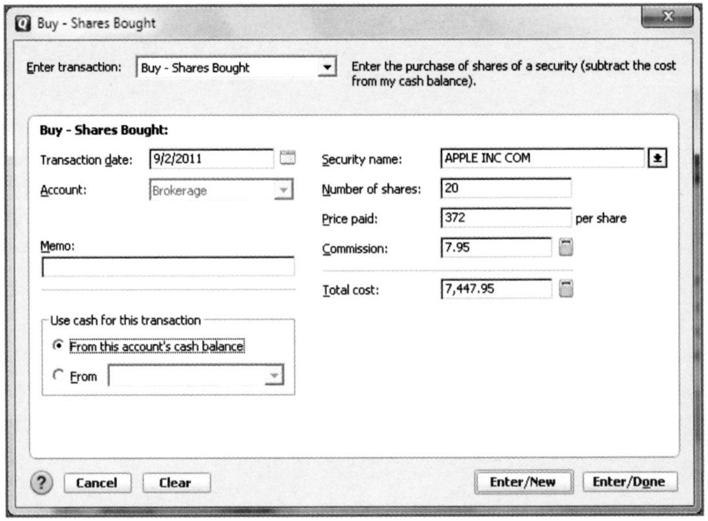

Figure 7-2: ***Use the Buy - Shares Bought dialog box to enter transactions into your investment account.***

UPDATING PRICES MANUALLY FROM A PAPER STATEMENT

After you have reconciled an investment account, Quicken gives you the opportunity to update the prices of your securities directly from your statement. After you have finished the reconciliation and returned to the investment account's Transaction List:

1. Click the **Investing** tab, and click the **Portfolio** button.

   –Or–

   Press **CTRL+U**.

   Either way, your portfolio appears.

2. Change the **As Of** date to the date of the paper statement.

3. Click in the **Quote/Price** column for each security, and enter the price shown on the statement.

Name	Quote/...
▼ 401 k	
⊞ APPLE INC COM	384.83

2. Enter each purchase transaction listed on your statement. Click **Enter/New** to move to a new transaction. If asked, enter or look up the ticker symbol, click **Next**, and verify the symbol is correct. As you enter the buys and sells, you can use the Share Bal column to monitor the total share balance of each security to ensure your entries are accurate. When you are finished, click **Done**.

3. For sale transactions, click the **Enter Transaction** down arrow, and click **Sell – Shares Sold**. Type the information requested, and click **Enter/New** to move to another transaction.

4. Click **Enter/Done** when you have entered all of the transactions shown on the statement. You are returned to the Transaction List for the account.

Update 401(k) Accounts

401(k) accounts are tracked a bit differently from other investment accounts. If you have Quicken Deluxe, Premier, Home & Business edition, or Quicken Rental Property Manager, you can track actual shares or dollar amounts. If your financial institution offers it, you can even download your transaction details. You can also manually enter the information from a paper statement or use the 401(k)/403(b) Update dialog box. The easiest method to use is the download option; however, the 401(k)/403(b) Update lets you track the performance of funds in your 401(k) or 403(b) account.

USE THE 401(K)/403(B) UPDATE

1. From the Account Bar's Investing section, click the account with which you want to work.

2. Click **Account Actions** and then click **Update 401(k) Holdings**. The 401(k)/403(b) Update dialog box appears. If you have an online-enabled 401(k) account, there is no update holdings option; instead, select **Update Transactions** to download them from your financial institution.

🔍 Find	Account Actions ▼
Transactions	
⚡ Set Up Download	
⚡ Update 401(k) Holdings	
⚡ Update Quotes only	

3. Enter the date of the statement in the This Statement Ends field.

4. Click either **Yes** or **No** in response to the question Does Your Statement Show How Many Shares Of Each Security You Own?, depending on which is correct.

Update 401(k)/403(b) Account: Exc 401(k)

Welcome to 401(k)/403(b) Update.

Use your most recent statement to update this account.

The previous statement ended: 7/30/2011

This statement ends: 8/31/2011

Does your statement show how many shares of each security you own?
○ No ● Yes

Did you take out a new loan against this account during the last statement period?
● No ○ Yes

Cancel | Next

5. Click either **Yes** or **No** in response to the question Did You Take Out A New Loan Against This Account During The Last Statement Period?, and then click **Next**.

6. Enter the amount of the employee contributions and employer-matching contributions, as shown on the statement.

7. If needed, click in the **Other Contributions And Payments** field, and enter those amounts from the statement. Quicken will add all of these transactions, which should match your paper statement.

8. Click **Next**. The Total Withdrawals This Period dialog box appears. Enter the amounts in each of the fields from the statement that are applicable to you. Quicken shows the total, which should match the statement. Click **Next**.

9. If you took out a loan during this period, you are asked to enter the purpose of the loan and the loan amount. You may also choose to set up an account to track the loan balance. Enter the relevant information, and click **Next**.

10. The Loan Repayments dialog box appears. Enter the amount of principal and interest paid, as shown on the statement, and then click **Next**.

11. The name of each security held in the account is displayed in the next dialog box. Click the check mark next to a security if it is no longer in your portfolio, and click **Add New Security** if there is a security on the statement that does not appear on this list. Otherwise, click **Next**.

UNDERSTANDING HOW QUICKEN WORKS WITH 401(K)/403(B) ACCOUNTS

When you add a 401(k)/403(b) account in Quicken Deluxe, Premier, Home & Business, and Rental Property Manager editions, Quicken adds a special tax-impact account. This account is not visible on the Account List, but you can see it on tax reports. (Learn more about taxes in Chapter 10.) This tax account tracks any transaction in this retirement account that may have an effect on your income taxes, such as early withdrawal of funds. Quicken uses the information in this hidden account in both reports and its tax planning tools. To ensure your tax planning tools and reports are as accurate as possible, do not change or remove any of the transactions in this account, or the account itself.

NOTE

Some companies allow loans of up to 50 percent of your 401(k) account. However, the interest on these loans is not deductible on your income tax.

NOTE

If your home has increased in value or your boat's value has decreased and you want to enter the increase or decrease, check with your tax professional for a category.

12. Click either **No** or **Yes** in response to the question Did You Move Any Money From One Security To Another?. If you clicked Yes, enter the number of transfers on the statement in the How Many Transfers Appear On Your Statement? field. Click **Next**.

13. If you selected Yes in step 4, enter the number of ending shares shown on your statement. If you selected No in step 4, you do not have that option. Enter the value in the Market Value field from the statement for each security in the account. Click **Next**.

14. Verify that the amount in the Total Market Value field shown on the statement matches the 401(k)/403(b) Update Summary.

15. Click **Done**.

Reconcile Property and Debt Accounts

You may note that asset and liability accounts are called property accounts in the Account Bar. Each of these accounts can be reconciled or updated in much the same way as other accounts. If you choose to update an asset account based on current market value, you can use documentation such as a property tax statement or valuation summary from a commercial appraisal. You may get monthly statements from a financial institution showing loan balances and loan payments due so that these accounts can be updated. While you can update these accounts without documentation, it is usually best to wait until you have written proof of your change before you make it. You can include the written proof as an attachment in Quicken, as described in Chapter 4.

Update a Property or Debt Account

You use the same process to update either an asset or a liability account.

1. From the Property & Debt section on the Account Bar, click the account you want to update.

   –Or–

   Click the **Property & Debt** tab, and click either **Property** or **Debt**. From the list of accounts, click the account name you want to update.

   In either case, the account's transactions register appears.

2. Click **Account Actions** and click **Update Balance**. The Update Account Balance dialog box appears.

3. In the Update Balance dialog box, click in the **New Balance** field, and enter the balance from the statement or other documentation. For an asset, this is the current value of the asset. For a loan, this is the balance due on the loan.

4. Click in the **Adjustment Date** field, and enter the date of the documentation.

5. Click **OK** to return to the account's transaction register showing that the adjustment has been added to the account.

Use the Find And Replace Dialog Box

When you need to locate a number of transactions for one payee, one category, or one amount, Quicken has a useful Find utility.

1. Click the **Edit** menu, and click **Find/Replace** or press **CTRL+H**. The Find And Replace dialog box appears (see Figure 7-3).

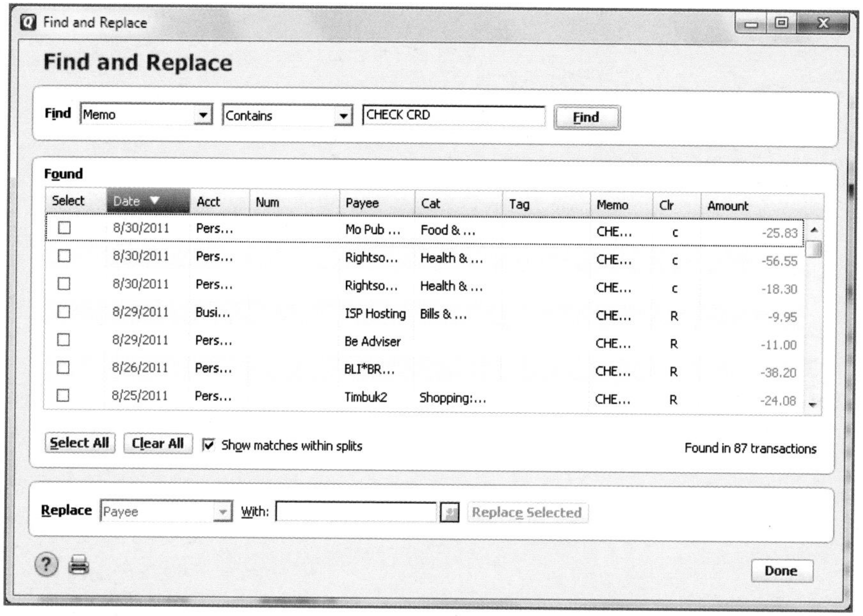

Figure 7-3: *Use the Find And Replace utility to locate transactions for one payee, category, or amount.*

2. Click **Any Field** or its down arrow, and click the field where Quicken is to look for the information you want to find.

3. Click **Contains** or its down arrow, and click the type of match.

4. Click in the text box to the right of the others, and enter the information for which you want to search. Depending on the field you selected in step 2, you may be able to select a memorized payee, a category from the Category list, or enter a tag.

5. Click **Find**. A list of all matching transactions is displayed in the Found List. (You will not see matching transactions in hidden accounts unless you have selected to view hidden accounts from the Account List.)

6. Click **Show Matches Within Splits** if it is not already selected and you want Quicken to include information shown in the Split Transactions window.

7. Click **Select All** to select all the items on the list, or choose only the transactions you want to change by clicking in the check boxes to the left of the transactions.

CAUTION

If you are replacing a number of transactions, categories, or payees, you may want to do a backup first in case you accidently replace something you did not intend.

8. Click the **Replace** down arrow, and choose a field whose contents you want to replace.

9. Click in the **With** text box and type the replacement text, or choose it from the drop-down list. Then click **Replace All** or **Replace Selected** to change the transactions depending on if you have selected all the Find results or just a subset of the Find results.

10. Click **Done** to close the dialog box.

Chapter 8

Managing Your Investments

Your investments help shape your financial future. Whether you are saving for a new home, your children's education, or your own retirement, Quicken can help you with your investments in many ways. You can obtain a quick online quote for a specific security or learn the historical value of your portfolio. You can use Quicken to monitor prices on securities you already own or are thinking about purchasing. You can download information from your broker, analyze your asset allocation, estimate your capital gains, or use other sophisticated analysis tools included with Quicken. Whatever your financial position today, Quicken can help you strengthen it for tomorrow. The Investing tab not only gives you access to all of your investment accounts, it also provides links for downloading transactions, online quotes, and other investment services. You can set alerts and establish a Watch List, track the performance of both individual securities and your mutual funds, and get an analysis of your entire portfolio.

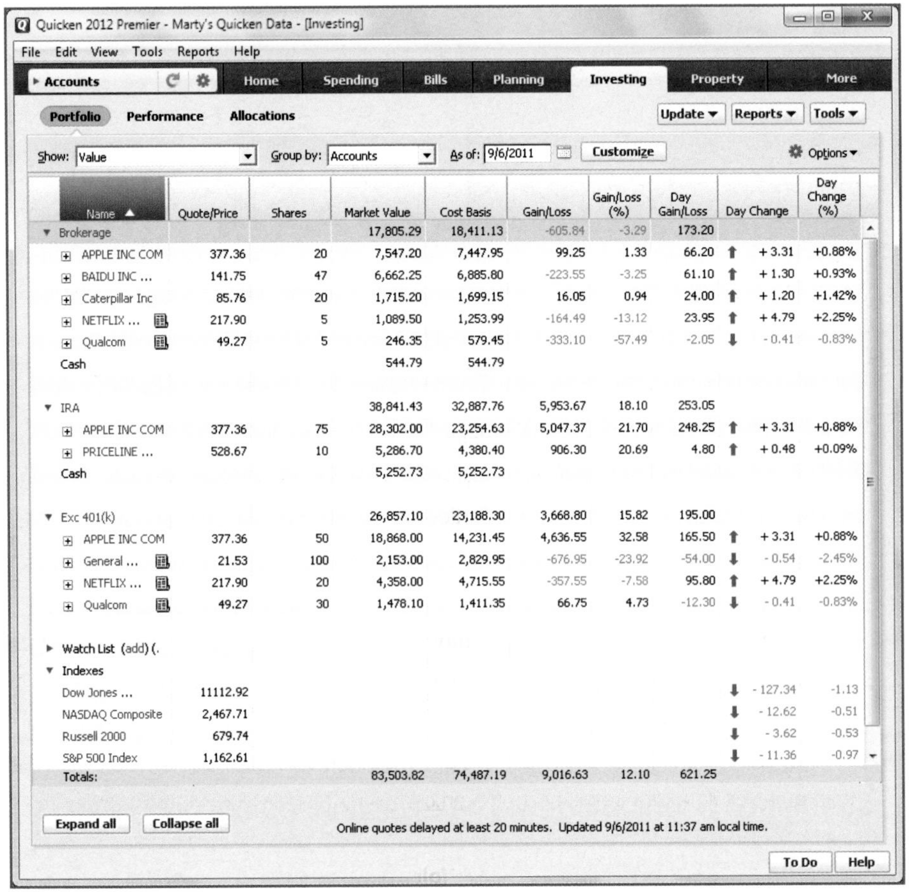

Understand the Investing Tab

When you first click the Investing tab, it opens to the Portfolio view. This view lists all of your investment accounts as well as the securities you have told Quicken to watch for you in the Quicken Watch List. To open the Portfolio view:

1. Click the **Investing** tab, and then click the Portfolio view, if it isn't already selected, as shown in Figure 8-1. Listed first are the investment and retirement accounts you have entered, showing the cost basis of the investment, the historical gain or loss in both dollars and percentages, and the daily gain or loss in dollars and percentages.

2. To work with any of the accounts, click that account name.

Download Current Quotes

Quicken provides the means to ensure you have up-to-date information about your investments. With an Internet connection, Quicken will download the most current *quotes*, or prices, for all of the securities in your portfolio, provided they are publically traded securities and are

Figure 8-1: *Use the Portfolio view to look at your current investments as well as securities you are watching.*

available from the price data provider. (A quote is the highest price being offered by a buyer or the lowest price being asked by a seller for a security at a given point in time.) To download quotes from the Investing tab's Portfolio view:

1. In the Investing tab, click the **Update** button, and click **Quotes**.

2. Once you are connected to the Internet, the Quicken Update Status dialog box appears. The latest quotes for your selected securities are downloaded to your computer.

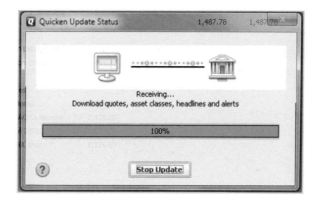

3. If you are having trouble connecting and downloading, click **Help** to display Quicken Help.

4. Click **Stop Update** to stop the download before it is complete.

5. When all of your quotes have been downloaded, the Quicken Update Status dialog box closes and you are returned to the Portfolio view.

Set Up Quicken.com

When you registered Quicken, you may have created a Quicken.com account. With this account, you can keep an eye on your investments from any computer with Internet access. To set up Quicken.com for your investment information:

1. Ensure you are connected to the Internet. In the address box of your browser, such as Internet Explorer or Firefox, type quicken.com and press **ENTER**. The Quicken.com website will open.

2. Click **Sign In** and click **Investment Portfolio** to set up and work with an investment portfolio at Quicken.com.

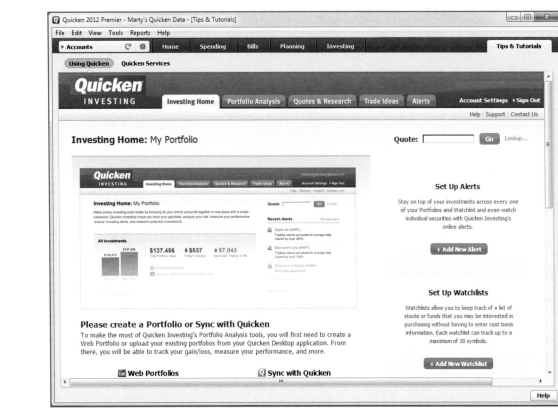

Figure 8-2: *Quicken.com provides a number of features to assist in your investing.*

3. The Quicken.com registration dialog box appears. If you have already registered, enter your member ID and password, and click **Sign In**.

4. If you have not yet created a Quicken .com account, click **Continue** to create one.

5. At the registration dialog box, enter your information and click **Submit**.

The Quicken Investing home page opens to My Portfolio, as you can see in Figure 8-2.

Use Quicken.com

Once you have registered with Quicken .com, you can use the investing tools available online from any computer with an Internet connection. You can upload your portfolio in Quicken to Quicken.com.

UPLOAD A PORTFOLIO TO QUICKEN.COM

The easiest way to work with investment data on Quicken.com is to first create a portfolio in Quicken by downloading the information from your brokerage and then uploading it to Quicken.com. Assuming you already created a portfolio in the Quicken program on your desktop and you have an Internet connection, then from that program:

1. Click the **Tools** menu, and click **One Step Update**. The One Step Update Settings dialog box will open.

TIP

If you use Quicken.com frequently, you can add a shortcut to it on the toolbar. See the "Customizing the Quicken Toolbar" QuickSteps in this chapter, and click **Show All Toolbar Choices**.

CUSTOMIZING YOUR QUICKEN TOOLBAR

In Chapter 1, you learned to turn on the Quicken Toolbar and use the default tools. However, you can customize it as well. To customize the Quicken Toolbar:

1. Click **View** and click **Show Toolbar**. The default tools appear, as discussed in Chapter 1.

2. Right-click anywhere in the Toolbar, and click the **Customize Toolbar** button.

   –Or–

   Click the small gear icon at the far-right end of the Toolbar.

   In either case, the Customize Toolbar dialog box appears.

3. Click any of the popular choices in the Available Toolbar Buttons list, and click **Add** to add them to the Quicken Toolbar. To see many more choices, click **Show All Toolbar Choices**.

4. To remove a tool, select that tool in the Your Toolbar Buttons list, and click **Remove** to return it to the Add To Toolbar list.

5. Select a tool in the Your Toolbar Buttons list, and click **Move Up** or **Move Down** to move that tool within the list of tools on the toolbar.

6. To restore all the default tools and eliminate any changes, click the **Reset To Default** button.

Continued . . .

2. If it is not already checked, click the **Quicken.com** check box and then click **Select Quicken.com To Update**. The Preferences dialog box opens displaying the preferences for your Quicken.com portfolio. On the right, click the accounts to view online or click **Select All** and click **OK**.

3. Click **Update Now**. If you are asked to register Quicken, follow those instructions. When asked, click **Yes** and either create a new Quicken.com account or enter your Quicken.com user ID and password, click **Sign In**, and then click **Finished** when requested. You are returned to the One Step Update Summary dialog box where you should see the message under Quicken.com shown in the illustration.

4. Click **Close**. In Quicken click **Tips & Tutorials**. Click **Sign In**, click **Investment Portfolio**, if needed, enter your user ID and password, and then click **Sign In** again. Your portfolio will be displayed.

CREATE A PORTFOLIO IN QUICKEN.COM

To create a new portfolio on Quicken.com:

1. If this is the first time you have accessed Quicken.com, at the Quicken Investing Home tab, scroll down and click **Add New Portfolio**. Otherwise, click **Manage Web Portfolios & Watchlists**, and click **Add New Portfolio**.

2. The Create New Portfolio dialog box appears. Type a name for this portfolio, accept or change the display currency, and click **Save Changes**.

3. The Manage Web Portfolio dialog box appears, displaying your new portfolio, as shown in Figure 8-3. Click **Make This My Default Portfolio** if you choose.

CUSTOMIZING YOUR QUICKEN TOOLBAR (Continued)

7. To create a keyboard shortcut for any toolbar button, select the button in the Your Toolbar Buttons list, and then click **Edit Shortcut Or Label**. In the Edit Shortcut Or Label dialog box that appears, change the label and/or add a letter to the keyboard shortcut combination displayed. Click **OK** to save your changes and close the dialog box. Click **Cancel** to cancel any changes and close the dialog box.

8. At the bottom of the Customize Toolbar dialog box, click **Show Icons And Text** to display both text and icons for each tool button, or click **Show Icons Only** to display only the icons.

9. Click **Show Global Search** to remove the check mark and the Find Payment Or Deposit search box from the Toolbar.

10. Click **Add Or Remove Saved Reports** to select reports you want to include on the Quicken Toolbar.

11. After you have made all of your changes, click **OK** to close the Customize Toolbar dialog box.

NOTE

You might see a different number of accounts created on Quicken.com if you selected more than one account for upload in the preferences dialog. You also might not see the message at all if you have selected in preferences to only see the One Step Update Summary when there is an error.

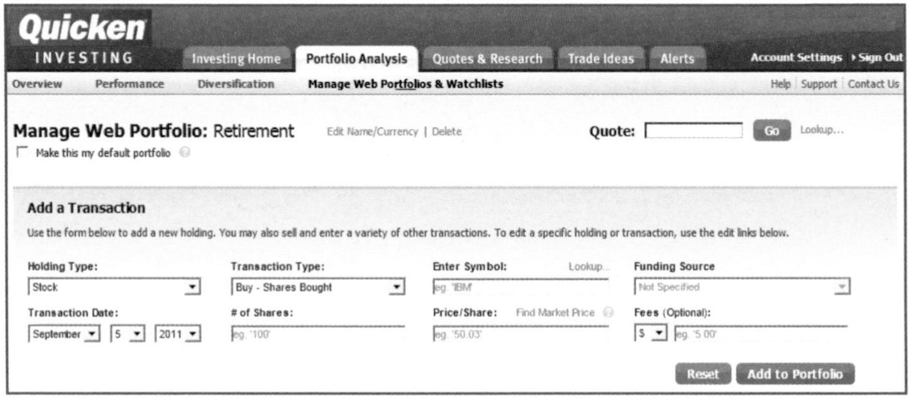

Figure 8-3: *You can create one or more personal web portfolios at Quicken.com.*

4. Click **Edit Name/Currency** to open the Edit Name/Currency dialog box.

5. Click **Delete** to delete this web portfolio.

6. Click the **Holding Type** down arrow to begin entering your web portfolio holdings.

7. Click **Transaction Type** to choose a type of transaction from the drop-down list.

8. Click **Enter Symbol** to enter the ticker symbol for your new holding. If you do not know the correct symbol, click **Lookup** to open the Quicken Symbol Lookup dialog box.

9. Click **Transaction Date** to enter the date of the transaction you are entering.

10. Continue through the dialog box, entering the number of shares, what you paid per share, and any fees. Click **Add To Portfolio** to complete the process. Your holdings information appears in the Transactions For *your portfolio* section of the webpage.

11. To add holdings, repeat steps 6 through 10.

SIGN OUT OF QUICKEN.COM

After you have completed your work online at Quicken.com, be sure to sign out. This is especially important if you are working from a public computer, such as at a library, or if you are working on your own laptop in a public place. To exit Quicken.com:

1. Click **Sign Out** at the upper-right corner of the window.

2. Ensure the Quicken registration dialog appears. Click **Close**.

QUICKSTEPS

UNDERSTANDING QUICKEN.COM TOOLS

Once you have set up a web portfolio, Quicken.com offers a number of tools to help you reach your investing goals. Each tab within Quicken.com Investing helps you look at your information in different ways:

- The Portfolio Analysis tab has four sets of tools:

  - In the Overview section, Quicken.com displays graphs on how your portfolios are performing, their risks and returns, and more, as you can see in Figure 8-4.

  - The Performance section charts your portfolio's values.

  - In Diversification, you can compare your portfolio's risk versus returns.

  - From the Manage Web Portfolios And Watchlists tab, you can add new portfolios and new Watch Lists, and perform detailed analysis on both.

- The Quotes & Research tab offers a variety of informational and analytical devices to help you invest wisely. In addition to showing your current portfolio's position, it displays current industry positions, the latest headlines that affect your holdings, and the One-Click Scorecard. See "Use Online Research Tools" later in this chapter.

- The Trade Ideas tab presents strategies from some top investment analysts.

- In the Alerts tab, you can manage both price and portfolio alerts to ensure you are staying on top of your market position.

Figure 8-4: *The portfolio analysis capability of Quicken.com is quite powerful.*

Explore the Performance View

Another useful tool is the Investing tab's Performance view. To use this tool:

Click the **Investing** tab, and click the **Performance** view. The Performance tools display, as seen in Figure 8-5.

Use and Customize the Performance View

The Performance view has two graphs and a tabular listing. All are controlled by three drop-down lists and the Update button. To use and customize this view:

1. At the top of the Performance view, in the left drop-down list, click one of the Account group options—**All Accounts**, **Investment Only**, or **Retirement Only**—or choose an individual account from the drop-down list to tell Quicken which accounts to include in the graph. Or, choose **Customize** and select the desired accounts via the Customize dialog.

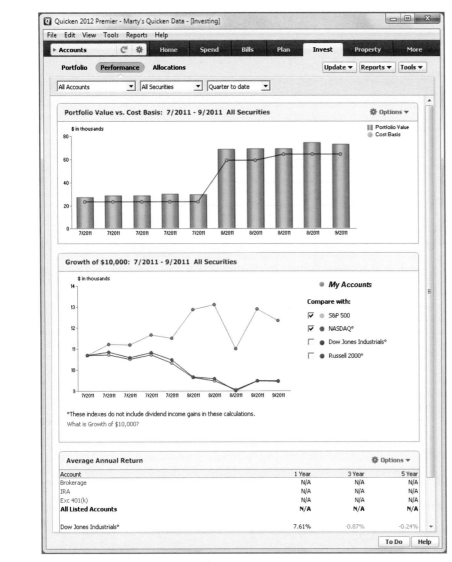

Figure 8-5: *The Growth Of $10,000 analysis tool, along with several others, shows the performance of your investments graphically.*

2. In the middle drop-down list, choose the securities you want included—**All Securities** or **Customize**. With the latter choice, the Customize dialog box appears. Select the securities you want to compare in the graph.

   a. Click **Select All** to choose all the securities in the Security List, or click **Clear All** to clear all selections and choose just a few.

   b. Click **OK** to close the dialog box and return to the graph.

3. In the right drop-down list, choose the time period you want plotted. Last 12 Months is the default.

4. Click the **Update** button, and click **Historical Prices**. The Get Historical Prices dialog box appears.

   a. Click the **Get Prices For The Last** down arrow, and click **Month**, **Year**, **Two Years**, or **Five Years**, depending on the time period for which you want to download prices.

   b. Select the securities for which you want to download prices, or click **Mark All** to include all of your securities. Click **Clear All** to start again.

   c. Click **Update Now** to download the information. When the information has been downloaded, the One Step Update Summary dialog box appears.

   d. Click **Close** to return to the graph.

USE THE PORTFOLIO VALUE VS. COST BASIS GRAPH

You can see how the value of your portfolio compares to your cost basis in the Portfolio Value vs. Cost Basis graph at the top of the Performance view. To work with this graph:

1. At the top of the graph, click **Options** and then click **Go To Full Screen View** to show the graph on a full screen.

2. Click **Show Value/Cost Basis Report** to show the information in report (text) form.

3. Click **Go To Full Portfolio** to show the Portfolio tab view.

QUICKSTEPS

CUSTOMIZING THE DATE RANGE

The default view for the Growth Of $10,000 snapshot is the last 12 months; however, you can customize the date range.

1. In the Investing tab, click the **Performance** view.

2. Click the right drop-down list, choose the time period you want plotted, and click the **Date Range** down arrow to see the list of possibilities; or click **Custom Dates** to open the Date Range dialog box.

Quarter to date
Earliest to date
Last 7 days
Last 30 days
Last 12 months
Quarter to date
Last quarter
Year to date
Custom dates

3. Enter the from and to dates you want to use, and click **OK** to close the dialog box.

USE THE GROWTH OF $10,000 UTILITY

Quicken has a utility called the Growth Of $10,000 that you can use to see how your portfolio compares to the main market indexes. This utility shows the value of $10,000 invested in your selected accounts compared to the same $10,000 invested in one or more of the market indexes over the same time period.

Download the necessary historical information as described in "Use and Customize the Performance View" earlier in this chapter, and then click the names of market indexes to select them for comparison.

FILTER THE AVERAGE ANNUAL RETURN ANALYSIS

The third analysis tool in the Performance view is the Average Annual Return tool. This shows the return on your investments as an annualized figure. To filter and customize this:

1. Set the account, securities, and time period options as described earlier in "Use and Customize the Performance View."

2. In the Average Annual Return title bar, click **Options** and click **Show Security Performance**. The Security Performance window appears. Click **Customize**, select the columns you want, and click **OK**. Click **Close** when you are finished with the Security Performance dialog box.

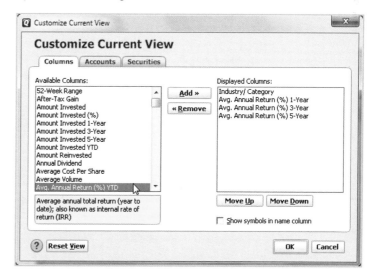

3. Click **Options** in the Average Annual Return title bar, and click **Show Security Performance Comparisons** to work with industry comparisons. You can customize this view as well. Click **Close** when you are finished.

4. Click **Options** and click **Historical Prices** to open the Get Historical Prices dialog box. Click **Update Now** to download these prices. When the One Step Update Summary dialog box appears, click **Close**.

Allocate Your Assets

Quicken provides an Asset Allocation Guide to help you structure your portfolio. The Investing tab Allocations view provides tools to help you allocate your assets appropriately. To work with the allocation of your assets:

1. Click the **Investing** tab, and then click the **Allocations** view. Your current allocations display in several graphical displays.

2. Click **Show Allocation Guide** at the bottom of the Asset Allocation snapshot. The Asset Allocation Guide displays the How Can Quicken Help With Asset Allocation? dialog box. Click **Print** to print a page of the guide. Figure 8-6 shows the first page. If you have downloaded quotes or other information from your brokerage firm or Quicken.com, this page displays your current asset allocation. If you don't see your asset allocation, click the **Replace It With An Example** or **Set Up Quicken So You Can** link.

3. On the left side of the Asset Allocation Guide, click **How Do I Update Asset Classes** to display the next page.

4. Click **Go Online And Update Asset Classes** to open the Download Security Asset Classes dialog box.

   a. Click to the left of each security name for which you want the asset class downloaded, or click **Mark All** to choose each security in the list.

   b. Click **Update Now** to update your asset classes. After the transmission window has closed, the One Step Update Summary dialog box may display what was downloaded. If you don't need to see this summary each time, click **Show This Dialog Only If There Is An Error**. In any case, click **Close** to return to the Asset Allocation Guide.

NOTE

You can access the Asset Allocation Guide from the Investing tab's Tools button by clicking **Asset Allocation Guide**.

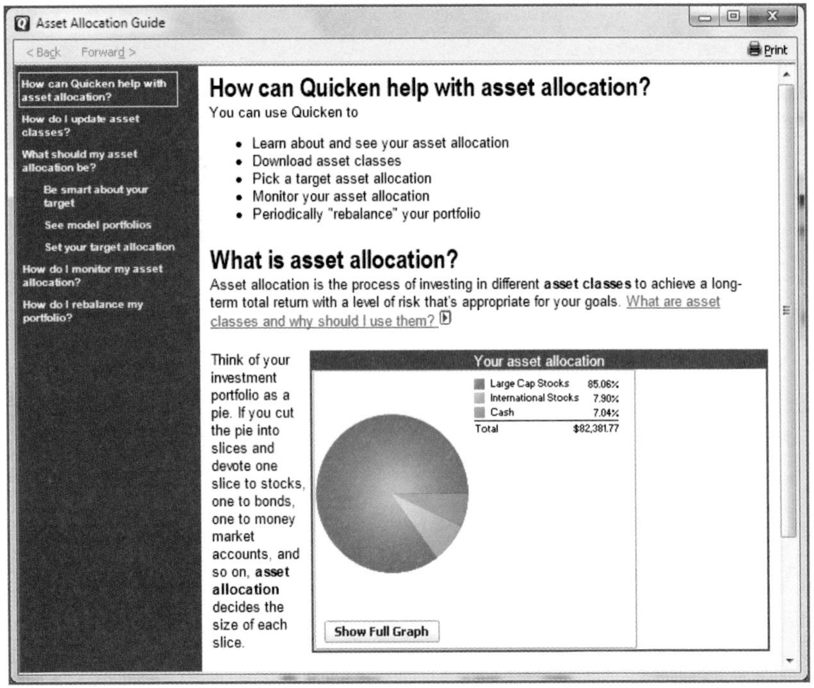

Figure 8-6: The Asset Allocation Guide shows you how to determine if your securities meet your risk-and-return objectives.

NOTE

If your preferences are set to automatically minimize screens, you may have to click the Asset Allocation Guide entry in the bottom of the Quicken screen to open the Asset Allocation screen.

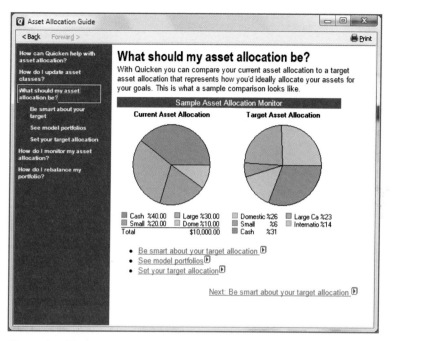

Figure 8-7: *The What Should My Asset Allocation Be? page of the guide helps you set your allocation.*

c. Click **Common Questions About Downloading Asset Classes** to display a list of frequently asked questions.

d. Click **Back: How Do I Update Asset Classes?** to return to that page.

e. Click **Next: What Should My Asset Allocation Be?** to continue. On this page of the guide, two sample asset allocation graphs are displayed: a current allocation and a target allocation, as shown in Figure 8-7.

f. Click **Be Smart About Your Target Allocation** or **See Model Portfolios** to read advice about your allocation.

g. After you have read the material, click **Set Your Target Allocation**.

h. Click **Set**. The Set Target Asset Allocation dialog box appears.

i. Click **Percentage** for each of the various asset classes to enter the percentage you want to achieve. Click **OK** when finished.

CAUTION

Remember that investments in mutual funds are composed of several asset classes. While the allocation of classes within the fund changes from time to time, you really have no control over that mixture, and it may not meet your target allocation.

j. If this is the first time you've allocated your assets, click **How Do I Rebalance My Portfolio**. *Rebalancing* means moving money between investments so that your total investments are allocated in the best way for you to achieve your goals, as shown in Figure 8-8. Goal setting and planning is discussed in Chapter 9. Follow the instructions on the page to rebalance your assets.

Asset Allocation Guide

< Back   Forward >   🖶 Print

How can Quicken help with asset allocation?

How do I update asset classes?

What should my asset allocation be?

   Be smart about your target

   See model portfolios

   Set your target allocation

How do I monitor my asset allocation?

How do I rebalance my portfolio?

What is rebalancing?

Rebalancing your portfolio means moving money between investments to more closely match your target allocation.

1. Decide which adjustments (if any) to make. Use adjustment information as a guideline only! Always consider taxes and brokerage fees before buying or selling investments. When should I rebalance my portfolio?
2. Double-click a pie slice in Current Asset Allocation, below, to see investments in an asset class. What if I have mutual funds?
3. Search for new investments, or evaluate potential investments.

Asset class	Current %	Target %	Current Value	Off by % points	Adjustment to reach target
Domestic Bonds	0	10	$ 0	10	$ 8,248 MORE
Global Bonds	0	0	$ 0	0	
Large Cap	85.1	55	$ 70,176	30.1	$ 24,813 LESS
Small Cap	0	15	$ 0	15	$ 12,372 MORE
International	7.9	10	$ 6,504	2.1	$ 1,744 MORE
Cash	7	10	$ 5,798	3	$ 2,450 MORE
Other	0	0	$ 0	0	
Unclassified	0	0	$ 0	0	
Total			$ 82,478		

Actual   **Target**

Total: 82,478.07   Change Target

	Actual	Target	Difference
Domestic Bonds	0.000%	10%	-10.000%
Large Cap Stocks	85.085%	55%	30.085%
Small Cap Stocks	0.000%	15%	-15.000%
International Stocks	7.886%	10%	-2.114%
Cash	7.029%	10%	-2.971%
Expected Return	7%	6%	
Expected Risk	High (14%)	High (10%)	

Figure 8-8: Periodically reviewing how your investments are balanced can help you better achieve your goals and objectives.

QUICKSTEPS

SCHEDULING ONE STEP UPDATES

The One Step Update utility allows you to download your quotes at the same time you update information from your financial institutions. You can schedule the updates so that Quicken will update your information at a time most convenient for you.

1. In the Investing tab, click the **Update** button, click **One Step Update**, and, if needed, enter your Vault password and click **OK**. The One Step Update Settings dialog box appears.

2. Click the **Schedule Updates** button at the bottom. The Schedule Updates dialog box will appear.

3. Click **Update Quotes, Asset Classes, Headlines And Alerts** to instruct Quicken to download the most current quotes for your securities, along with headlines and alerts.

4. Click the financial institutions that you want to update.

5. Click the **Update My Portfolio On Quicken.com** check box to do that, and then click **Select Quicken.com Data To Update** if you want to select just some of that data.

Continued . . .

k. Click **How Do I Monitor My Asset Allocation** to understand more about your asset allocation.

l. Click **Close** to close the guide.

Work with the Portfolio Tab

The Investing tab's Portfolio view displays all of your investment information. By customizing the way you see this information, you can make educated decisions about the performance of each investment. To see the Portfolio view, press **CTRL+U**.

Customize Your Portfolio View

Quicken has nine standard views for the portfolio, and you can customize up to nine others. All of the views can use any of the column headings. Before you

---

Schedule Updates

Update these Financial Institutions
- ☑ TD Ameritrade
- ☑ Wells Fargo Bank

Schedule

On: ☐ Mon ☐ Tue ☐ Wed ☐ Thu
☐ Fri ☐ Sat ☐ Sun

At: [▼] Updates will run within 15 minutes of time specified.

Passwords

Prompt for Password Vault password:
- ⦿ before each scheduled update
- ○ at Windows startup

☐ Update quotes, asset classes headlines and alerts
Select symbols to update -optional

☐ Update my Portfolio on Quicken.com
Select Quicken.com data to update -optional

ⓘ You must store your financial institution password(s) in a Password Vault in order to use Schedule Updates to update your transactions and balances.

Learn more about security in Quicken

[OK] [Cancel]

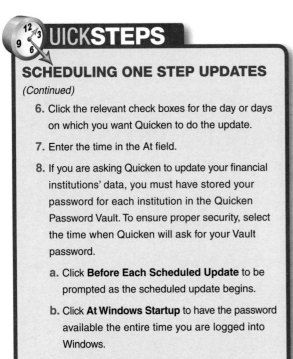

SCHEDULING ONE STEP UPDATES

(Continued)

6. Click the relevant check boxes for the day or days on which you want Quicken to do the update.

7. Enter the time in the At field.

8. If you are asking Quicken to update your financial institutions' data, you must have stored your password for each institution in the Quicken Password Vault. To ensure proper security, select the time when Quicken will ask for your Vault password.

   a. Click **Before Each Scheduled Update** to be prompted as the scheduled update begins.

   b. Click **At Windows Startup** to have the password available the entire time you are logged into Windows.

9. Click **OK** to close the Schedule Updates dialog box.

create a customized view, make sure you download both the latest quotes and historical prices. To customize a view in your portfolio:

1. In the Portfolio view, click the **Show** down arrow to select the view you want to customize.

2. Click the **Customize** button to open the Customize Current View dialog box. The name of the current selected view is displayed in the Name Of This View field. Type a new name for this view if you want.

3. Click the **Accounts** tab, and click to either add or remove the check mark on the left of the accounts to indicate which you want to include or not, respectively. Click **Show (Hidden Accounts)** to include hidden accounts.

4. By default, your accounts are displayed alphabetically. If you want to change this, click an account, and then click **Move Up** or **Move Down** to change that account's position in the list.

5. To choose all of the accounts in the list, click **Select All**; or click **Clear All** to start over.

6. Click the **Securities** tab, and click to add or remove the check mark on the left of the securities to indicate which you want to include. Click **Show (Hidden Securities)** to include hidden securities. The securities are displayed in alphabetical order and cannot be changed.

SETTING OPTIONS IN YOUR PORTFOLIO VIEW

The Investing tab's Portfolio view allows you to set the display options for each view you display. From your Portfolio view:

1. Click **Options** on the top-right corner of the Portfolio view, and then click **Portfolio Preferences**. The Portfolio View Options dialog box appears.

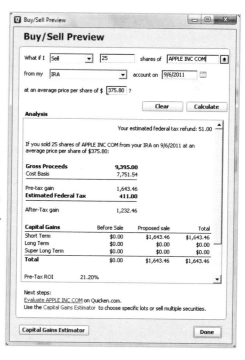

2. Click **Earliest Available Date** to include all transactions for your securities. This is the default setting. The alternative is to click the lower option and enter a beginning date from which to display the information. The ending date is always today's date.

3. Click the **Tax Rate Used In Portfolio View** down arrow to choose a tax rate. The tax rate for short-term gains is shown first, and the rate for long-term gains is shown second. For example, (15%/5%) indicates that short-term gains are calculated at a 15-percent tax rate and long-term gains are calculated at a 5-percent tax rate.

4. Click **OK** to close the dialog box.

7. Click the **Columns** tab. The columns that appear by default for this view are shown in the Displayed Columns list. To add a column, click a column in the Available Columns list, and click **Add**.

8. To remove a column, click its name in the Displayed Columns list, and then click **Remove**. The column heading moves from the Displayed Columns list to the Available Columns list.

9. Click a column in the Displayed Columns list, and click **Move Up** or **Move Down** to change its position in the list.

10. Click **Show Symbols In Name Column** to display the ticker symbol rather than the name of your security.

11. Click **Reset View** if you want to return to the original default settings.

12. Click **OK** when you are finished.

Work with Investing Tools

In the Investing tab, Quicken provides a number of useful tools for your investing analysis. Each tool gives you a slightly different perspective on your investments or potential investments.

Use the Buy/Sell Preview Tool

1. In the Investing tab, click the **Tools** button, and click **Buy/Sell Preview** to open the Buy/Sell Preview dialog box.

2. In the What If I text box, choose **Buy** or **Sell** from the drop-down list.

3. Complete the rest of the information as appropriate. You must select an account that actually contains the shares and the appropriate quantity you want to sell.

8

4. Click **Calculate** to have Quicken calculate the tax and capital gains effects.

5. Click **Clear** to add new information or **Close** to return to the Investing tab.

Estimate Capital Gains

The Capital Gains Estimator helps you determine how much tax you might have to pay if you sell a security.

1. In the Investing tab, click the **Tools** button, and click **Capital Gains Estimator**. The Capital Gains Estimator wizard appears. If you have previously used the Capital Gains Estimator, the screen may open to the What If scenarios.

2. Click **Let's Get Started** at the bottom of the Welcome message to start the wizard.

3. You can create up to three scenarios for comparison. Click one of the scenarios, and then click **Next** to continue.

4. Click to the left of the account name(s) you want to include in the scenario. Click **Next**.

5. Continue through the Estimator by clicking **Next** and entering all relevant information.

6. Click the goal you want to achieve, such as **Maximize After-Tax Return And Minimize Fees** or **Balance My Year-To-Date Capital Gains**. The default is **Maximize After-Tax Returns And Minimize Fees**.

7. Click **Search** to have Quicken find the best way to meet your goal. When the Search dialog box has reached 100 percent, click **View Results**. The What Should I Sell? dialog box may appear and notify you that Quicken could not complete the scenario as you requested. Click **OK** and click **Settings**. Then:

   a. Click in the **% Of Your Target Goal** text box, and enter a percent of your target goal. Ten is the default percentage.

   b. Click in the **Seconds** text box, and enter the maximum number of seconds you want Quicken to try to meet your goal.

   c. Click in the **Optimal Solutions** text box, and enter the maximum number of possible solutions.

   d. Click **Stop As Soon As The First Acceptable Answer Is Found** to have Quicken end the search when any answer is found matching your criteria.

   e. Click **Quick Search** to choose one best method, or click **Exhaustive Search** to have Quicken merge a number of searches to give you a result.

   f. Click **OK** to return to the Search dialog box, and click **Start**.

Capital Gains Estimator

Step 1 Please select the securities or individual lots you plan to sell:

Current Holdings:

	Name	Price	Shares Held	Gain/Loss	Holding Period
⊟	APPLE INC COM	375.80	95	$4,998	
	└ Lot 9/2/2011	372	20	$68	ST to 9/3/2012
	└ Lot 8/4/2011	309.9951	75	$4,930	ST to 8/5/2012
⊟	BAIDU INC SPON ...	141.75	47	-$224	
	└ Lot 8/4/2011	146.40	47	-$224	ST to 8/5/2012
⊟	Caterpillar Inc	85.76	20	$16	
	└ Lot 9/5/2011	84.56	20	$16	ST to 9/6/2012
⊟	NETFLIX INC COM	217.90	5	-$164	

Step 2 Next, specify how many shares to sell, and at what price:

Proposed Sales:

	Name	Shares to Sell	Sale Price	Gain/Loss	Gross Proceeds
⊟	PRICELINE COM INC COM NEW	10	528.67	$906	$5,287
	└ Lot 8/4/2011	10		$906	$5,287
	Total			**$906**	**$5,287**

Step 3 View the results of your proposed sales:

Taxable Gains from Proposed Sales:

Type of Income	Gain	Loss	Total
Short Term Cap Gain	$906		$906
Total			**$906**

Total Gross Proceeds from Proposed Sales:	$5,287
Estimated Federal Tax Impact	$136
Estimated State Tax Impact	$0
Net Proceeds from Proposed Sales:	$5,151

Figure 8-9: The Capital Gains Estimator helps you figure out what stocks to sell with the minimum tax impact.

8. In the Capital Gains Estimator that opens after a successful search (see Figure 8-9), the Current Holdings area will indicate with a check mark the security it is recommending be sold. If you have several lots of this holding, the recommended lot or lots to sell will be checked.

9. In the Step 2 area, the Shares To Sell column, located opposite the stock to sell, will display the recommended number of shares to sell.

10. In the Step 3 area, view the potential taxable gains from your proposed sale. Read the bottom of the page to see detailed information about the proposed sale.

11. Click **Close** to return to the Investing tab.

Use Online Research Tools

Quicken.com has a number of additional investment tools, as mentioned in the "Understanding Quicken.com Tools" QuickFacts earlier in this chapter.

1. With an Internet connection to your computer, click the **Tips & Tutorials** tab. Click **Sign In** and click **Investment Portfolio**.

2. Click the **Quotes & Research** tab to display the Snapshot view of a single stock, which is initially Intuit, the creators of Quicken.

3. To analyze a specific security, type its symbol in the **Quote** text box in the upper-right area, and click **Go**. (The Quote text box has Type Ahead and will list symbols that match the letters you type. If you select a match from the Type Ahead list, there is no need to click Go.)

4. If you don't know the symbol for a security, click **Lookup**, type the company name and click **Search**, scroll if needed to find the symbol you are looking for, and click the symbol.

5. Review the various sections in the Snapshot view that appears (see Figure 8-10). Under Overview and above the chart, click the various time periods to redisplay the chart over those periods.

*Figure 8-10: **Quicken.com provides several tools to analyze possible investments.***

WORK WITH THE ONE-CLICK SCORECARD

From within the Quicken.com Investing Quotes & Research tab, there is a powerful tool called the One-Click Scorecard. To use this tool:

1. Click the **One-Click Scorecard** view of the Quotes & Research tab. The One-Click Scorecard view opens.

2. If you have not already selected the company you want to analyze, click in the **Quote** text box, and enter the ticker symbol of the security you want to research.

3. Click **Go** to see the report. Quicken creates a report showing the opinions of several industry experts about this security.

4. From the report window, you can do the following:

   - Click **Add To Watchlist** to include this security in your Quicken Watch List.

   - Click **Set Alert** to open a dialog box where you can choose to be alerted when any of a number of events related to the security occur.

   - Read comments from financial analysts about this security.

   - Scroll down to view graphs reporting how the security has performed and a grade for each of several different categories.

REVIEW THE EVALUATOR AND HEADLINES

Once you have selected a stock in the Quicken.com Investing Quotes & Research tab, there are two other views you can use in your research: Evaluator and Headlines.

1. Click the **Evaluator** view of the Quotes & Research tab. Review the Growth Trends, Financial Health, Management Performance, Market Multiples, and Intrinsic Value sections to see how the security is evaluated by Quicken (or rather, by a computer).

2. Click the **Headlines** view of the Quotes & Research tab, and scan the recent headlines for the company you are analyzing.

3. When you are ready, click **Sign Out** and then click **Close** to return to the Investing tab of Quicken.

Manage Your Security List

Once you have entered your investment accounts, you may want to work with the individual securities in them. When you created your investment accounts

> **TIP**
>
> Make signing out of Quicken.com a habit even when using your home computer. This way, you won't forget to sign out when using a public computer.

Use the **Look Up** button to change the symbol of a security rather than typing it yourself in the Symbol field to ensure you have correctly entered the new symbol. You will need to copy and paste the symbol once you have found it using the Look Up button.

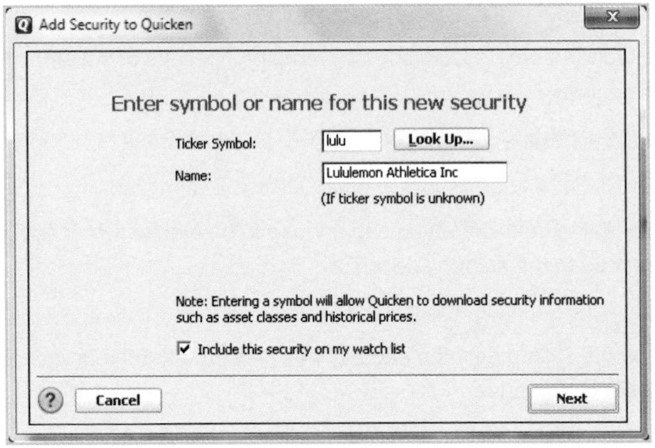

and told Quicken which securities were included in them, Quicken created a list of these securities in its data file. To access your Security List:

1. Press **CTRL+Y** to open your Security List. The Security List window appears as shown in Figure 8-11. From this list, you can add, edit, hide, and delete specific securities or add securities to your *Watch List*. (The Watch List is a special snapshot that allows you to track on a daily basis the performance of securities you own or may purchase. See the QuickSteps "Working with Your Watch List" later in this chapter.)

2. To add a new security to your Security List, click **New Security**. The Add Security To Quicken dialog box appears.

   a. Click in the **Ticker Symbol** field, and type the ticker symbol for this security. If you don't know the symbol and have Internet access, enter the company name, and click **Look Up**.

   b. Click **Include This Security On My Watch List** if you want to monitor its daily performance without owning it.

   c. Click **Next** to continue. The Quicken One Step Update window opens briefly, and information about this security is downloaded into Quicken.

   d. A summary window displays the name of your security, its ticker symbol, security type, asset class, and whether you have chosen to include this security on your Watch List. If the information is correct, click **Done**. The new security is displayed on your Security List in alphabetical order by name.

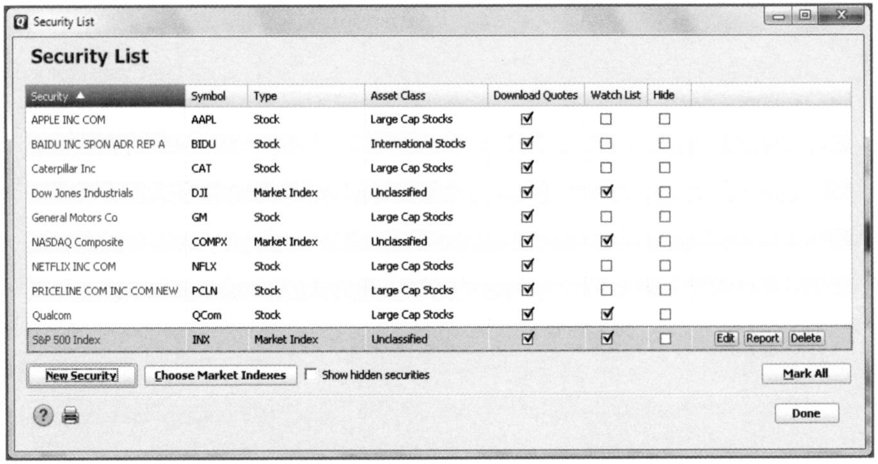

Add Security to Quicken

Enter symbol or name for this new security

Ticker Symbol: lulu Look Up...

Name: Lululemon Athletica Inc
(If ticker symbol is unknown)

Note: Entering a symbol will allow Quicken to download security information such as asset classes and historical prices.

☑ Include this security on my watch list

Cancel   Next

Security List

Security ▲	Symbol	Type	Asset Class	Download Quotes	Watch List	Hide	
APPLE INC COM	AAPL	Stock	Large Cap Stocks	☑	☐	☐	
BAIDU INC SPON ADR REP A	BIDU	Stock	International Stocks	☑	☐	☐	
Caterpillar Inc	CAT	Stock	Large Cap Stocks	☑	☐	☐	
Dow Jones Industrials	DJI	Market Index	Unclassified	☑	☑	☐	
General Motors Co	GM	Stock	Large Cap Stocks	☑	☐	☐	
NASDAQ Composite	COMPX	Market Index	Unclassified	☑	☑	☐	
NETFLIX INC COM	NFLX	Stock	Large Cap Stocks	☑	☐	☐	
PRICELINE COM INC COM NEW	PCLN	Stock	Large Cap Stocks	☑	☐	☐	
Qualcom	QCom	Stock	Large Cap Stocks	☑	☑	☐	
S&P 500 Index	INX	Market Index	Unclassified	☑	☑	☐	Edit Report Delete

New Security   **Choose Market Indexes**   ☐ Show hidden securities   **Mark All**

Done

*Figure 8-11: **Quicken's Security List provides a single location for seeing all the securities you either have in your portfolios or in a Watch List.***

3. To edit an existing security, click anywhere on the security listing other than the name to select it, and then click **Edit** on the right of the entry. The Edit Security Details dialog box appears. Click in and edit the fields you want to change, and then click **OK** to save your changes and return to the Security List.

4. To permanently delete a security on your Watch List (in this list you can't delete a security for which you have transactions), click the security and click **Delete**. A warning dialog box appears, telling you that you are about to permanently delete a security. Click **OK** if you want to continue.

5. To hide a security so that its information is available but not included in totals or reports, click its name and then click the **Hide** check box. To include hidden securities in the Security List, click **Show Hidden Securities**. To restore a hidden security, select it and click the **Hide** check box again.

6. Click **Choose Market Indexes** to display a list of market indexes, which you can include as part of your Security List and your Watch List. By including these indicators, you can compare their short-term performance to those of your securities.

Add Security to Quicken

Select market indexes to display in Quicken.

Name	Symbol
☑ Dow Jones Industrials	DJI
☑ NASDAQ Composite	COMPX
☑ S&P 500 Index	INX
☐ Russell 2000	IUX
☐ AMEX Composite	XAX.X
☐ Dow Jones Composite	COMP
☐ Dow Jones 20 Transportation	TRAN

Note: Except for S&P 500, these indexes do not include dividend income in the rate of return calculations. For most indexes, this will impact returns less than 1%. It will have greater impact for the Dow Jones Industrial Average.

Cancel — Done

a. Click in the check box of each index you want to include. A small check mark is displayed.

b. Click **Done** to close the dialog box.

QUICKSTEPS

WORKING WITH YOUR WATCH LIST

The Watch List in the Investing tab's Portfolio view provides a convenient way to see the current performance of securities you may want to purchase in the future. From the Watch List you can add and edit securities on your Security List and perform other functions that are available in the Portfolio view. To work with the Watch List:

1. From the Investing tab's Portfolio view, scroll down until you see the Watch List. If it is not open, click the folder icon on the left to open your Watch List, as shown in Figure 8-12.

2. Click **Add** opposite Watch List to open the Add Security To Quicken dialog box, or click **Edit** to display the Security List. In either case refer to the steps in "Manage Your Security List" earlier in this chapter.

3. Click **Update** and click **Quotes** to download the latest quotes for your holdings. The last date and time you downloaded appears as a note at the bottom of the Portfolio view.

4. Click an individual security to get a detail view and chart for that security. Click **Close** to return to the Portfolio view's Watch List.

5. Point at the **News** icon to the right of the security name to get current news about that security.

6. If you have set up an alert for a particular security and it is triggered, an alerts icon (an exclamation point) will appear to the right of the security name. Pointing at it will display the alert message.

7. To create a report on your purchases and sales of a security, click the name of the security, and click **Report**. Click **Close** to exit the report and return to the Security List.

8. Click the **Print** icon to print the Security List.

9. Click **Close** to close the Security List.

Figure 8-12: *The Watch List gives you a place to keep track of securities you don't own.*

TIP

If you don't see the Watch List on the selected view, either switch to another portfolio view that includes the Watch List or customize the view to include the Watch List.

Chapter 9

Making Plans for Your Future

Why should you plan for your financial future? It has been said that anyone who fails to plan, plans to fail. Gaining control over your finances, a debt-free lifestyle, college for your children, a house you fully own, a once-in-a-lifetime cruise, retirement, or a vacation cabin are all major financial events. Will you have the money to fund them? By budgeting and using the planners in Quicken, you can better manage your current finances and create a road map that will help you achieve your goals for the future. In this chapter you will learn how to create a budget and use the various professional planning tools available in Quicken to help reach your goals.

Use Budgets to Control Spending

Most people can't just buy anything they want due to limits in the amount of money they have, so the question is, what can they afford. That is the role of budgeting. A budget is simply a spending plan that looks at your income and identifies how you will spend it among the various items that you need or want to spend it on. Whether you scribble it on the back of an envelope or create color-coded spreadsheets and graphs, a budget helps you understand where your money comes from, where it goes, and plan for things and events in the future.

Create a Budget

Quicken provides tools you can use to create a budget simply and quickly using the data you have already entered into your various accounts. You have two options for creating a budget:

- **Automatic Budget** in which Quicken uses your spending data to create a budget for your top five categories, which you can customize.

- **Advanced Budget** where Quicken uses all your spending categories to create a more detailed budget, which you can customize.

To set up your budget in Quicken:

1. Click the **Planning** tab and then, if it isn't already selected, click **Budgets**. The Budgets view opens. Click the **Get Started** tab to begin.

2. Either accept the default budget name, Budget 1, or type a new name of your own.

GENERATE AN AUTOMATIC BUDGET

The Automatic Budget provides a quick way to start managing your money.

1. Accept the default **Automatic Budget** and click **OK**. Quicken looks at your spending for up to 12 months, determines your top five spending categories, calculates the average monthly spending in those categories, and displays the current monthly spending against that average, which is considered your budget, as you can see in Figure 9-1.

Figure 9-1: Quicken's Automatic Budget compares your current spending against your average spending over the last several months in the five categories where you have spent the most.

2. Given that you are in the current month, adjust the budget in each of the categories by hovering your mouse over the budget amount on the right of a category and then clicking either the right or left arrow to raise or lower, respectively, the budget amount.

| | Food & Dining:**Groceries** | 288 | 312 left | Edit 599 |

3. Add a category to the initial five automatically selected by clicking **Add Category To Budget** in the lower-left corner of the page to open the Add A Budget Category dialog box.

Add a budget category

Add a budget category

⚖ **Bills & Utilities**

I plan to spend about

$ [0] 🖩 [Monthly ▼]

Monthly Average

📊 $204

click to see graph

(?) [Cancel] Advanced Setup [Back] [Done]

4. Click the drop-down arrow, click the category you want to add, and click **Next**. Enter the budget amount you want to use and the period it is for, and click **Done**.

5. Add a budget for all the categories not otherwise listed by clicking the plus sign in a green circle opposite Everything Else. Enter the amount you want for all other categories, and click **Done**.

6. Delete a category by hovering the mouse on a category, clicking the minus sign in a red circle on the left of the category, and then clicking **Remove**.

7. Repeat steps 2 through 6 as needed to complete your budget.

8. Hover over a bar within a category that has both dark and light green areas. You'll see an explanation that the dark green is actual expenditures, while the light green is reminders of planned expenditures.

		$197	=	$187	+	$10		
Auto & Transport:Gas & Fu		**Total Spending**		Actual		1 Reminder	3 left	184
⊖	**Bills & Utilities (Total)**	187	7 left	◄	Edit 204	►

9. Click the green bar within a category to see the actual transactions that created the bar. Click the **History** tab to see a bar chart of your spending history in that category.

History	**Transactions**

Expenses		
Pay to	Date	Amount
Texaco	Jun 1	**67.65**
Costco Gas	Jun 8	**42.72**
Arco	Jun 10	**43.63**
Arco	Jun 23	**61.32**
Arco	Jul 1	**60.72**
Arco	Jul 6	**41.08**
Arco	Jul 8	**29.38**
Arco	Jul 11	**35.66**
Texaco	Jul 18	**56.05**
Chevron	Jul 22	**31.47**
Arco	Jul 26	**57.12**
Arco	Jul 29	**48.67**
Total		**$727.34**

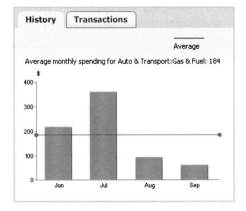

History | Transactions

Average

Average monthly spending for Auto & Transport:Gas & Fuel: 184

10. Click **Close** in the upper-right corner to close the spending history dialog box.

Compare Figure 9-1 to Figure 9-2, in which one category was added (Bills & Utilities), one category was deleted (Misc.), and Everything Else was converted to a category that was being tracked.

UNDERSTANDING QUICKEN'S BUDGETING

Both the Automatic Budget and the Advanced Budget are built by using up to the most recent 12 months of transactions in all spending accounts. Partial months on either end of the set of months are discarded, as are categories with only a couple of transactions over a period of months. For example, if you have seven months of transactions with the first month having no transactions before the seventh of the month and a last month that is the current incomplete month, Quicken will use the middle five months. It then eliminates all categories with only a couple of transactions and calculates the average by summing up all the transactions in the remaining categories and dividing by the number of good months, five in this case.

Figure 9-2: *The Automatic Budget can be easily modified to give you the ability to quickly manage the most important categories.*

If you have already created an Automatic Budget, selecting **Advanced Budget Setup** at either the bottom-right corner of the Automatic Budget display or from the Budget Actions menu simply gives you further detail of the five categories you displayed with the Automatic Budget. To get a full budget covering all the categories you are using, you must click **Budget Actions** and click **Create New Budget**.

BUILD AN ADVANCED BUDGET

If you would like to build a detailed budget incorporating all the categories you are using, then use Quicken's Advanced Budget Setup. You must do this while creating a new budget.

1. Click the **Planning** tab and then, if it isn't already selected, click **Budgets**. The Budgets view opens. If you haven't already created an automatic budget, click **Get Started** to begin. Otherwise, click **Budget Actions** and then click **Create New Budget**.

2. Either accept the default budget name or type a new name of your own. Click **Advanced Budget** and click **OK**. The Advanced Budget Setup opens as you see in Figure 9-3.

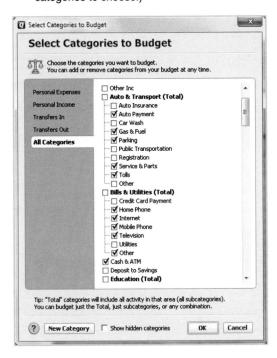

Advanced Budget Setup

Select any budget line below for advanced budgeting options
- Add more categories to your budget
- Click the graph icon to see past activity for the category

12 MONTH SUMMARY   BUDGETED EXPENSE 91,296

Select Categories to Budget	AMOUNT	YOUR BUDGET	PERIOD	2011 SEP	OCT	NOV	DEC	2012 JAN	FEB
▸ Everything Else	Average	$ 0	Monthly	0	0	0	0	0	0
▾ Expenses		91,296	per year						
Auto & Transport:**Auto Payment**	Average	356	Monthly	356	356	356	356	356	356
Auto & Transport:**Gas & Fuel**	Average	184	Monthly	184	184	184	184	184	184
Auto & Transport:**Parking**	Average	5	Monthly	5	5	5	5	5	5
Auto & Transport:**Service & Parts**	Average	378	Monthly	378	378	378	378	378	378
Auto & Transport:**Tolls**	Average	119	Monthly	119	119	119	119	119	119
Bills & Utilities	Average	222	Monthly	222	222	222	222	222	222
Bills & Utilities:**Home Phone**	Average	19	Monthly	19	19	19	19	19	19
Bills & Utilities:**Internet**	Average	24	Monthly	24	24	24	24	24	24
Bills & Utilities:**Mobile Phone**	Average	307	Monthly	307	307	307	307	307	307
Bills & Utilities:**Television**	Average	94	Monthly	94	94	94	94	94	94
Cash & ATM	Average	82	Monthly	82	82	82	82	82	82
Education:**Books & Supplies**	Average	173	Monthly	173	173	173	173	173	173
Education:**Student Loan**	Average	175	Monthly	175	175	175	175	175	175
Entertainment	Average	4	Monthly	4	4	4	4	4	4
Entertainment:**Amusement**	Average	11	Monthly	11	11	11	11	11	11
Entertainment:**Movies & DVDs**	Average	19	Monthly	19	19	19	19	19	19
Entertainment:**Music**	Average	13	Monthly	13	13	13	13	13	13
Entertainment:**Newspaper & Maga...**	Average	8	Monthly	8	8	8	8	8	8
Fees & Charges:**ATM Fee**	Average	3	Monthly	3	3	3	3	3	3
Fees & Charges:**Service Fee**	Average	5	Monthly	5	5	5	5	5	5
Financial	Average	164	Monthly	164	164	164	164	164	164
Food & Dining	Average	444	Monthly	444	444	444	444	444	444
Food & Dining:**Fast Food**	Average	12	Monthly	12	12	12	12	12	12
Food & Dining:**Groceries**	Average	599	Monthly	599	599	599	599	599	599

Options ▼   Done

Figure 9-3: The Advanced Budget built by Quicken provides a detailed framework for building a budget.

3. To begin the process of customizing an Advanced Budget, click **Select Categories To Budget** to open its dialog box. The categories that are automatically budgeted are initially checked. Add and remove check marks to select the categories you want included in your budget, and click **OK** when you are finished. (As an earlier Note mentioned, the Spending By Category report can help you decide which categories to choose.)

4. To change the amounts in a category, click anywhere within a category's line to select it, and then click the **Average** down arrow. Leave Average selected if you want the same amount in every month, or click **Specific** to specify a unique amount in each month.

Food & Dining	Specific ▼	per month	T	444	444	444	444	444

NOTE

The principle difference between the Automatic Budget and the Advanced Budget is where you start. With the Automatic Budget you start with the top five categories and can add more as desired. With the Advanced Budget you start with all the categories you are using and can delete ones that are not important to you.

5. If you are using the Average method for a category, click in the **Your Budget** amount field, type an amount you want in every month, and press **ENTER**.

–Or–

If you want to enter a daily, weekly, quarterly, or yearly amount, type it, click the down arrow opposite **Monthly**, and select the period you want to use.

6. If you are using the Specific method for a category, click in each of the monthly fields and type the amount you want for that month.

Food & Dining	▬	Specific	3,768	per year	54	313	54	313	54	313
⊖ Food & Dining:**Fast Food**	▬	Average ▾	$ 500	Yearly ▾	42	42	42	42	42	42

7. In a given category, click the blue chart icon to the left of what, by default, is "Average." The same list of transactions and bar chart that was described in "Generate an Automatic Budget" earlier in this chapter is available here.

8. To delete a category, hover over the category, and click the white bar in a red circle on the left of a category.

9. When you have made all the changes to your budget, click **Done** in the lower-right corner of the page. A detailed budget chart will open as shown in Figure 9-4. This can be used and modified as described in "Generate an Automatic Budget" earlier in this chapter.

CREATE ADDITIONAL BUDGETS

After you have created your original budget, you can add, copy, edit, or delete other budgets.

1. From the Planning tab, click **Budget Actions**. You have a choice of several alternatives:

```
            Budget Actions ▾
  ✎  Advanced budget…
  ✎  Edit budget name…
  ▣  Budget Reports        ▸
  ⊖  Delete this budget
  ⊕  Duplicate this budget…
  ⊕  Create new budget
```

● Click **Advanced Budget** to open the Advanced Budget Setup window for the currently selected budget, where you can add and delete categories and change amounts as described previously.

The Advanced Budget screen (Figure 9-4)

▸ Accounts C ⚙ Home Spending Bills **Planning** Investing Property More

Budgets Debt Reduction Lifetime Planner Tax Center | Planning Tools ▾ Tax Tools ▾ Reports ▾

Budget 3 ▾ Monthly ▾ ◀ September 2011 ▶ Budget Actions ▾

September 2011

Budget: **$6,908** ⚠

TOTAL SPENDING $4,321 left
Today ▲

		Budget
▾ EXPENSES	2,095 → 4,321 left	6,908
Auto & Transport:**Auto Payment**	356 left	356
Auto & Transport:**Gas & Fuel**	61 → 123 left	184
Auto & Transport:**Parking**	5 left	5
Auto & Transport:**Service & Parts**	378 left	378
Auto & Transport:**Tolls**	119 left	119
Bills & Utilities (Other)	50 / 179 → 53 left	282
⊖ Bills & Utilities:**Home Phone**	38 left ◀ Edit 38 ▶	
Bills & Utilities:**Internet**	10 → 35 left	45
Bills & Utilities:**Mobile Phone**	232 → 25 left	257
Bills & Utilities:**Television**	137 / 72 → 94 over	116
Cash & ATM	150 left	150
Financial (Other)	164 left	164
Food & Dining (Other)	47 → 7 left	54
Food & Dining:**Fast Food**	42 left	42

⊕ Add Category to Budget ⚙ Advanced Budget Setup

*Figure 9-4: **The Advanced Budget***

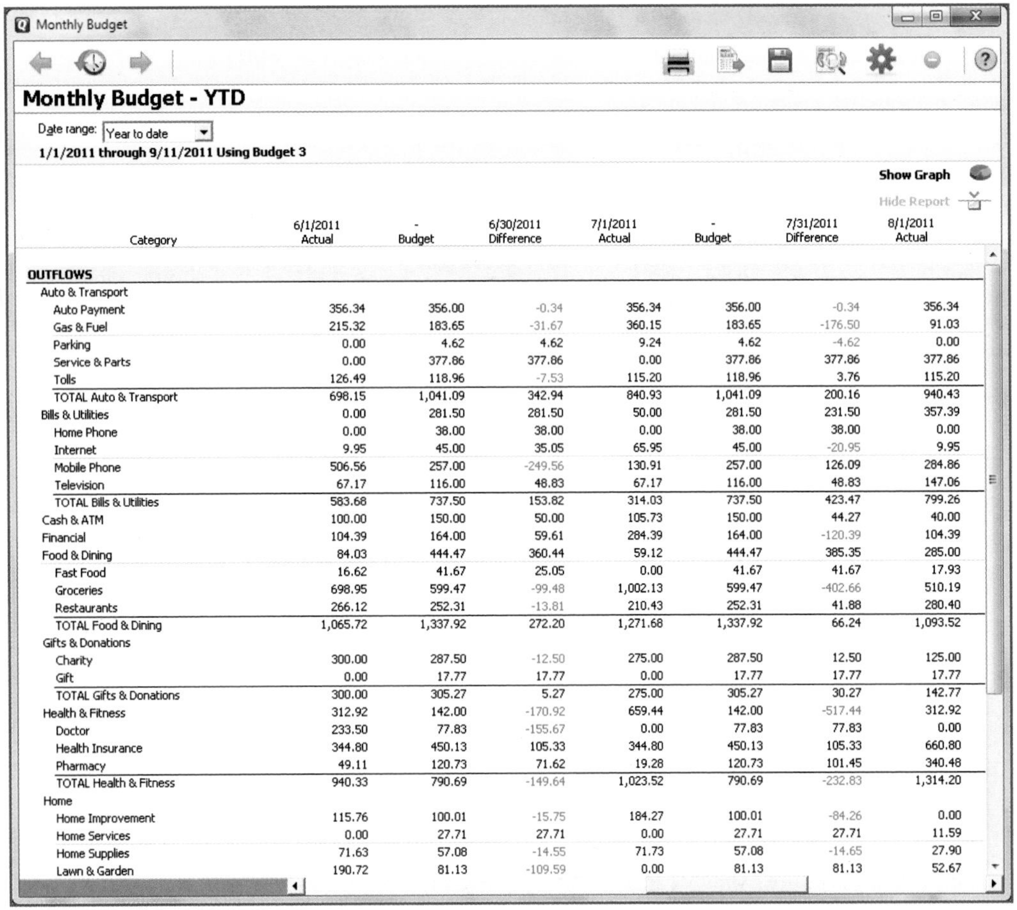

Category	6/1/2011 Actual	- Budget	6/30/2011 Difference	7/1/2011 Actual	- Budget	7/31/2011 Difference	8/1/2011 Actual
OUTFLOWS							
Auto & Transport							
Auto Payment	356.34	356.00	-0.34	356.34	356.00	-0.34	356.34
Gas & Fuel	215.32	183.65	-31.67	360.15	183.65	-176.50	91.03
Parking	0.00	4.62	4.62	9.24	4.62	-4.62	0.00
Service & Parts	0.00	377.86	377.86	0.00	377.86	377.86	377.86
Tolls	126.49	118.96	-7.53	115.20	118.96	3.76	115.20
TOTAL Auto & Transport	698.15	1,041.09	342.94	840.93	1,041.09	200.16	940.43
Bills & Utilities	0.00	281.50	281.50	50.00	281.50	231.50	357.39
Home Phone	0.00	38.00	38.00	0.00	38.00	38.00	0.00
Internet	9.95	45.00	35.05	65.95	45.00	-20.95	9.95
Mobile Phone	506.56	257.00	-249.56	130.91	257.00	126.09	284.86
Television	67.17	116.00	48.83	67.17	116.00	48.83	147.06
TOTAL Bills & Utilities	583.68	737.50	153.82	314.03	737.50	423.47	799.26
Cash & ATM	100.00	150.00	50.00	105.73	150.00	44.27	40.00
Financial	104.39	164.00	59.61	284.39	164.00	-120.39	104.39
Food & Dining	84.03	444.47	360.44	59.12	444.47	385.35	285.00
Fast Food	16.62	41.67	25.05	0.00	41.67	41.67	17.93
Groceries	698.95	599.47	-99.48	1,002.13	599.47	-402.66	510.19
Restaurants	266.12	252.31	-13.81	210.43	252.31	41.88	280.40
TOTAL Food & Dining	1,065.72	1,337.92	272.20	1,271.68	1,337.92	66.24	1,093.52
Gifts & Donations							
Charity	300.00	287.50	-12.50	275.00	287.50	12.50	125.00
Gift	0.00	17.77	17.77	0.00	17.77	17.77	17.77
TOTAL Gifts & Donations	300.00	305.27	5.27	275.00	305.27	30.27	142.77
Health & Fitness	312.92	142.00	-170.92	659.44	142.00	-517.44	312.92
Doctor	233.50	77.83	-155.67	0.00	77.83	77.83	0.00
Health Insurance	344.80	450.13	105.33	344.80	450.13	105.33	660.80
Pharmacy	49.11	120.73	71.62	19.28	120.73	101.45	340.48
TOTAL Health & Fitness	940.33	790.69	-149.64	1,023.52	790.69	-232.83	1,314.20
Home							
Home Improvement	115.76	100.01	-15.75	184.27	100.01	-84.26	0.00
Home Services	0.00	27.71	27.71	0.00	27.71	27.71	11.59
Home Supplies	71.63	57.08	-14.55	71.73	57.08	-14.65	27.90
Lawn & Garden	190.72	81.13	-109.59	0.00	81.13	81.13	52.67

Figure 9-5: ***The Monthly Budget Report provides a detailed look at how you are doing against your budget.***

- Click **Edit Budget Name** to rename your current budget, leaving its data as is.
- Click **Budget Reports** and select either the Budget Report, which you can tailor to give you a budget comparison for a single period, or the Monthly Budget Report, where you can compare budgeted and actual numbers by month, as shown in Figure 9-5.
- Click **Delete This Budget** to open a dialog box stating that you are about to delete the current budget and all associated information. If that is what you want to do, click **Delete** to complete the task; otherwise, click **Cancel** to keep the budget and its data.
- Click **Duplicate This Budget** to copy the current budget so that you can change it without changing the original.
- Click **Create New Budget** to create a totally new budget with a new name and the ability to choose between the Automatic Budget and the Advanced Budget, as described earlier in this chapter.

2. If you have created two or more budgets, you can select the one you want to view and possibly work with by clicking the **Budget** drop-down list in the upper-left corner of the Planning tab Budgets view.

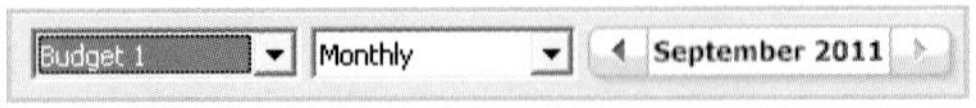

3. Clicking the second drop-down list in the upper-left corner of the Planning tab Budgets view allows you to select the time period you want to view and possibly work with. The default Monthly view also allows you to select a month to display.

TIP

Once you have created a budget, you can also view it at the bottom of the Home tab if you have not customized the Main View of the Home tab.

Plan for Your Future

After setting up budgets for managing the immediate months and years, you'll want to look ahead and plan for your future. This is the job of Quicken's Lifetime Planner, which is based on a set of assumptions that you create. You can change or add to these assumptions at any time. Quicken uses the data you have already entered to help you with your long-term plans, but if you have not yet entered all your data, you can enter it while you are creating your plans.

Describe Your Family

You begin by telling Quicken some information about yourself. Then you continue by including information about your income, tax rate, savings, investments, other assets, any debt, and living expenses. Quicken uses this information—along with the financial data you have already entered and a large database of financial resources—to help you create a plan. To begin your plan:

NOTE

If you have previously entered only some information into the Lifetime Planner, you may see a slightly different message in the Plan Results section indicating that you have not entered enough information for Quicken to analyze your life plan.

1. Click the **Planning** tab, and click **Lifetime Planner**. In the Plan Assumptions section, click **About You** to begin entering information in the Quicken Planner, as seen in Figure 9-6.

```
┌─────────────────────────────────────────────────────────────────┐
│ ▶ Accounts        ↻ ⚙   Home    Spend    Bills    Plan    More ⌄ │
│ ( Lifetime Plann... ▾ )              Tools ▾  Tax ▾  Reports ▾    │
│ [ Change Assumptions ] [ Explore What If's ]                     │
│                                                                   │
│  Plan: Results                                    ⚙ Options ▾    │
│                                                                   │
│  Quicken will help you establish a financial plan made up of     │
│  your life events.                                                │
│  Click here to begin planning.                                    │
│                                                                   │
│  Plan Assumptions                                 ⚙ Options ▾    │
│  Click on the links below to set or change your plan assumptions. │
│                                                                   │
│  About You            Tell Quicken about yourself and your family.│
│  Income               Enter your salary and other income.         │
│  Tax Rate             What tax rate do you expect to pay?          │
│  Inflation            How much inflation do you expect?            │
│  Savings & Investments  How much do you save and invest?          │
│  Homes and Assets     Do you own a home or car?                   │
│  Loans and Debt       Do you have any loans?                      │
│  Expenses             Enter your living expenses and plan for      │
│                       future expenses.                            │
│                                              [ To Do ]  [ Help ]  │
└─────────────────────────────────────────────────────────────────┘
```

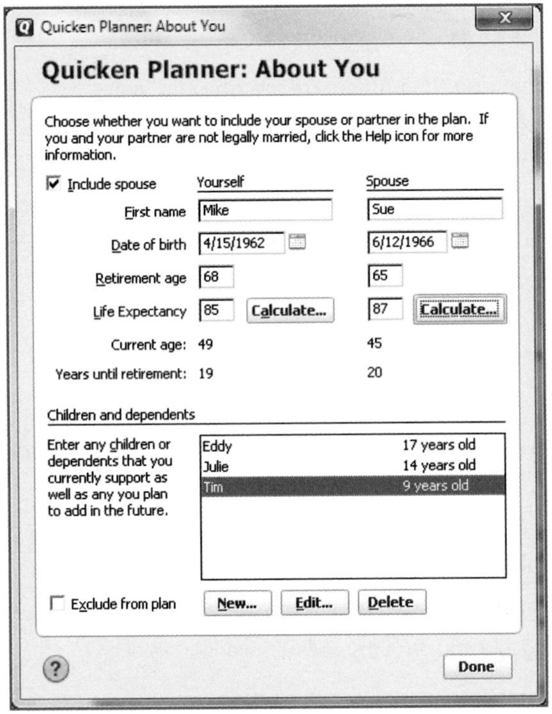

Figure 9-6: *The Quicken Planner: About You dialog box is used to enter age-related information about you, your spouse, and your children.*

TIP

You can include or exclude a dependent or a spouse at any time when making your assumptions.

CAUTION

If you support a parent or other family member who was born before 1930, you must enter all four digits in the year, for example, 1929. Otherwise, Quicken will use 2029 as the date of birth.

2. Click **Include Spouse** if you want to include your spouse in the assumptions.

3. Under Yourself, click in the **First Name** field, and type your first name. If you are including your spouse, under Spouse, click in the **First Name** field, and type your spouse's first name.

4. Continue through the dialog box, entering all relevant information. The maximum life expectancy or retirement age is 150 years, and the earliest birth date for you or your spouse is 1901.

5. If you want to include information about children and other dependents, click **New** at the bottom of the dialog box. The Add Child/Dependent dialog box appears. This information can include children that you plan to have.

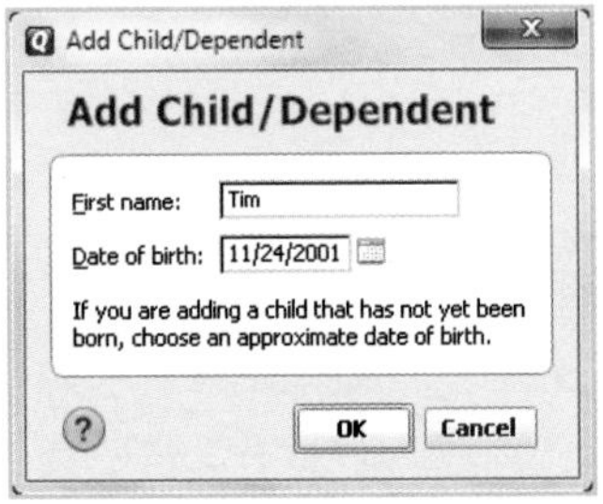

6. Click in the **First Name** field, and enter the first name of your child.

7. Click in the **Date Of Birth** field, and enter the child's date of birth. You can use the format MM/DD/YY. Quicken will change the year to four digits.

8. Click **OK** to close the Add Child/Dependent dialog box and return to the Quicken Planner: About You dialog box.

9. Click the name of a dependent, and click **Exclude From Plan** if you don't want Quicken to include dependents in the financial assumptions.

10. Click **Done** when you have entered all of your information and are ready to return to the Plan Assumptions section of the Lifetime Planner view.

The Plan Assumptions section now displays your name, your spouse's name if you included one, and the number of dependents you chose to include in your plan. If you want to change any of the assumptions that display, click the **Change Assumptions** button at the top of the Lifetime Planner view to open the Planning Assumptions dialog box. From that dialog box, click **Edit** to change any of the information. (You can also click the links in the Plan Assumptions

UNDERSTANDING YOUR SOCIAL SECURITY RETIREMENT AGE

Each year, you get a statement from the Social Security Administration showing your estimated benefits based on the current laws. This statement shows your benefits based on three dates: early retirement at age 62, full retirement age (which depends on your date of birth), and retirement at age 70. In addition to this annual statement, the Social Security Administration provides a website (www.ssa.gov) where many retirement-benefit questions are answered. The site provides benefit calculators and other tools to help you make retirement decisions based on potential Social Security benefits.

CAUTION

The Quicken Planner supports only U.S. dollars. Even if you have enabled multicurrency support in Quicken Preferences and do not use U.S. dollars as your main currency, U.S. dollars needs to be in the currency list with the current exchange rate.

pane. For example, to change the About You info, click the **About You** link in the Plan Assumptions pane.)

Assumptions	About you		
		Mike	Sue
About you	Age	49 years old	45 years old
Income	Life Expectancy	85	87
Salary	Retirement Age	68	65
Retirement benefits	Retirement Date	4/2030	6/2031
Other income	Years Until Retirement	19	20
Taxes & Inflation	Years In Retirement	17	22
Taxes			
Inflation	Children and dependents		Age
Savings & Investments	Eddy		17 years old
Savings	Julie		14 years old
Investments	Tim		9 years old
Rate of Return			
Homes & Assets			

Enter Income and Taxes

The next item in the Plan Assumptions section pertains to information about your income. This includes regular salaries, self-employment income, retirement benefits, and other income, such as child support or alimony.

ENTER SALARIES AND SELF-EMPLOYMENT INCOME

1. In the Planning tab Lifetime Planner view, Plan Assumptions section, click **Income** to begin entering salary and other information in the Quicken Planner.

2. In the Salary tab enter salary information for yourself and your spouse, if you are including a spouse in your planning assumptions.

3. Click **New** in the middle of the dialog box under Salary. The Add Salary dialog box appears.

   a. Click **You** or **Spouse** in response to "Who Earns This Salary?".

   b. Click in the **Name Or Description Of The Salary** field, and type the relevant information.

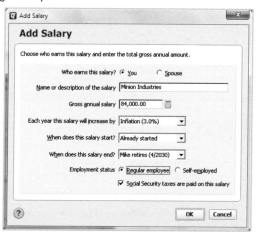

c. Click in the **Gross Annual Salary** field, and type the amount in U.S. dollars.

d. Continue through the questions, entering all relevant information.

e. Click **OK** when you are finished. You are returned to the Quicken Planner: Income dialog box. The information you entered for the starting and ending dates for this salary appear in the Adjustments To Salary section.

4. If you have other adjustments to your salary, such as a promotion, changing jobs, or an expected bonus, click **New** under Adjustments. The Add Salary Adjustment dialog box appears. Enter any relevant information in the appropriate fields. The data you can enter changes based on the adjustment type selected on the left side of the dialog box.

5. Click **OK** to save your adjustment and return to the Income dialog.

USE THE RETIREMENT BENEFITS TAB

If you have a retirement plan through your employer or want to include Social Security benefit information in your plan, use the Retirement Benefits tab in the Quicken Planner: Income dialog box (see "Enter Salaries and Self-Employment Income" to open this dialog box).

1. Click the **Retirement Benefits** tab to enter information about retirement income.

2. Click **Social Security Starting Age** to enter the age at which you expect to start collecting Social Security benefits. It must be between 62 and 70. If you don't know, click the **Estimate** button. The Estimate Social Security Benefits dialog box appears.

3. Continue through the fields, entering information that pertains to your situation. When you are ready, click **OK** to save your Social Security estimate and return to the Retirement Benefits tab.

4. In the Pension Benefits section, click **New** to add information about any pension that you or your spouse may receive. The Add Pension dialog box appears. Enter all of the information that pertains to the pension, and click **OK** when you are finished.

5. If you want to change a pension that you have already entered, select that pension benefit, and click **Edit** to change that benefit, or click **Delete** to remove it from your list. If you want to exclude a specific pension benefit from your plan, select it from the list, and click **Exclude From Plan**.

Quicken Planner: Income

| Salary | Retirement Benefits | Other Income |

If you or your spouse are already receiving Social Security benefits, enter the amounts below. Otherwise, click the "Estimate" button to estimate future benefits.

Social Security	**Yourself**	**Spouse**
Starting age:	88 Estimate...	65 Estimate...
Annual benefit:	18,585.00	13,302.00

If you think that Social Security benefits may be reduced in the future, lower the annual amount you expect to receive.

Reduce the estimated benefit amount? ⊙ No ○ Yes, by 0 %

Pension Benefits

Click the "New" button below to enter information about any pensions you or your spouse are receiving or will receive in the future.

Pension Plan	Start Age	Yearly Amount	COLA
My pension	68	$60,000	3.0% per ...

New... Edit... Delete   □ Exclude from plan

ENTER OTHER INCOME

The Other Income Tab in the Quicken Planner: Income dialog box is for gifts, inheritances, royalties, and other miscellaneous income you expect to receive. (See "Enter Salaries and Self-Employment Income" to open the Quicken Planner: Income dialog box.)

1. Click the **Other Income** tab, and then click **New**. The Add Other Income dialog box appears.

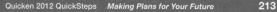

Add Other Income

Income Type: Inheritance

Description: Sue's Parents

Start date: Specific date: 2/12/2020

Income period: ● One-time event
　　　　　　　　○ Multiple-year income: [ ] years

Income amount: 150,000.00 (today's value)

Annual growth: Inflation (3.0%)

Tax rate: Normal rate

Use for income: ● Save it and invest in your taxable portfolio.
　　　　　　　　○ Use it to pay expenses (none will be saved).

OK　Cancel

2. Click the **Income Type** drop-down list, and select the type of income you want to include.

3. Continue through the Planner, entering the relevant information. If you have chosen one of the specific types of income, this name appears in the field.

4. Click **OK** to close the Add Other Income dialog box and return to the Quicken Planner: Income dialog box.

5. Click **Done** to close the Quicken Planner: Income dialog box and return to the Planning tab's Lifetime Planner.

DETERMINE YOUR TAX RATE

Quicken takes your tax liability into account when helping you create your plan. To tell Quicken what rate to use:

1. In the Planning tab Lifetime Planner, Plan Assumptions section, click **Tax Rate**. The Quicken Planner: Average Tax Rate dialog box appears.

Quicken Planner: Average Tax Rate

Your average tax rate is the best measure of the taxes you pay. It is your total taxes divided by your total income, and is typically lower than your marginal rate.

If you have your most recent tax returns, click "Tax returns" to base your average tax rate on your actual taxes. If not, click "Demographic average" to use the average tax rate paid by people in your income bracket in your state.

● Demographic average　　○ Tax returns

What state do you live in? Arizona

Approximate combined annual income: $100,000.00 to $150,000.00

Based on the demographic average, the average tax rate for people in your income bracket is 21%.

Adjust the rate if you want it to be higher or lower than the estimate: 21 %

If you are certain your income will decline after retirement, enter a lower after-retirement tax rate. To be conservative, use the same rate you entered above. For more information, click "Help".

What is your estimated after-retirement tax rate? 21 %

Done

NOTE

You can always enter a higher tax rate for Quicken to use in its planning calculations.

QUICKSTEPS

ESTIMATING INFLATION FOR YOUR PLAN

Quicken uses an average inflation rate of 3 percent. *Inflation* is a rise in the price of goods or services when consumer spending increases and supplies or services decrease. For the last 50 years, inflation in the United States has ranged from 0 to 23 percent, with an average of 2 to 3 percent per year. As you make your assumptions in Quicken, you may choose to be conservative and increase the default inflation rate to 3 percent, or be more optimistic and decrease the rate. To change the rate of inflation used by Quicken:

1. In the Planning tab Lifetime Planner, Plan Assumptions section, click **Inflation**. The Quicken Planner: Estimated Inflation dialog box appears.

2. Click in the **What Inflation Rate Do You Want To Use In Your Plan?** field, and type the number you want to use.

3. Click **OK** to close the dialog box.

2. Click **Demographic Average** if you want Quicken to calculate your average tax rate based on the average rate of people in your income category in your state.

   a. Click the **What State Do You Live In?** down arrow, and click the name of your state.

   b. Click the **Approximate Combined Annual Income** ("Approximate Annual Income" if you are single) down arrow, and click the approximate annual income for you and your spouse.

3. Alternatively, click **Tax Returns** if you want to enter information from your most recent tax return. A different set of questions appears.

   a. Enter the total income from Form 1040.

   b. Enter the total federal taxes from Form 1040.

   c. If your state has a state income tax, enter the total state taxes from your state tax form.

4. The average tax rate for your income bracket in your state appears in the Adjust The Rate If You Want It To Be Higher Or Lower Than The Estimate field. Enter any change in the estimated tax rate you want Quicken to use.

5. This same rate appears in the What Is Your Estimated After-Retirement Tax Rate? field. Enter any change you want Quicken to use.

6. Click **Done** when you have entered all of the information to return to the Planning tab's Lifetime Planner.

Consider Savings, Investments, and Rate of Return

Quicken can use the information you entered for your checking, savings, and investment accounts in its assumptions for planning. You can choose to have Quicken include or exclude any account from its computations, designate the use for each account, and indicate what contributions will be made to these accounts in the future.

INCLUDE CHECKING AND SAVINGS ACCOUNTS

To tell Quicken how to use your checking and savings accounts:

1. In the Planning tab Lifetime Planner, Plan Assumptions section, click **Savings & Investments**. The Quicken Planner: Savings And Investments dialog box appears.

Quicken Planner: Savings and Investments

2. Click the **Savings** tab to display a list of your checking and savings accounts. If you have not yet entered all of your accounts, now is a good time. Click the **New** button to add a new account, and follow the directions in Chapter 3.

3. Click an account and click **Exclude From Plan** to exclude that account from the plan. Click **Show Excluded Accounts** if you want them to be displayed in the list even if they are not included in the plan.

4. Click **Details** to open the Account Details dialog box for the selected account.

   a. Click the **Account Will Be Used For** down arrow, and select the purpose for this account. If you have used any of the specific planners, such as the Home Purchase Planner or the Retirement Planner, you will have that choice included; otherwise, your only choice is the default: General Expenses.

   b. Click **OK** to return to the Quicken Planner: Savings And Investments dialog box.

5. If either you or your spouse regularly puts money in any of these bank accounts, click **New** underneath Contributions To for the account you have selected. The Add Contribution dialog box appears.

6. Enter the relevant information for your situation, and click **Next** to go to the next section.

7. Click **Done** to return to the Quicken Planner: Savings And Investments dialog box.

QUICKSTEPS

ENTERING YOUR EXPECTED RATE OF RETURN

The *rate of return* is how much you get back each year on your investments expressed as a percentage. For example, if you make $100 on a $2,000 investment, your rate of return is 5 percent ($100 divided by $2,000). You can use different rates for taxable and tax-deferred investments. Before retirement, your investments must grow enough to ensure that you have funds available to you even when you are not earning a salary. After retirement, your funds must grow to keep pace with inflation and fund your living expenses. A conservative rule of thumb for return on investments is between 5 and 7 percent. To enter your estimated rate of return on your investments:

1. In the Planning tab Lifetime Planner, Plan Assumptions section, click **Savings & Investments**. The Quicken Planner: Savings And Investments dialog box appears.

2. Click the **Return** tab.

Continued . . .

QUICKSTEPS

ENTERING YOUR EXPECTED RATE OF RETURN

(Continued)

3. Click **Use Separate Rates Of Return For Taxable And Tax-Deferred Accounts**, if applicable.

   - Enter the information in taxable accounts before retirement and after retirement.

   - Enter your tax-deferred rates both before retirement and after retirement.

   - Enter your spouse's tax-deferred rates both before retirement and after retirement.

4. If you did *not* choose Use Separate Rates Of Return For Taxable And Tax-Deferred Accounts in step 3, click in the **Rate Of Return** field under Before Retirement, enter the return you expect on your investments before you retire, click in the **Rate Of Return** field under After Retirement, and enter your expected after-retirement return.

5. In the How Much Of Your Taxable Return Will Be Subject To Taxes Each Year? field, enter an appropriate percentage. In most cases, all of the return may be taxable. Check with your financial professional to learn what you should enter.

6. Click **Done** to return to the Planning tab.

INCLUDE INVESTMENT ACCOUNTS

The Investments tab shows all of the investment accounts you have entered. You can include or exclude any of these accounts from your plan and tell Quicken about any regular contributions you make to any of them.

In the Quicken Planner: Savings And Investments dialog box, click the **Investments** tab, and follow the procedure in "Include Checking and Savings Accounts" earlier in this chapter.

Work with Homes and Other Assets

You can include your home and other assets in your plan, both those you currently own and those you plan on purchasing.

INCLUDE CURRENT ASSETS

To work with the Homes And Assets Planner:

1. In the Planning tab Lifetime Planner, Plan Assumptions section, click **Homes And Assets**. The Quicken Planner: Homes And Assets dialog box appears.

2. Click the **Asset Accounts** tab to display a list of the accounts you have created so far in Quicken, including homes, vehicles, real estate, and so on. The list shows a description of the asset, its purchase date, a planned sale date (if any), and its current value, as shown in Figure 9-7.

3. Click **New** to add a new account, follow the directions in Chapter 3, and return to the Quicken Planner: Homes And Assets dialog box.

4. Select an asset and click **Exclude From Plan** if you want Quicken to ignore this asset in your plan.

Quicken Planner: Savings and Investments

| Savings | Investments | **Return** |

Enter the average rate of return that you and your spouse expect to achieve before and after retirement. For more information, click "Help".

☑ Use separate rates of return for taxable and tax-deferred accounts

	Before retirement	After retirement
Taxable accounts:	7%	5%
Your tax-deferred:	8%	6%
Spouse's tax-deferred:	8%	6%

If you are invested mostly in stocks that do not pay dividends or interest, less than 100% of your gain may be taxed each year. To be conservative enter 100% or click "Help" for more information.

How much of your taxable return will be subject to taxes each year? 100%

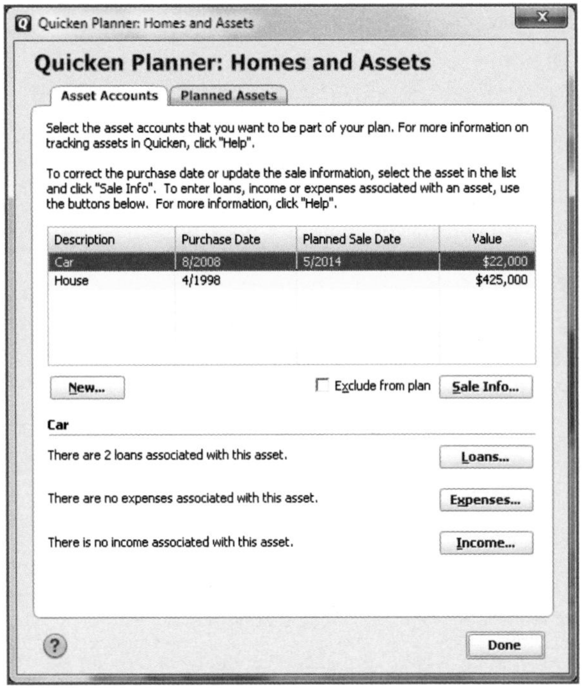

Quicken Planner: Homes and Assets

Figure 9-7: The Asset Accounts tab lists each asset you have entered, its purchase date, and its current recorded value.

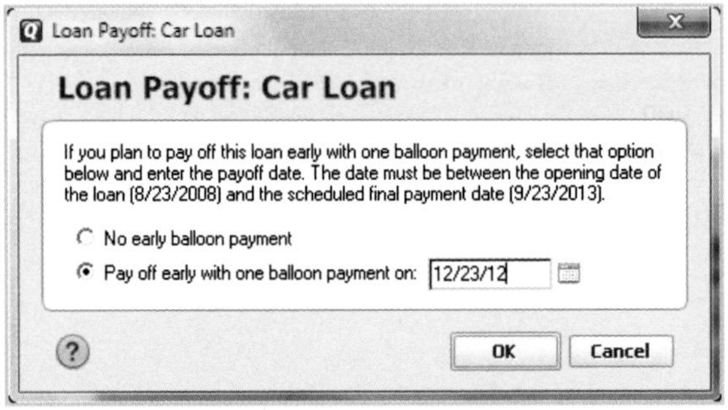

Loan Payoff: Car Loan

5. Click **Sale Info** to open the Asset Account Sale Information dialog box. Click in each of the fields, and select or type the requested information, clicking **Next** as needed.

Asset Account Sale Information

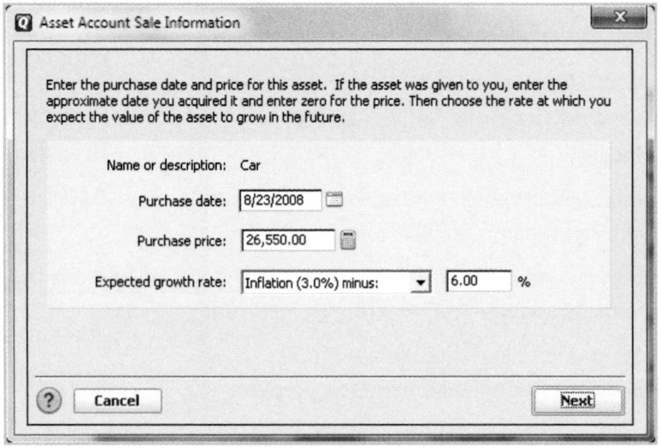

6. Click **Done** to return to the Quicken Planner: Homes And Assets dialog box.

7. Click the **Planned Assets** tab to enter any large assets you plan to purchase in the future. Click **New** to open the Add Planned Asset dialog, and type the requested information, clicking **Next** as needed.

8. Click **Done** when you have finished entering the information to return to the Quicken Planner: Home And Assets dialog box.

CONSIDER LOANS ON ASSETS

If you intend to add, pay off, or change a loan using one of your assets, either existing or planned, as collateral:

1. Click the name of the asset, and then click the **Loans** button to open the Quicken Planner: Loans dialog box.

2. Click the **Loan Accounts** tab to display the current loans associated with this asset.

3. To enter early payoff information about a loan associated with an asset, select the loan and click **Payoff** to open the Loan Payoff dialog. Enter the appropriate information, and click **OK** when you are done.

4. Select a loan and click **Exclude From Plan** if you want to exclude that loan from your plan.

Add Planned Loan

Enter when the loan will start, the amount borrowed, and the amortized length of the loan (even if you plan to pay it off early).

Name or description: Loan for Car

Opening date: Specific date: 6/15/2014

Amount borrowed: 15,000.00

Loan length: 5 years

If you will be making payments on a regular basis, select the period from the list. Otherwise, choose "Other period" and enter the number of payments you will make each year.

○ Standard payment period: Monthly

○ Other period: ___ payments per year

[?] [Cancel] [Next]

Add Asset Expense

Enter the details about the amount and duration of the expense.

Start of expense: Specific date: 9/1/12

Duration of expense: ○ one-time expense
○ multiple-year expense: ___ years
○ as long as you own the asset

Expense amount: 100,000.00

(enter the amount you expect to pay when the expense occurs)

[?] [Cancel] [Back] [Next]

5. To enter loans you plan for the future, click the **Planned Loans** tab, and click **New**. The Planned Loans dialog box appears. Click in each of the fields, and select or type the information that is correct for your loan. Click **Next** to move through the sections.

6. Click **Done** to return to the Quicken Planner: Loans dialog box. The details of this planned loan are displayed at the bottom of the dialog box. Click **Done** again to return to the Quicken Planner: Homes And Assets dialog box.

ENTER EXPENSES ASSOCIATED WITH AN ASSET

Many assets have expenses associated with them that must be included in the plan, such as taxes, insurance, and maintenance on a house. You can include them here with their associated asset or include them later in the "Figure Your Living Expenses" section of this chapter. To include expenses with their associated asset, either existing or planned:

1. In the Quicken Planner: Homes And Assets dialog box, click the asset with which you want to work.

2. Click the **Expenses** button toward the bottom of the dialog box. The Quicken Planner: Asset Expenses dialog box appears.

3. Click in the **How Much Tax Do You Pay On This Asset?** field, and enter the tax amount, if any, that you pay.

4. If there are other expenses, such as homeowner association fees, moorage fees, maintenance fees, or gardening expenses, click **New**. The Add Asset Expense dialog box appears.

5. Click in the **Name Or Description** field, and type a name for this expense if you want a name different from the default Quicken supplies. Click **Next** to continue. Click in each of the fields, and select or type the information that is appropriate for this expense, clicking **Next** as needed and clicking **OK** to return from any subsidiary dialog box you open.

6. Click **Done** to return to the Quicken Planner: Asset Expenses dialog box. Click **Done** again to return to the Quicken Planner: Homes And Assets dialog box.

7. Click **Done** a third time to return to the Planning tab Lifetime Planner.

Part of your future retirement may come from income you earn by renting an asset you own, such as a motor home, boat, cabin, or real property. You can include this information for both existing assets and planned assets in your Quicken Planner: Homes And Assets dialog box.

1. In the Planning tab Lifetime Planner, Plan Assumptions section, click **Homes And Assets**. The Quicken Planner: Homes And Assets dialog box appears.

2. Click the name of the asset from which you earn income, and click **Income** at the bottom of the dialog box.

3. Click **New** to open the Add Other Income dialog box. Click in each of the fields, and select or type the information that is requested.

4. Click **OK** to return to the Other Income dialog box.

5. Click **Done** to return to the Quicken Planner: Home And Assets dialog box.

6. Click **Done** again to return to the Planning tab Lifetime Planner.

Add Other Income

Enter the information about this income generated by the asset "House".

Description:	Income from House
Start date:	Tim is (years old): 18
Income period:	○ One-time event
	○ Multiple-year income: years
	● As long as you own the asset
Income	4,800.00 (today's value)
Annual growth:	Inflation (3.0%)
Tax rate:	Normal rate (21%)
Use for income:	● Save it and invest in your taxable portfolio.
	○ Use it to pay expenses (none will be saved).

OK   Cancel

Use the Loans And Debt Planner

To have a comprehensive plan, you need to include your liabilities (loans and debts), as well as your assets.

1. In the Planning tab Lifetime Planner, Plan Assumptions section, click **Loans And Debt**. The Quicken Planner: Loans And Debt dialog box appears.

2. Click the **Loan Accounts** tab to display a list of all the loans you have entered. You can select loans and exclude them from your plan, change the payoff date, and add new loans.

3. Click the **Planned Loans** tab to display a list of any loans you plan to take out in the future. You may have entered these loans in the Quicken Planner: Homes And Assets section. You can edit, delete, and exclude these loans from the plan, as well as add new ones.

4. Click **Done** to close this dialog box.

Figure Your Living Expenses

Expenses are a critical part of your plan. To figure what your expenses will be:

1. In the Planning tab Lifetime Planner, Plan Assumptions section, click **Expenses**. The Quicken Planner: Expenses dialog box appears.

2. In the Living Expenses tab, you are prompted to enter your regular living expenses, such as food, transportation, rent, medical insurance payments, and utility bills. Quicken offers you two methods of entering these items: by rough estimate or by category detail.

3. Click **Rough Estimate** to let Quicken calculate an annual estimate of your expenses based on the transactions in your registers. You must have several months' worth of transactions for Quicken to do this.

   ● Click **Yearly Living Expenses**, and, if needed, modify the amount.

   ● Click in the **What Percent Of Surplus Cash Do You Want To Sweep To Savings?** field, and enter

> **CAUTION**
>
> Do not include amounts in your living expenses that are entered elsewhere, such as regular mortgage payments. Conversely, do not forget to include credit card and loan payments you make regularly.

a percentage if you feel you will be spending less than your income. The most conservative amount to select is 0 percent.

Living Expense Category Detail

Select the categories that you use for your living expenses and, if you wish, enter or change the monthly amount. Clicking in the first column will select and de-select categories to use. The categories displayed with a checkmark will be used to determine your living expenses.

The values in the "Estimate" column were calculated from your Quicken transactions in date range 9/2010 to 8/2011. Click the "Estimate" button to obtain new values.

Use	Category	Estimate	Monthly Amount
✔	Entertainment:Movies & DVDs	3	25
✔	Entertainment:Newspaper & Mag...	1	10
✔	Shopping	12	400
✔	Shopping:Clothing	33	200
	Shopping:Books		
✔	Shopping:Electronics & Software	41	100
	Shopping:Hobbies		
	Shopping:Sporting Goods		
✔	Personal Care	0	50
	Personal Care:Hair		
	Personal Care:Spa & Massage		
	Monthly Totals:	**$1,180**	**$4,417**

☐ Only show living expense categories.   [Estimate...]

[OK] [Cancel]

Quicken Planner: Expenses

| Living Expenses | Adjustments | College Expenses | Special Expenses |

Enter your living expenses below. Do not enter expenses that are specified elsewhere in the plan, such as taxes, savings contributions, loan and debt payments, or home and asset expenses. For more information click "Help".

Select "Rough estimate" to enter an estimate of all your living expenses. Select "Category detail" to track expenses individually by category.

What method do you want to use? ⦿ Rough estimate   ◯ Category detail

A conservative estimate of living expenses assumes that you spend all money that does not go to loans, debt, savings or taxes.

Yearly living expenses: 48,000.00

If you have cash flow surpluses in some years, you may be able to save more. If you are confident that these are true surpluses, you may elect to "sweep" a percentage of each surplus into your savings. To be conservative, enter zero.

What percent of surplus cash do you want to sweep to savings? 50 %

[Done]

4. Click **Category Detail** if you want to track your expenses by category. Click **Detail** and select the categories you want to enter, review the estimate, and enter the monthly expenses for that category. When you have completed all of the categories, click OK.

ENTER ADJUSTMENTS

The Adjustments tab is used to enter major changes to your living expenses. This could be due to a layoff from work, a new baby, or an illness.

1. Click the **Adjustments** tab, and click **New**. The Add Living Expense Adjustment dialog box appears.

2. Click **No Specific Person** if this is a general adjustment, such as the cost of a new water heater. Click **A Plan Member**, and choose the member from the drop-down list if the change affects one of the persons in your plan. The members are you, your spouse, and any dependents you listed as being included in the plan.

3. Click in the remaining fields that are applicable, and select or type the appropriate information.

4. Click **OK** to close the dialog box.

ENTER COLLEGE EXPENSES

The College Expenses tab helps you enter information about the costs of college. See the "Use Planners, Calculators, and Other Tools" section later in this chapter for information about calculating the costs you will enter here.

1. Click the **College Expenses** tab, and click **New**. The Add College Expense dialog box appears.

2. Click **This Expense Is For**, and choose a name from the drop-down list.

3. Make any necessary changes in the remaining fields, and click **Next**.

4. Enter an amount in the **Tuition & Fees** field, and continue through the dialog, adding fees as necessary.

5. Click **Next** to enter any anticipated financial aid and other help the student will receive. Click in each field to enter the applicable information.

6. Click **Next** to display a dialog that describes how you will fund these college costs. Make any changes that are necessary.

7. Click **Done** to return to the College Expenses tab. Click **New** to add another person's expenses.

8. To change information about a person's expenses, select the name from the list, and click **Edit** to open the Edit College Expense dialog. To remove a person's name from the list (and your plan), select the name and click **Delete**.

PLANNING TO PAY FOR COLLEGE

When you are planning for your children's college education, consider the following:

- How old is the child, and when will he or she actually start college? For most students, it is the fall after they graduate from high school.

- What are their options as to the type of school?

- Consider community or junior college so that the child can complete any lower-level requirements. Some community college programs guarantee entry into a four-year state school if the student graduates with an associate's degree.

- Community college tuition is usually much less expensive than a four-year institution.

- State colleges and universities usually charge less tuition to residents of that state than to out-of-state students.

- Many schools are now offering a large number of classes online. This saves room and board as well as transportation costs.

- How can the student receive grants or scholarships?

- Look for scholarships or grants early. Use the Internet to search on the Web, and contact friends or family members in organizations that offer scholarships.

Continued . . .

ENTER SPECIAL EXPENSES

Special expenses are those expenses that are not part of regular living expenses but should be included in your plan. An example of a special expense might be an extended vacation, a 50th wedding anniversary party, or some other elaborate event.

1. Click the **Special Expenses** tab to open the dialog box.

2. Click **New** to open the Add Special Expense dialog box.

3. Enter all the applicable information, clicking **Next** as needed, and click **Done** when you are through to return to the Quicken Planner: Expenses dialog box.

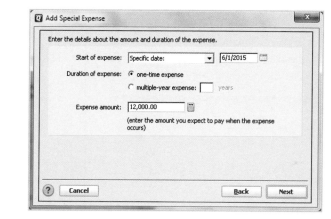

4. Click **Done** to close the dialog box. You are returned to the Lifetime Planner view of the Planning tab with a graphic displaying the results of your plan, as seen in Figure 9-8 later in this chapter.

Understand the Plan Results

After you have entered all of your assumptions, the result of your hard work is displayed in graphical format in the Plan: Results section of the Planning tab. The graph shows if your plan is working and how much money you will have in retirement. A list of major events is displayed under the graph, as shown in Figure 9-8.

1. Click **Options** in the upper-right corner of the Plan: Results section of the Planning tab's Lifetime Planner view to see how you can change the graph.

PLANNING TO
PAY FOR COLLEGE *(Continued)*

- Check to see if your state offers a guaranteed education account. Many universities and colleges, both state and private, now offer a prepayment plan for parents that allows you to pay over a longer period at a reduced cost and ensure a four-year education at the state or private school offering such a plan.

- Talk to your tax professional about IRAs and other savings plans designed to fund education.

The earlier you begin answering these questions, the more completely you can plan and handle this very substantial expense when it occurs.

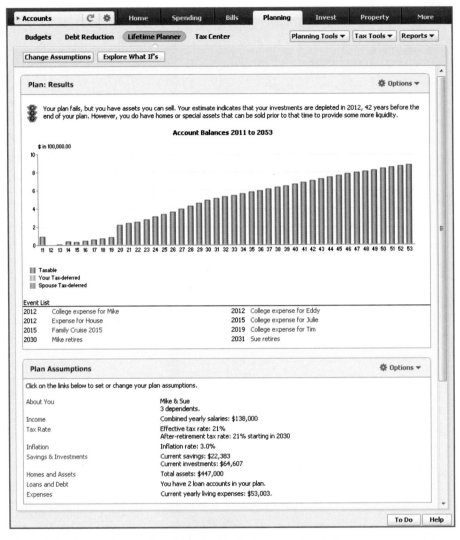

Figure 9-8: *After you have entered all of your plan's assumptions, Quicken displays the results.*

Planning assumptions

About you

	Mike	Sue
Age	49 years old	45 years old
Life Expectancy	85	87
Retirement Age	68	65
Retirement Date	4/2030	6/2031
Years Until Retirement	19	20
Years In Retirement	17	22

Children and dependents		Age
Eddy		17 years old
Julie		14 years old
Tim		9 years old

Salary

Your Salary	Amount	Annual Increase	Self Emp.	Pay SS Tax
Minion Industries (Alrea...	$84,000	Inflation	No	Yes

Your spouse's Salary	Amount	Annual Increase	Self Emp.	Pay SS Tax
CyberDisplay (Already s...	$54,000	Inflation	Yes	Yes

Retirement benefits

Your Social Security Benefits	
Age you elected to start collecting	68

Assumptions
- About you
- Income
  - Salary
  - Retirement benefits
  - Other income
- Taxes & Inflation
  - Taxes
  - Inflation
- Savings & Investments
  - Savings
  - Investments
  - Rate of Return
- Homes & Assets
  - Current homes & assets
  - Future homes & assets
- Loans & Debt
  - Current loans
  - Debt reduction
  - Future loans
- Expenses
  - Living expenses
  - Adjustments
  - College expenses
  - Special expenses

2. Click **Show Amounts In Future Value** to display the graph in future (inflated) dollars. Click **Options** and click **Show Amounts In Today's Value** to change it back.

3. Click **Options** and click **Review Or Change Plan Assumptions** to open the Planning Assumptions dialog box. Each assumption you entered is displayed with its result. Scroll through the dialog box, or click an area on the left to ensure that you entered everything correctly. If you did not, click **Edit** on the right of the title of each section to open the relevant dialog box and change the information. You can also access this dialog box by clicking the **Change Assumptions** button in the upper-left corner of the page, under the Budgets button of the Planning tab. Click **Close** to return to the Planning tab.

4. Again, click **Options** on the Plan: Results title bar, and click **What If I Did Something Different** to open the What If dialog box (see the "Using What If's" QuickSteps in this chapter). This allows you to temporarily change any assumption by clicking the assumption area on the left and seeing the result. If you like the change, keep it; if not, close the dialog box without saving your changes. You can also open this dialog box by clicking the **Explore What If's** button to the right of the Change Assumptions button at the top of the Lifetime Planner view. Click **Close** to return to the Planning tab.

QUICKSTEPS

USING WHAT IF'S

As you spend time creating plans for your financial future, Quicken provides a utility that allows you to quickly see the result of a possibility or a different path. The What If scenarios allow you to change assumptions or make changes in each of the four different goal types: College, Home Purchase, Retirement, and Special Expense. You can either save the new scenario or close the What If dialog box without saving your changes. To use the What If dialog box:

1. In the Planning tab's Lifetime Planner view, click **Explore What If's** at the top of the view.

Continued . . .

Choose a goal type
Retirement

What If I
- Change retirement age?
- Save more or less?
- Adjust my lifestyle?
- Sell a home or asset?
- Adjust rate of return?
- Live longer?
- Work in retirement?

Or, change any assumption:
- About you
- Salary
- Retirement benefits
- Other income
- Tax rate
- Inflation
- Savings
- Investments
- Rate of return
- Current homes & assets
- Future homes &

You can temporarily change any of your assumptions or goals (and even exclude goals) to see the effect. If you like the changes, you can save them.

Reset What If | Save What If as Plan | Close Without Saving

Your plan is working! You estimate that you will have 539,671 (today's value) in investments at retirement. According to your estimate, you should have enough money to fund all your life event goals and your expenses in retirement.

Account Balances 2011 to 2053
$ in 100,000.00

- Taxable
- Your Tax-deferred
- Spouse Tax-deferred

Use Planners, Calculators, and Other Tools

Quicken provides planners, financial calculators, and additional tools to help you plan for and achieve your financial goals. In addition to the Lifetime Planner, Quicken offers the Debt Reduction Planner and several calculators that provide a quick look at your financial situation for a particular event without having to enter all the data in plan assumptions.

QUICKSTEPS

USING WHAT IF'S *(Continued)*

–Or–

Click **Options** on the right of the Plan: Results section, and choose **What If I Did Something Different?**

2. Click the **Choose A Goal Type** down arrow, and select one of the four options. Each option has a different set of What If scenarios with which you can work.

3. Click a **What If I** option. A Quicken Planner dialog box will appear.

4. Click the area that might change and make any needed adjustments; or click **Edit** in the appropriate area to open its dialog box, make any needed adjustments, and click **OK** to close that dialog box.

5. Repeat steps 3 and 4 for other What If scenarios or changes in assumptions. When you are ready, click **Done** to close the Quicken Planner dialog box. The result of this change is displayed in the Plan Results graph in the What If dialog box.

6. Click **Reset What If** to revert to your original settings or assumptions.

7. If you want, click **Save What If As Plan** to keep the change you entered and return to the Lifetime Planner view of the Planning tab. Otherwise, click **Close Without Saving**.

You can use these tools to enter information rather than use the Plan Assumptions dialog boxes or to make changes to the data you entered in those assumptions.

Work with the Debt Reduction Planner

The Debt Reduction Planner helps you plan to get out of debt, as seen in Figure 9-9. To work with the Debt Reduction Planner:

1. Click the **Planning** tab, click the **Debt Reduction** view, and click **Get Started**.

2. Hover your mouse over each debt and choose whether to include or remove the debt from the plan. When you have selected the debts you want in the plan, click **Next**.

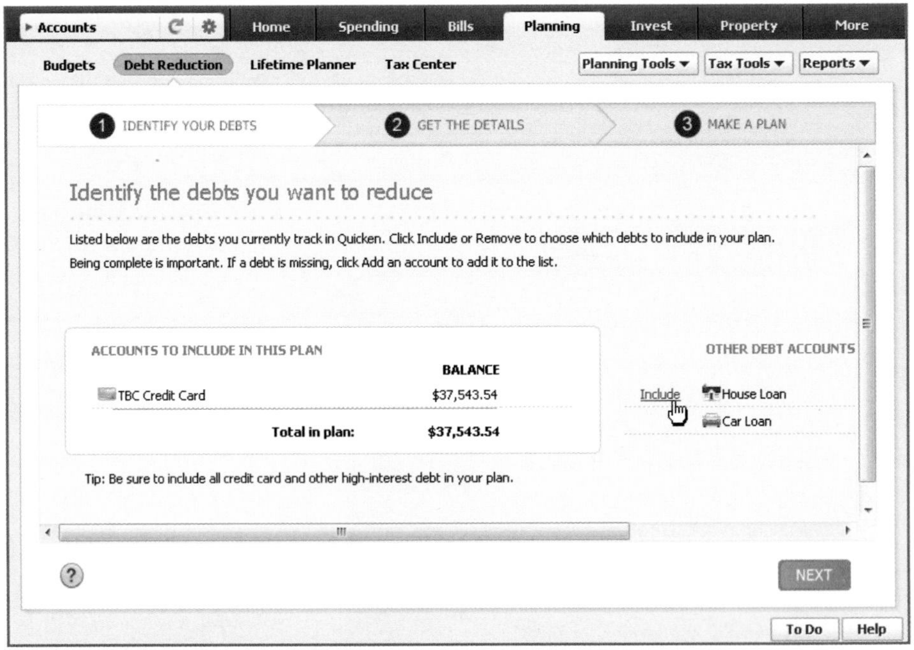

Figure 9-9: *The Debt Reduction Planner allows you to choose which debts to include in the plan.*

Get the details

A good debt reduction plan requires a few critical details about your debts.
Being accurate is important. It's best not to guess or "ballpark" this step.

	INTEREST RATE (APR)	MINIMUM PAYMENT
Car Loan	6.00 %	$310
TBC Credit Card	12.90 %	$780

Tip: Review your statements or visit your financial institutions' web sites to get the correct numbers.
For credit cards, look for a "Purchases" or "Standard APR" to find the interest rate.

3. Enter or correct the interest rates and minimum payments of all of the debts in the plan, and then click **Next**.

4. In the Make A Plan step, which displays a suggested plan and its benefits (see Figure 9-10), you can drag the slider in the yellow payment bar at the top of the graph to increase or decrease the monthly payment and see the result.

5. You can also choose to make a one-time payment to kick-start your plan by either dragging the slider below the graph or typing an amount in the text box on the right of that slider.

6. When you have the plan you want to use, decide whether you want to start this month or next, and then click **Next** to display the final results of your plan.

Get Quick Answers with Calculators

The five Quicken calculators—Retirement, College, Refinance, Savings, and Loan—help you to quickly calculate your current position without having to enter all of your assumptions. Each calculator has different questions but performs in the same manner. This section uses the Retirement Calculator as an example.

The Retirement Calculator lets you quickly see where you stand in your retirement preparations, as shown in Figure 9-11. To use it:

1. Click the **Planning** tab, click **Planning Tools**, and click **Retirement Calculator**.

2. Click in each of the fields, and select or type the information that is requested.

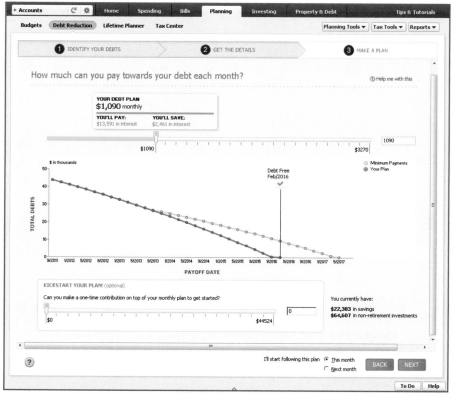

Figure 9-10: *Quicken's Debt Reduction Planner provides an interactive tool you can use to see the result of changing your monthly payment.*

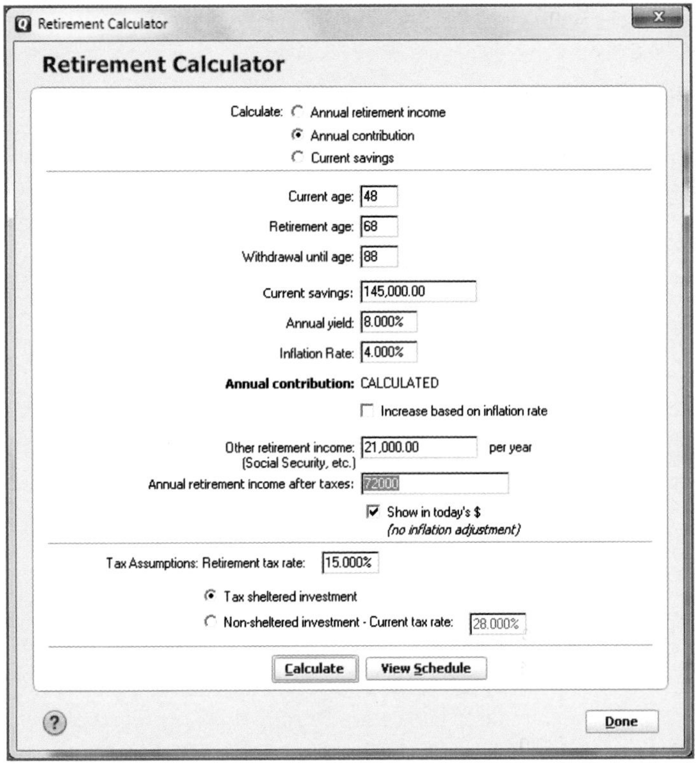

Figure 9-11: *The Retirement Calculator helps you see how you will fare in retirement.*

3. Click **Calculate** to complete any calculations, and click **View Schedule** to display an annual schedule of the amounts produced by the calculator.

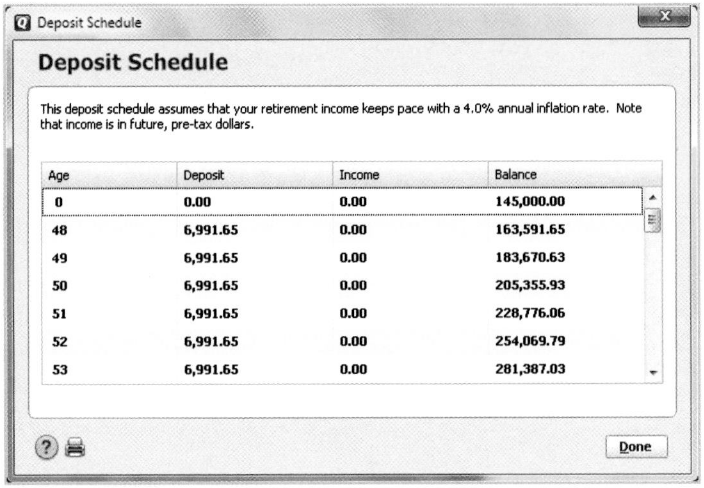

4. Click **Done** when you have finished with your calculations.

SET A SAVINGS GOAL

Writing down a goal is often the best way to achieve it. The Savings Goal dialog box lets you plan for some future event, such as a world cruise or a vacation home, and save for it systematically. This is *not* a real bank account—it is just a way to track your savings (and hide it from yourself). To start from scratch to set a savings goal:

1. In the Planning tab, click **Planning Tools** and click **Savings Goals**.

2. When the Savings Goals dialog box appears, click **New** in the menu bar at the top. The Create New Savings Goals window opens.

3. Click in the **Goal Name** text box, and type the name of your goal. Press **TAB** to continue.

4. Type what you want to save toward the goal in the Goal Amount text box.

Create New Savings Goal

Goal Name: Kitchen Remodel

Goal Amount: 30,000.00

Finish Date: 10/1/16

5. Type the date by which you want to achieve this goal in the Finish Date text box, and click **OK** to create the goal.

6. Click **Contribute** to add funds to your goal. Quicken computes the projected monthly contribution you must make to achieve the goal by the finish date you entered. Select the account from which the money will come, the date of the transaction if different from today, and the amount you want to set aside if different from what Quicken calculated. Click **OK** to return to the Savings Goals window.

Contribute To Goal: Kitchen Remodel

From Account: Personal Checking

Date: 9/11/2011   Amount: $ 1000

Current Personal Checking Balance: 7,710.23

7. In the Savings Goals window you can change the goal and the start and finish dates. Also, at the bottom of the window is a progress bar, which you can use to track your savings.

8. Click **Close** to return to the Planning tab.

Savings Goals

New   Edit   Delete   Contribute   Withdraw   Report   Print   How Do I?

Goal Name	Goal Amount	Finish Date	Current Savings
Family Cruise	12,000.00	7/14/2012	2,000.00
Kitchen Remodel	12,000.00	10/1/2016	1,000.00

Kitchen Remodel Progress   Goal: 12,000.00

1,000.00

Start: 9/11/2011   Finish: 10/1/2016

Projected Monthly Contribution: 177.41

Chapter 10

Getting Ready for Tax Time

Tax preparation can be stressful and frustrating. You have to locate and organize your financial records, read complex publications, and fill out forms that are difficult to read, much less understand. In many cases, it means writing a check to the federal and/or state government taxing authority and worrying about how much more you will owe next year. Quicken can lessen the burden. With its organizational features, it can help you be ready well before the tax due date. Quicken also has a Tax Planner, a tool that helps you determine which deductions you can take, and another tool to help you decide how much withholdings you should claim. You can access additional tools online through the links provided in the Tax Center view of the Planning tab. With Quicken, April 15 can be just another day in your smooth financial life.

NOTE

Most of the tasks performed with the Tax Planner and the other Quicken tax-related tools are easily done with *worksheets* in which Quicken fills in numbers it knows about, you enter other numbers or correct the ones Quicken automatically entered, and then Quicken summarizes these amounts and does the necessary calculations.

Use the Tax Planner

The basis for all of your tax information can be entered into the Tax Planner. The Planner helps you evaluate your income tax position. It bases its estimates on numbers you give it, on the data you've entered into Quicken, or on last year's TurboTax return. It covers such areas as your employment income, interest and dividends you receive, deductions and exemptions, withholding, and other taxes or credits for which you may be liable. Figure 10-1 shows an example of the Tax Planner Summary worksheet. If you entered information earlier, the Tax Planner starts with that information; however, you can change it at any time.

Enter the Tax Planner Options

Begin using the Tax Planner by checking and correcting, if necessary, your tax marital status in the upper-left area of the Tax Planner.

1. If needed, click the **Planning** tab to display it. Click the **Tax Center** view, and click **Show Tax Planner** at the top-left corner of the view, as seen in Figure 10-2.

2. Click **Year** in the upper-left area of the Tax Planner to open the Tax Planner options in the right pane, and select the year you want to use. While you can click the **Year** down arrow to choose another year for which to plan, there is only one instance in which you want and can do it—the first quarter of a year in which you may still be working with the previous year. The default is the current year. If you try to change to a future year, a message box appears telling you that Quicken cannot display tax values for a future year. Click **OK** to return to the Tax Planner options.

3. Click the **Filing Status** down arrow to change your income tax filing status, if necessary. If you are not sure of your status, consult your tax professional.

4. Click the **Scenario** down arrow to create a new scenario. You can create up to three additional scenarios in the Tax Planner. For example, if you are thinking of starting a small business, you could enter information about your projected income in a second scenario to see how it would affect your tax situation.

NOTE

The Tax Planner is only available in Quicken Deluxe, Premier, Home & Business, and Rental Property Manager editions.

NOTE

You may also open the Tax Planner from the Tax Tools button in the Planning tab.

TIP

The warning message about Quicken's inability to display future years' tax values tells you that you cannot display *projected* tax values for a future year. You can use one of the other three scenarios to estimate your taxes for next year using the current tax rates.

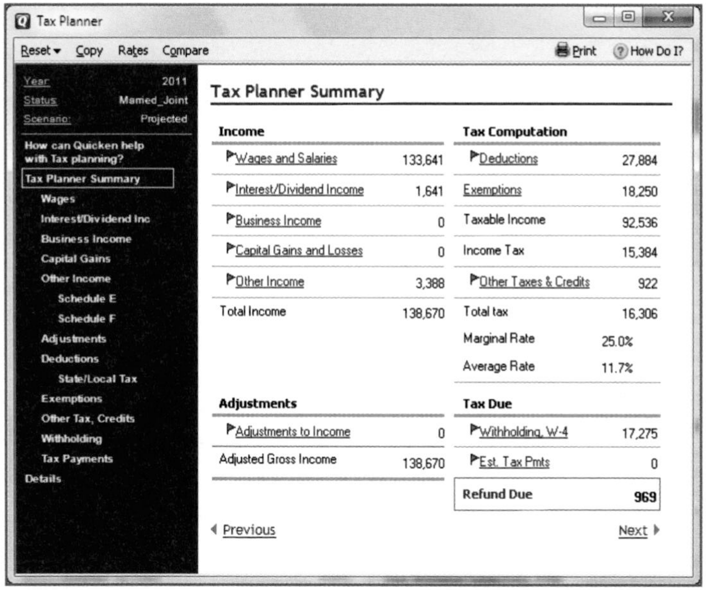

Figure 10-1: The Tax Planner Summary worksheet displays information from Quicken or TurboTax, or that you enter yourself.

Figure 10-2: Quicken provides a number of tools for managing your taxes, including the Tax Center and the Tax Planner.

5. Click **Next**. The How Can Quicken Help With Tax Planning page is displayed. If you see the Tax Planner Summary instead, which means that the Tax Planner has been used in the past, click **How Can Quicken Help With Tax Planning** in the left pane.

6. If you are not already at the Tax Planning Summary, when you are finished with the How Can Quicken Help With Tax Planning page, click **Let's Get Started**. The Tax Planner Summary appears. Unless you have an existing scenario that either you built or Quicken built out of your current year's data, the Tax Planner Summary should be mainly blank and you need to begin by filling it in.

TIP

If you create more than one scenario, you can compare them. Click **Compare** in the toolbar in the Tax Planner after you have entered data into two different scenarios.

TIP

From the left pane of the Tax Planner, click **Details** (only available with the Projected scenario) to display detailed information about an element of your tax plan. When you are finished, click **Return To The Tax Planner Summary** (enlarge the window if you don't see this button in the lower-right area) or click the **Tax Planner Summary** option on the left.

NOTE

Items that Quicken does not consider complete are flagged with a small red flag icon.

If you have set up a paycheck or downloaded investment transactions that contain interest, dividends, or sales of securities, you may already have info in the Tax Planner. As you go through the Tax Planner, check the Details area at the bottom of each pane to see what data is already available and its source. It may make more sense to make your entries in the Details area, rather than in the summary area. For example, if you have scheduled your paycheck, the Wages pane should show your year-to-date salary and the projected salary for the remainder of the year with Quicken Data (from 2011) as the source. You can fine-tune the projection by selecting from Scheduled Bills And Deposits, Estimate Based On YTD Daily Average, or No Projected Amount and by entering an adjustment.

7. From the Tax Planner Summary, click **Next** to continue to the Wages worksheet, as shown in Figure 10-3.

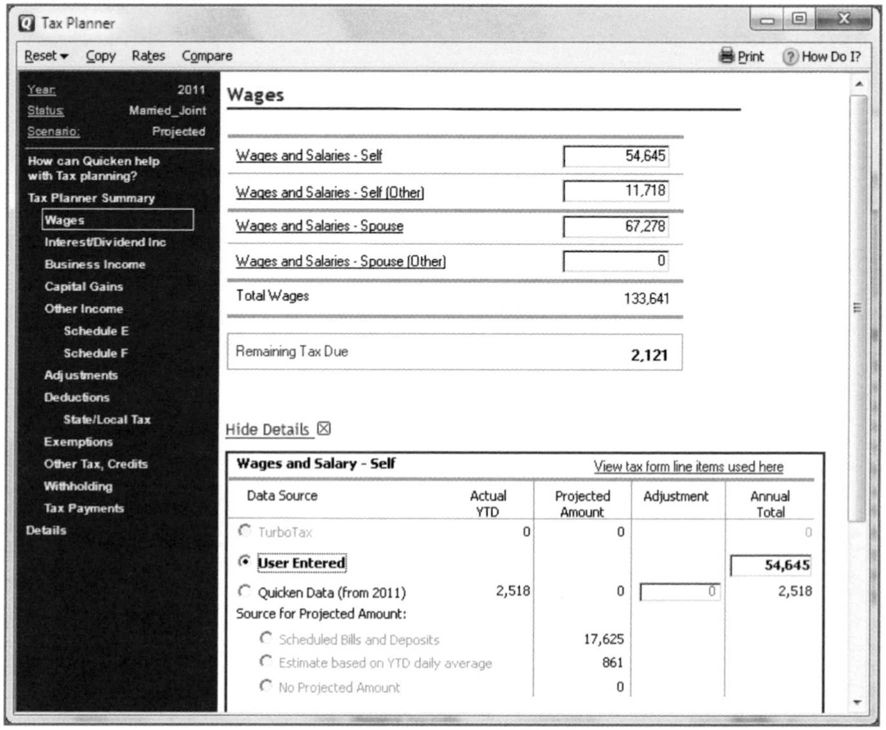

Figure 10-3: The first step in tax planning is entering information into the Wages worksheet.

NOTE

If you are entering a projected-values scenario, you have the option of showing the details about where the information came from. To show the detail information, click one of the underlined text entries, or click **Show Details** if they are not shown. If you are using an alternate scenario, you do not have this option.

QUICKSTEPS

USING THE TAX LINE IN CATEGORIES

You have the option to include tax information when entering a new category.

1. Click the **Tools** menu, and click **Category List**.

2. Click **New** in the lower-left area of the window to enter a new category; or select an existing category, and click **Edit**. If you are entering a new category, type its name and select whether it is an income, expense, or a subcategory of another selected category.

3. Click the **Tax Reporting** tab, and then click the **Tax Line Item For This Category** down arrow to display a list of possible tax-line items. These items are arranged by IRS form number and schedule letter, but they aren't in any logical order. You may need to scroll all the way to the bottom of the list to find the item you are looking for. Check with your

Continued . . .

Set Up Category

| Details | Tax Reporting |

Complete this form to use the category in tax related features. (learn more)

☑ Tax related category

○ Standard line item list
○ Extended line item list

Tax line item for this category (optional)

Schedule C:Gross receipts or sales ▼

Tax Line Item Description:

Gross receipts or sales from a business before deducting adjustments for returns and allowances and cost of goods sold.

OK   Cancel

Enter Income into the Tax Planner

Start the Planner by entering your income information.

1. In the Tax Planner Wages worksheet, displayed in Figure 10-3, click in the **Wages And Salaries – Self** text box. Enter the amount of wages or salary you expect to earn for the year. After you enter the information, your projected tax due or refund due is computed and displayed. (Although you can fill out the Tax Planner this way, it is much easier to set up a paycheck and let the paycheck entry do this work for you.)

2. Click in the **Wages and Salaries – Self (Other)** text box, and enter the taxable amounts from other income sources, such as Employee Stock Purchase Plan (ESPP) sales. Check with your tax professional to find out if this option applies to you.

3. Click in the **Wages And Salaries – Spouse** text box, and enter your spouse's wages.

4. Click in the **Wages And Salaries – Spouse (Other)** text box, and enter any other income amounts. The total wages for the both of you are displayed in the Total Wages field.

5. Click **Next** to continue to the Interest And Dividend Income worksheet.

Enter Interest, Dividend, and Business Income

To determine your interest, dividend, and business income, use information from your financial institutions, such as 1099-INTs or partnership K-1s, if you have it. Otherwise, enter estimates in this area.

1. In the Tax Planner, click **Interest/Dividend Inc** in the left pane.

2. Click in the **Taxable Interest Income** text box, and enter the amount of taxable interest you will receive for the year from savings, money market accounts, or other loans you have made.

3. Click in the **Dividends** text box, and enter all the amounts reported on 1099-DIV and K-1 forms from mutual funds, stocks, partnerships, estates, trusts, or S corporations. If you have not yet received a 1099-DIV or K-1 form, estimate the amount that you received.

4. Click **Next** to display the Business Income worksheet.

5. If you have a small business, use this worksheet to enter the information from your Schedule C (see Figure 10-4) or from a profit-and-loss statement.

Year:	2011	Business Income or Loss - Schedule C		
Status:	Married_Joint			
Scenario:	Projected			
			SELF	SPOUSE
How can Quicken help with Tax planning?		Revenue	12,648	0
Tax Planner Summary		Cost of Goods Sold	4,856	0
Wages				
Interest/Dividend Inc		Gross Margin	7,792	0
Business Income		Meals/Entertainment Expense	268	0
Capital Gains				
Other Income		Deductible Meals/Entertainment	134	0
Schedule E		Deductible Business Mileage	312	0
Schedule F				
Adjustments		Other Allowable Expenses	2,271	0
Deductions				
State/Local Tax		** Unspecified Business Expenses **	0	0
Exemptions		Total Expenses	2,717	0
Other Tax, Credits				
Withholding		Exp. for Business Use of Home	0	0
Tax Payments		Business Income or Loss	5,075	0
Details				
		Remaining Tax Due		975

Figure 10-4: If you operate a small business, enter the data from a financial statement.

6. Click in the **Revenue Self** text box, and enter the total revenue for your business. Click in the **Revenue Spouse** text box, and enter the revenue for your spouse's business, if applicable.

7. Click in the **Cost Of Goods Sold** text box, and enter the costs of the items you sold for each business.

8. If you have associated any expense category with a Tax Schedule C line, that amount will appear in the appropriate fields. Click in the **Other Allowable Expenses** and the **Unspecified Business Expenses** text boxes to enter any additional amounts. After you have entered the amount for these expenses, Quicken calculates your total expenses.

9. Click in the **Exp. For Business Use Of Home** text box, and enter the amount you allot for the business use of your home. The total business income or loss amount is displayed for each business, as well as the total remaining tax due.

10. Click **Next** to display the Capital Gains And Losses worksheet.

Enter Capital Gains

Before you can enter information into the Capital Gains And Losses worksheet, you must know whether a gain is a short-term or a long-term gain. See the QuickFacts "Determining the Type of Capital Gain" later in this chapter. A capital gain is the difference between the price for which you have sold an asset and the price you paid for it. You *realize,* or achieve, a capital gain when you sell an investment for more than you paid for it. (You may receive information from your broker that some of your investments have *unrealized* capital gains. That means an investment hasn't been sold yet but would give you a profit and tax consequences *if* you did sell it.) Capital gains are received on many types of investments, including mutual funds, bonds, stocks, homes, and businesses. If you sell an investment for less than you paid for it, you have a *capital loss.*

When you use the Capital Gains And Losses worksheet, make sure you understand which type of gain or loss, short-term or long-term, you are entering. In this, as in all areas, it is important that you consult with your tax professional.

1. If it is not already displayed, in the Tax Planner, click **Capital Gains** in the left pane.
2. Click in the **Short-Term Gains And Losses** text box, and enter the result you get when you subtract your short-term losses from any short-term gains.
3. Click in each of the remaining text boxes that are applicable to you, and enter the appropriate amounts.
4. Click **Next** to display the Other Income Or Losses worksheet.

Work with Other Income or Losses

The Other Income Or Losses worksheet allows you to enter information that affects your tax situation but that is not covered in other areas of the Tax Planner. These items include taxable state income tax refunds, alimony, taxable Social Security benefits, and so on. As with all items in the Tax Planner, review your entries and discuss them with your tax professional.

1. In the Tax Planner, click **Other Income** in the left pane. Figure 10-5 displays an Other Income Or Losses worksheet.

QUICK**FACTS**

DETERMINING THE TYPE OF CAPITAL GAIN

A capital gain can be either long-term or short-term, depending on the length of time you have owned an asset. Generally speaking:

- Any asset you have owned for one year or less is considered a short-term asset.

- Normally, a gain on a short-term asset is taxed at your regular income tax rate.

- Any asset you have owned for more than one year is deemed to be a long-term asset and any gain on it is taxed at a special rate, depending on your tax bracket.

- Additional information about how to determine whether an asset is short-term or long-term can be found in IRS publications or from your tax professional.

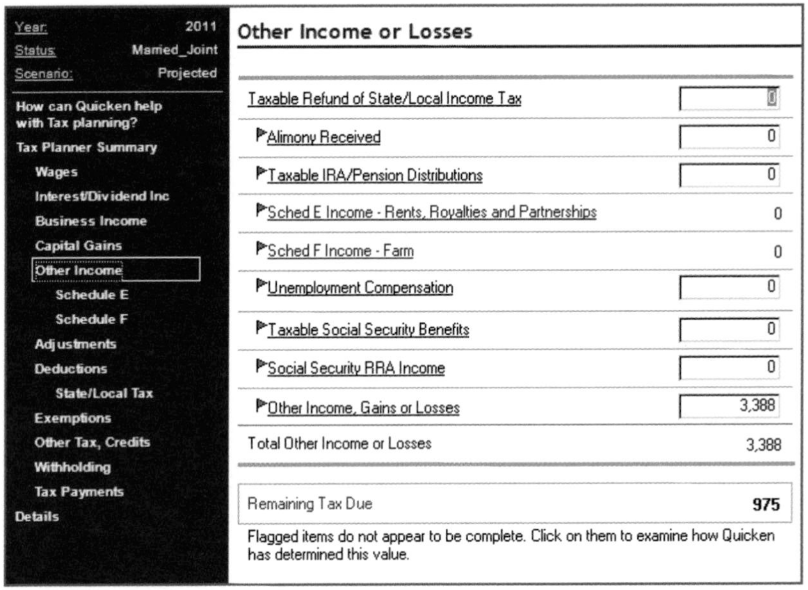

Year:	2011
Status:	Married_Joint
Scenario:	Projected

How can Quicken help with Tax planning?

Tax Planner Summary
- Wages
- Interest/Dividend Inc
- Business Income
- Capital Gains
- Other Income
  - Schedule E
  - Schedule F
- Adjustments
- Deductions
  - State/Local Tax
- Exemptions
- Other Tax, Credits
- Withholding
- Tax Payments
Details

Other Income or Losses

Taxable Refund of State/Local Income Tax	0
▶Alimony Received	0
▶Taxable IRA/Pension Distributions	0
▶Sched E Income - Rents, Royalties and Partnerships	0
▶Sched F Income - Farm	0
▶Unemployment Compensation	0
▶Taxable Social Security Benefits	0
▶Social Security RRA Income	0
▶Other Income, Gains or Losses	3,388
Total Other Income or Losses	3,388

Remaining Tax Due	**975**

Flagged items do not appear to be complete. Click on them to examine how Quicken has determined this value.

Figure 10-5: Enter other income, such as unemployment benefits, into the Other Income Or Losses worksheet in your Tax Planner.

2. If needed, click in the **Taxable Refund Of State/Local Income Tax** text box, and enter any refund of taxes that you deducted as an itemized deduction on your federal tax return in earlier years.

3. If applicable, click in the **Alimony Received** or **Taxable IRA/Pension Distributions** text boxes, and enter the appropriate amount.

4. If needed, click the **Sched E Income-Rents, Royalties, And Partnerships** link or click the **Sched F Income-Farm** link. A corresponding worksheet is displayed. In each of the categories where you have receipts, enter the appropriate amount. Quicken calculates your net income or loss and displays it at the bottom of the worksheet. Click **Previous** to return to the Other Income Or Losses worksheet.

Rents, Royalties, and Partnerships - Schedule E

Rents	5,400
▶Royalties	0
▶Partnership Income/Loss	0
Total Income	4,150
Depreciation	1,250
▶Expenses	895
Rental Property Mileage	0
*** Unspecified Rental Property Expenses ***	0
Net Income/Loss	3,255

Remaining Tax Due	**1,821**

Flagged items do not appear to be complete. Click on them to examine how Quicken has determined this value.

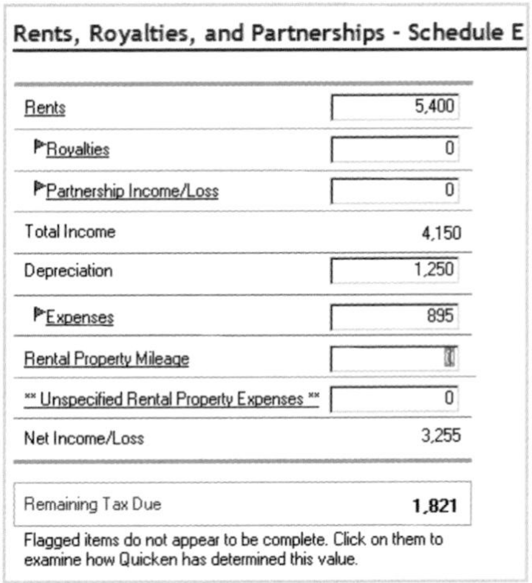

NOTE

The Tax Planner does not determine which, if any, of your Social Security or Railroad Retirement income is taxable. The instruction booklet that comes with your 1040 form has a worksheet to help you determine this. You can also consult your tax professional.

5. As appropriate, click in the remaining text boxes, and enter the amount you received (or will receive) for this year.

6. Click **Next** three times, or click **Adjustments** in the left pane, to display the Adjustments To Income worksheet.

Work with Income Adjustments and Deductions

After entering all your income, you need to consider those items that reduce your income before taxes. These are primarily income adjustments, deductions, exemptions, and tax credits.

ENTER ADJUSTMENT TO INCOME

Adjustments to income are those items that, while not deductible, reduce your income. They include Individual Retirement Account (IRA) contributions, health insurance paid by self-employed persons, Keogh or Simplified Employee Pension (SEP) contributions, alimony you have paid, moving expenses, and other adjustments.

1. In the Tax Planner, click **Adjustments** in the left pane.

NOTE

Quicken calculates the amount of self-employment tax that is an adjustment to income based on the information you entered for your business(es)' income and expenses.

2. Click in each text box, and enter the relevant amounts if any of these items pertain to you.

3. Click **Next** to display the Standard And Itemized Deductions worksheet.

ENTER STANDARD AND ITEMIZED DEDUCTIONS

According to the IRS, most people take the standard deduction to reduce their income tax bill.

Adjustments to Income	
Allowable IRA Deduction (Not all IRA Contributions are Deductible)	0
One-Half of Self-Employment-Tax	359
▶Allowable S.E. Health Insurance Deduction	0
▶Keogh/SEP Deduction	2,000
▶Penalty on Early Withdrawal of Savings	0
▶Alimony Paid	0
▶Moving Expenses	0
Other Adjustments	0
Total Adjustments	2,359
Remaining Tax Due	**1,301**

Flagged items do not appear to be complete. Click on them to examine how Quicken has determined this value.

However, if you pay high mortgage interest payments or have large medical bills, itemizing your deductions might reduce your tax liability even more.

Quicken provides a Deduction Finder to help you with this. See "Use the Deduction Finder" later in this chapter.

1. In the Tax Planner, click **Deductions** in the left pane.

2. Click in the **Medical And Dental Expense** field to enter all of your medical and dental expenses for the year. Quicken will compute the amount of your deduction, if you can take one, and display it in the Allowable Medical Deduction area. If you cannot take a deduction, the Allowable Medical Deduction area shows zero.

3. If your state or locality has an income tax, click **State & Local Income Tax** to display the State And Local Income Tax worksheet. If figures are already filled in from the paycheck detail you entered and you believe that it is correct, you can skip to step 4. Otherwise:

State and Local Income Tax

Projected Withholdings	SELF	SPOUSE
Withholdings To Date	9,834	8,247
Next Pay Date	09/15/11	09/15/11
Pay Period	Every 2 weeks	Every 2 weeks
Withholding per Pay Period	0	0
Projected Future Withholding	0	0
Projected Total Withholding	9,834	8,247
Projected Total Withholdings for Self and Spouse		18,081
►Estimated Taxes Paid to Date plus Projected Payments Through Year-End		0
►Tax Payments this Year for Last Year's State Tax		0
Total Tax Payments to Date plus Projected Withholding Through Year-End		18,081
Remaining Tax Due		**1,301**

Flagged items do not appear to be complete. Click on them to examine how Quicken has determined this value.

a. Click in the **Withholdings To Date** text box, and enter the state or local withholding amounts for you and your spouse through your last paychecks. This information should appear on your pay stubs.

b. Click in the **Next Pay Date** text box, and enter the date on which you will receive your next paychecks.

c. Click the **Pay Period** down arrow, and choose how often each of you is paid.

d. Click in the **Withholding Per Pay Period** text box, and enter the amount of state or local taxes withheld from your paychecks.

NOTE

If you pay your real estate taxes with your mortgage payment, your mortgage company will show the amount of real estate taxes paid on the Form 1098 they send you at the end of the year.

Standard and Itemized Deductions

Itemized Deductions (Schedule A)		Standard Deduction	
Medical and Dental Expense	1,336	☐ Taxpayer can be claimed as a dependent on another return.	
Allowable Medical Deduction	0		
▶State & Local Income Tax	18,081	SELF	
		☐ Blind ☐ 65 or Older	
Real Estate and Other Taxes	4,800	SPOUSE	
▶Deductible Investment Interest	0	☐ Blind ☐ 65 or Older	
Mortgage & Other Deductible Interest	3,678	Deduction 11,400	
▶Charitable Contributions	1,325	**Deduction**	
▶Deductible Casualty Losses	0	Larger of Itemized or Standard Deduction	
Misc. Deductions	568	27,884	
Less: Income-Related and Misc. Deduction Limitations	568		
▶Misc. Deductions (No Limit)	0	**Remaining Tax Due**	
Total Itemized Deductions	27,884	**1,301**	

Flagged items do not appear to be complete. Click on them to examine how Quicken has determined this value.

e. Click in the **Estimated Taxes Paid To Date Plus Projected Payments Through Year End** text box, and enter how much estimated tax you have paid to the state and local taxing authorities.

f. Click in the **Tax Payments This Year For Last Year's State Tax** text box, and enter any amounts you have paid in state income tax during this calendar year.

g. Quicken calculates what your total payments for state and local income taxes will be.

h. Click **Previous** to return to the Standard And Itemized Deductions worksheet.

4. Click in the **Real Estate And Other Taxes** text box, and enter the amount of real estate taxes you have paid or will pay for the current year.

5. Click in the **Deductible Investment Interest** text box, and enter the relevant amount.

6. Click in the **Mortgage & Other Deductible Interest** text box, and enter your mortgage interest, as shown on the Form 1098 you received from your mortgage company.

7. Click in the **Charitable Contributions** text box, and enter the amount of money you have given to charity for the current year. The Tax Planner will adjust your deduction to comply with IRS regulations.

8. Click in the **Deductible Casualty Losses** text box, and enter any losses in this category. To understand what you can deduct, consult your tax professional.

9. Click in the **Misc. Deductions** and **Misc. Deductions (No Limit)** text boxes, and enter any qualifying deductions. Quicken will calculate your total itemized deductions.

10. In the Standard Deduction column, click any check box that pertains to your situation. The amount of your standard deduction appears in the Deduction field. If your itemized deductions are larger than your standard deduction, the larger amount appears in the Larger Of Itemized Or Standard Deduction field.

11. Click **Next** twice to display the Exemptions worksheet.

12. Enter your number of dependents, and click **Next** to display the Other Taxes And Credits worksheet. The information you entered earlier regarding your self-employment income is already included on this worksheet. If your tax professional tells you that you are subject to the alternative minimum tax, enter any relevant information; otherwise, click **Next** to display the Federal Withholdings worksheet.

DEDUCTING STATE SALES TAX

Under current law, taxpayers may deduct state and local sales tax from their tax returns if they itemize their deductions. However, you should consider the following:

- To take the deduction, you must itemize deductions.

- If you live in a state that collects income tax, you must choose to deduct either the state (or local) income tax you paid or the sales tax deduction—you cannot deduct both.

- You can add up the sales tax you paid from your cash register and credit card receipts to determine your deduction. This requires that you keep these receipts with your income tax records for the year.

- Alternatively, you can use the appropriate amount from the sales tax tables created by the IRS. These tables are included in your Form 1040 packet and are also available online at the IRS website: www.irs.gov.

- You may want to consult your tax professional to see if you qualify for any of these deductions.

Update Your Federal Withholdings

The Withholdings worksheet may already display information you have entered, either from your paycheck setup or on earlier worksheets of the Tax Planner. If not, enter the information as needed.

In the center of the worksheet, the Tax Payment Summary displays your projected tax as well as your projected withholdings from the Total Withholdings To Date amount. Your estimated tax due or refund due has been calculated by Quicken, as shown in Figure 10-6.

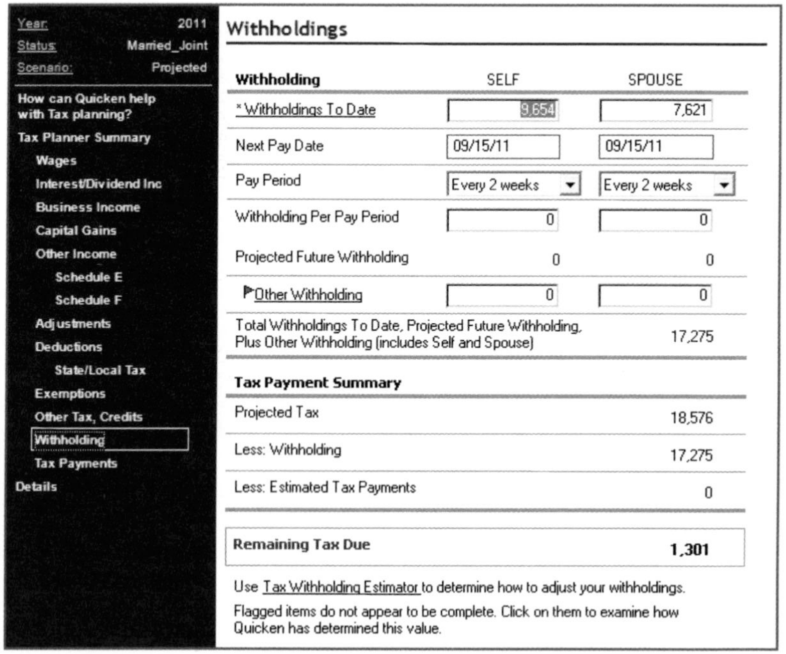

Figure 10-6: The Withholdings worksheet displays your projected withholdings as well as your current tax or refund due.

Estimated Tax Payments

Estimated Taxes (1040-ES) Paid to Date	0
▶Projected Future Estimated Tax Payments	0
▶Refund Applied from Prior Year Federal Tax Return	0
Total Estimated Tax Payments and Refunds Applied	0
Remaining Tax Due	1,301

Flagged items do not appear to be complete. Click on them to examine how Quicken has determined this value.

NOTE

The Tax Withholding Estimator helps you determine how much to withhold from your paycheck. See "Use the Tax Withholding Estimator" later in this chapter for more information.

NOTE

The Tax Calendar, which appears in the Tax Center, displays the important tax dates for the current taxing period.

TIP

The Projected Tax section of the Tax Center view displays the information you entered into Quicken or the Tax Planner. You can click any of the links to go to the relevant section of the Tax Planner.

ENTER ESTIMATED TAX PAYMENTS

You may enter your total estimated tax payments for the year in the Estimated Tax Payments worksheet.

1. In the Tax Planner, click **Tax Payments** in the left pane.

2. Click in the **Estimated Taxes (1040-ES) Paid To Date** field to enter the amount you have paid this year to date.

3. Click **Projected Future Estimated Tax Payments** to enter any amounts you plan on paying for this year.

4. Enter the amount of refund from prior years. Quicken will total your estimated payments.

PROVIDE TAX PLANNER DETAILS

If you are using the Projected scenario (it's not available with the other scenarios), you can review the details and make any changes to your Tax Planner information from the Tax Planner Details worksheet.

1. In the Tax Planner, click **Details** in the left pane, and click the **Form** down arrow to choose the form you want to change.

2. Click the **Item** down arrow to select the specific item with which you want to work.

3. Click **Return To Tax Planner Summary** when you have made all the changes you wish to make and you want to see the result of your entries into the Tax Planner. A sample Tax Planner Summary is shown in Figure 10-1.

4. Click **Close** to close the Tax Planner when you're ready.

Work with the Tax Center

The Tax Center view in the Planning tab provides an overview of your tax standing at any time during the year. It shows your projected tax, the Tax Calendar, any tax-related expenses, and all of your taxable income for the year. From the Tax Tools button, the Tax Center offers a variety of tools to help you plan. All of this information is based on data you have entered. You can adjust this data, add to it, and create reports based on it. While ultimately all

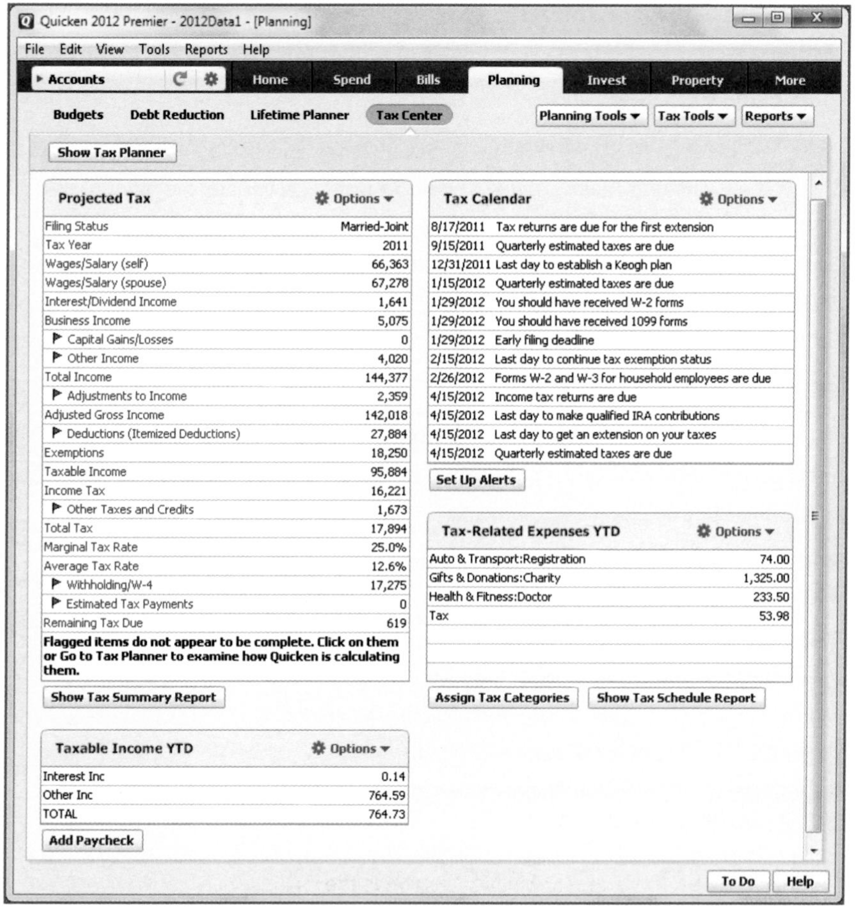

Figure 10-7: The Tax Center view gives an overview of your tax information and provides you with links to several tax tools.

tax questions should be reviewed with your tax professional, Quicken provides a host of useful tools and reports to help you. To see what information is currently available in the Tax Center:

Click the **Planning** tab, and click **Tax Center** to display your tax information, as shown in Figure 10-7.

Assign Tax-Related Expenses

The Tax-Related Expenses YTD section of the Tax Center helps you track any expenses that have a tax consequence. To assign a tax line to an expense category:

1. Click **Assign Tax Categories**, located below the Tax-Related Expenses YTD section, to open the Category List.

2. Select the category to which you want to assign a tax line, scroll to the right, and click **Edit** on the right of that category. This opens the Set Up Category dialog box, which is described in the "Using the Tax Line in Categories" QuickSteps earlier in this chapter.

3. Back in the Tax Center view, click **Show Tax Schedule Report** to display an itemized report of the information that relates to income tax schedules, as seen in Figure 10-8.

4. Close the Tax Schedule report. In the Tax Center, click **Options** in the title bar of the Tax Related Expenses YTD section to open a menu from which you can do the following:

   ● Find other deductions by using the Deduction Finder, as discussed later in this chapter.

   ● Learn how your deductions will change your income tax liability. This takes you to the Tax Planner Summary in the Tax Planner.

   ● Create a tax schedule report.

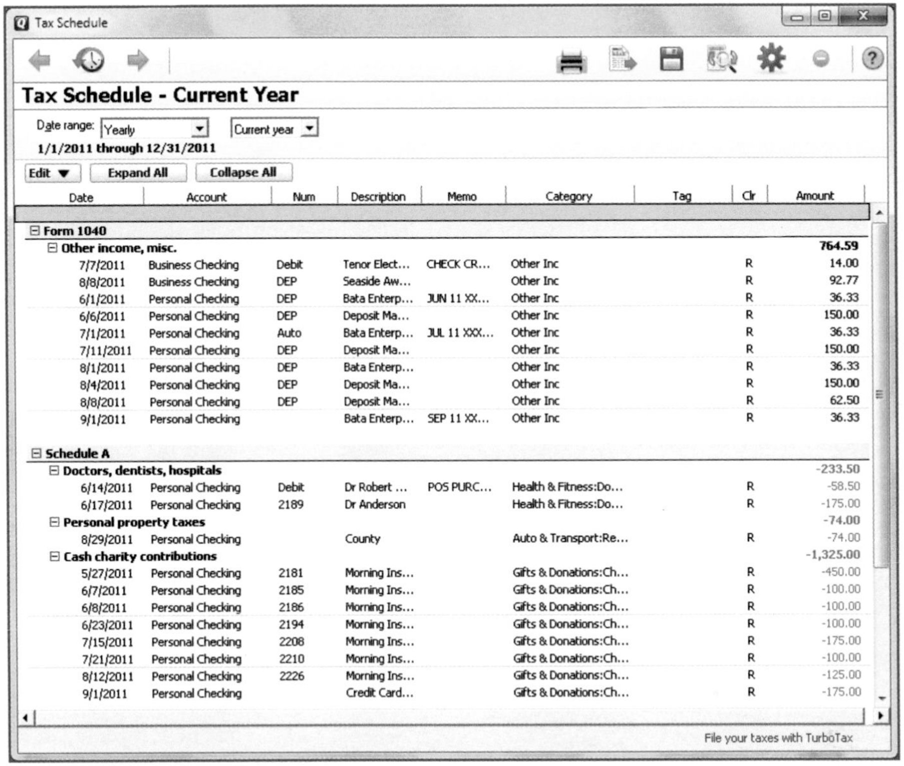

Figure 10-8: As you enter information into Quicken, you can run a report that shows the detail for each income tax schedule.

- Link categories to tax forms, which takes you to the Category List.
- Go to the Category List to make any tax-related or other changes.

See Your Taxable Income

The Taxable Income YTD section enables you to add a new paycheck, which is discussed in Chapter 1. From the Options menu in the Taxable Income YTD section, you can do the following:

- Click **Report My Net Worth** to create a net worth report for any time period.
- Click **How Will This Income Affect My Taxes?** to open the Tax Planner.
- Click **Go To Category List** to open the list if you want to make any changes.

QUICKSTEPS

CREATING TAX REPORTS

Click the **Reports** menu, and click **Tax** to display six reports that are designed specifically for taxes:

Reports	Help
Banking	▶
Comparison	▶
Investing	▶
Net Worth & Balances	▶
Spending	▶
Tax	▶
EasyAnswer	
Graphs	▶
Reports & Graphs Center	

Tax submenu:
- Capital Gains
- Schedule A-Itemized Deductions
- Schedule B-Interest and Dividends
- Schedule D-Capital Gains and Losses
- Tax Schedule
- Tax Summary

- **Capital Gains** creates a report that shows any gains Quicken believes you have realized from the sale of assets or securities.

- **Schedule A-Itemized Deductions** prepares a transaction report that is subtotaled by each item on Schedule A of Form 1040.

- **Schedule B-Interest And Dividends** creates a transaction report that is subtotaled by each item on Schedule B of Form 1040.

Continued . . .

Use Tax Tools

In the Planning tab, click **Tax Tools** to see tools you can use to help with your tax planning:

- The **Tax Planner**, which is covered earlier in this chapter, helps you determine how much you will owe in taxes.

- Click **Deduction Finder** to open this tool, discussed later in this chapter.

- The **Itemized Deduction Finder** opens a worksheet that helps you find additional itemized deductions, as discussed in "Use the Itemized Deduction Estimator" later in this chapter.

- The **Capital Gains Estimator** helps you determine the tax implications of selling assets and investments. This wizard gives you general information about potential sales, but does not substitute for a financial or tax advisor. You can create up to three scenarios that combine with the information you entered into the Tax Planner. This utility is discussed in Chapter 8.

- The **Tax Withholding Estimator**, which is covered at the end of this chapter, helps you determine whether you are having the appropriate amount withheld from your earnings.

- Click **Online Tax Tools** to work with tax calculators, get answers to common tax questions, and access state and federal income tax forms and federal tax publications. You must have an Internet connection to use this feature.

Planning Tools ▼	Tax Tools ▼
Tax Planner	
Deduction Finder	
Itemized Deduction Estimator	
Capital Gains Estimator	
Tax Withholding Estimator	
Online Tax Tools ▶	Tax Calculators and Common Tax Questions
TurboTax ▶	Tax Forms and Publications

- Click **TurboTax** to go online and use TurboTax, to order either a CD or downloaded version, or to import a current TurboTax file.

UICKSTEPS

CREATING TAX REPORTS *(Continued)*

- **Schedule D-Capital Gains And Losses** prepares a report of all gains and losses reportable on Schedule D.

- **Tax Schedule** prepares a report of all of your tax-related transactions that you might use in preparing your tax return.

- **Tax Summary** creates a report of all your tax-related transactions subtotaled by category.

Use the Deduction Finder

If you are not sure you have assigned tax-line items for all of your categories, or if you would just like to identify other potential deductions, you can use the Deduction Finder.

1. In the Planning tab, click **Tax Tools** and then click **Deduction Finder** to open the worksheet and the Introduction To Deduction Finder dialog box, which explains how it works. (If you have used the Deduction Finder before, you won't see the Introduction screen; the tool opens to the Deduction tab.) Click **OK** to continue.

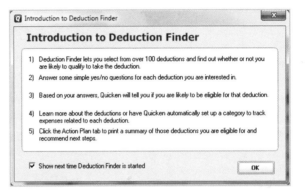

2. Click the **Choose A Deduction Type** down arrow, and click one of the six types of deductions from the drop-down list. A list of deductions appears on the left side of the window.

3. Click any item on the list to display questions about that possible deduction on the right side of the window. Click either **Yes** or **No** to answer each question, as shown in Figure 10-9.

4. After you have answered all the questions, a green check mark appears to the left of any deduction for which you may be eligible and a red X appears if you are not eligible. The result also is displayed at the bottom of the section.

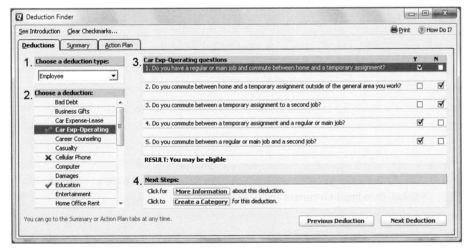

Figure 10-9: The Deduction Finder helps you find additional deductions for which you may be eligible.

TIP

Quicken will not tell you that you already have a standard category for a tax-line item and, unfortunately, you can't search the category list by tax-line item. You can print the category list to search it manually or bring it into Excel, but it might be worthwhile to ensure you don't end up with a bunch of nonstandard categories that duplicate what you already get from the standard categories.

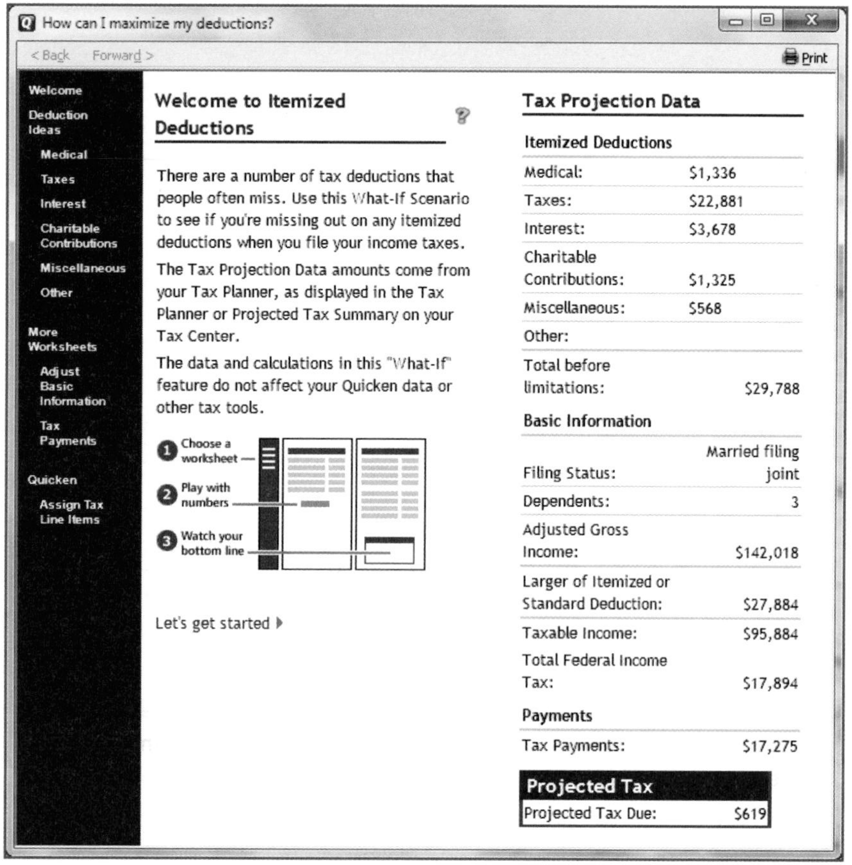

Figure 10-10: The Itemized Deduction Estimator can help you identify less well-known deductions.

5. Click **More Information** in the lower-middle area of the window if you want to learn more about this deduction. Click **Create A Category** to display an explanation about a potential new category for this deduction, and then click **Create** to do that.
6. Click **Next Deduction** to go to the next deduction on the list, or select one on the left that may pertain to your situation, and follow the same steps.
7. Click the **Summary** tab to see how many deductions are available for each deduction type, how many you have viewed and answered, and how many for which you are eligible.
8. Click the **Action Plan** tab to see the steps to take to use the deductions you have found.
9. Click **Clear Checkmarks** in the menu bar to clear all of your answers and start over.
10. Click **Close** to close the Deduction Finder.

Use the Itemized Deduction Estimator

You can take a wide variety of tax deductions, some of which are more common than others. Quicken provides the Itemized Deduction Estimator to ensure that you are deducting all to which you are entitled. It uses information from the Tax Planner and lets you create what-if scenarios. To use the Itemized Deduction Estimator:

1. In the Planning tab, click **Tax Tools** and then click **Itemized Deduction Estimator** to open the worksheet.
2. A welcome message appears, shown in Figure 10-10. The Itemized Deduction Estimator displays your projected data as you entered it in the Tax Planner.
3. Click **Let's Get Started** to begin the process.

4. The Medical Deductions worksheet is displayed. Each worksheet in this wizard displays the tax projection data on the right side so you can see any changes. As you make entries into the scenario, your projected tax bill changes if your scenario information decreases your liability.

5. Click in any of the text boxes that are applicable to you, and enter any costs you incurred.

6. Enter any other relevant items in this worksheet. Your total additional medical expenses appear in the Total area.

7. Click **Next** to display the Taxes worksheet.

ENTER REMAINING DEDUCTION WORKSHEETS

The remaining deduction worksheets follow a similar pattern to the Medical Deductions worksheet. Open the sheet by either clicking in the left column or clicking **Next** in the previous sheet. Then click in the text boxes that are applicable to you, and type the related amount. Close the Estimator when you are finished.

Use the Tax Withholding Estimator

The Tax Withholding Estimator allows you to determine how much you should have taken out of each paycheck. You can create a what-if scenario to ensure that you are not withholding too much or too little.

1. In the Planning tab, click **Tax Tools** and then click **Tax Withholding Estimator** to display the Tax Withholding Estimator, which is similar to the Itemized Deduction Estimator. Each worksheet has two parts. The left section allows you to enter possible changes. The right side displays the tax-projection data reflecting the current information you have entered into Quicken or into your Tax Planner. As you make changes on the left side, the right side displays the result of those changes.

2. Click **Let's Get Started** to display the Adjust Basic Information worksheet. Select each of the fields you want to change, and either select or type the information that is correct for you, clicking **Next** as needed.

3. When you have completed all of the worksheets, click **W-4 Worksheet** and click the **Print** icon to create a printed worksheet you can take to work and use to complete a new W-4.

CAUTION

Clicking the Reset To Tax Planner Values button clears all the entries you have made in all the Itemized Deduction Estimator screens, not just the screen you are currently working with.

TIP

If your tax situation has not changed, you probably don't need to do a new W-4 each January. But you can submit a new W-4 anytime your tax situation changes. If you live in a state that has state income taxes, you may also want to consider submitting a withholding form for the state as well.